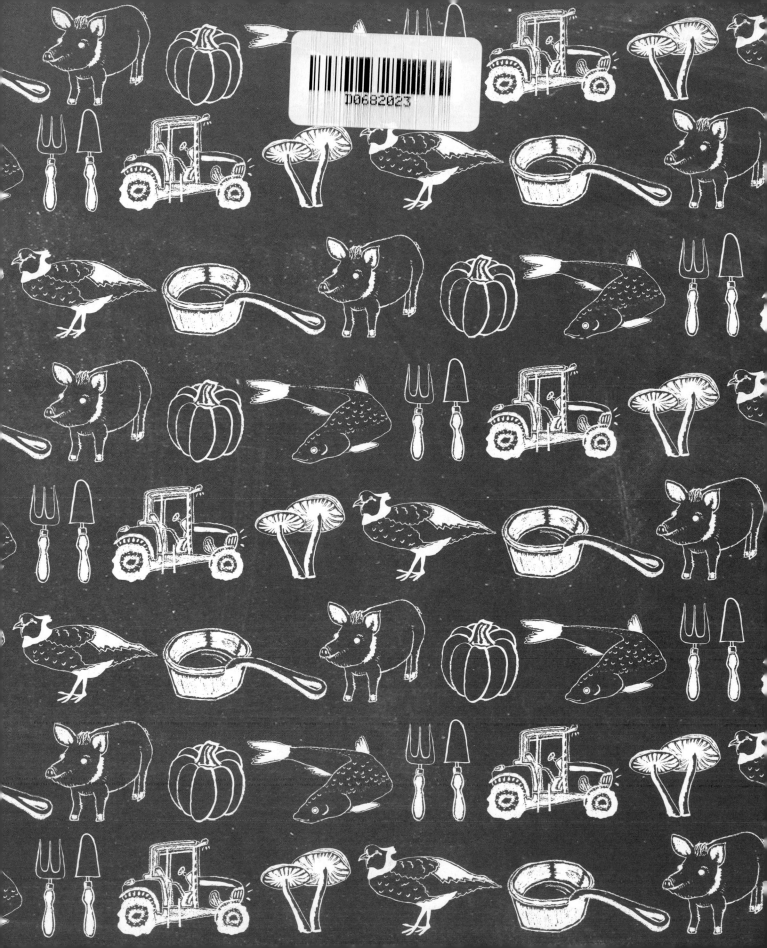

D0682023

THE SHED

THE COOKBOOK

To our dad, Peter Gladwin, who worked long and hard
putting these words together as well as training
each of us in our complementary career paths.

THE SHED

THE COOKBOOK

Original, seasonal
recipes for year-round
inspiration

Gregory, Oliver
& Richard Gladwin

Photography by Simon Wheeler

Kyle Books

First published in Great Britain
in 2014 by Kyle Books
an imprint of Kyle Cathie Limited
192–198 Vauxhall Bridge Road
London SW1V 1DX
general.enquiries@kylebooks.com
www.kylebooks.com

10 9 8 7 6 5 4 3 2 1

ISBN: 978 0 85783 253 5

A CIP catalogue record for this title is
available from the British Library

Gladwin Brothers Enterprises Ltd are hereby identified
as the authors of this work in accordance with Section 77
of the Copyright, Designs and Patents Act 1988.

All rights reserved. No reproduction, copy or transmission of this
publication may be made without written permission. No paragraph
of this publication may be reproduced, copied or transmitted save
with written permission or in accordance with the provisions of
the Copyright Act 1956 (as amended). Any person who does any
unauthorised act in relation to this publication may be liable to
criminal prosecution and civil claims for damages.

Text © Gladwin Brothers Enterprises Ltd 2014
Photographs © Simon Wheeler 2014
Illustrations © Emma Blecker 2014
Design © Kyle Books 2014

Editor: Vicky Orchard
Design: Helen Bratby
Photographer: Simon Wheeler
Stylist: Cynthia Inions
Illustrator: Emma Blecker
Copy editor: Catherine Ward
Production: Nic Jones and Gemma John

Colour reproduction by ALTA London
Printed and bound in China by C&C Offset Printing Co., Ltd.

CONTENTS

FOREWORD
HUGH FEARNLEY-WHITTINGSTALL

Celebrating great food, while also trying to forge stronger connections between the land, the sea, the seasons and our working kitchens, both domestic and professional, has been my life's work. It's a never-ending journey - and one that brings all kinds of pleasures and surprises along the way. One of the greatest recurring pleasures has been working with talented people who share my excitement about creating great dishes from well-sourced, seasonal ingredients. Oliver Gladwin stands out amongst them.

Ollie cooked with us for a couple of years at River Cottage, during which time he revealed himself as a brilliant young chef, full of enthusiasm, skill and bright ideas. Despite his tender years and relative lack of experience he quickly proved his worth, and was soon teaching on our courses as well as supporting our head chef Gill Meller in devising and preparing food for our events.

He completely understood and appreciated the River Cottage ethos - but also brought his own spirit to the food he cooked. That individual style and verve is writ large in this, his first cookbook, a draft copy of which I'm delighted to be holding in my hands. The pleasure I had working with Ollie is now fully matched by the pleasure of seeing what he has achieved since he left us.

The Shed, the vibrant eatery in Notting Hill that Ollie runs alongside his brother Richard, is a very exciting and fun place to be - and a very rewarding place to eat and drink. Using beautiful British produce, much of which is provided by the third Gladwin brother, Greg, Ollie produces gutsy, rustic, generous dishes - from tempting 'mouthfuls' that enable the greedy and the curious to sample many delicious things in one sitting, to more lavish roast meats, grilled veg, gloriously dressed salads and sumptuous puds.

I love Ollie's playful menus, his big, bold flavours, his unfussy but compelling and emphatic presentation, and his unbridled passion for the very best seasonal British ingredients. The recipes you'll find in these pages (my favourites include Wood Pigeon Saltimbocca, Pan-fried Cuttlefish with Black Beans, Paprika and Almonds and Apple and Marmalade Bakewell Tart), are certainly enticing, glamorous even, but they are also approachable and achievable. They will bring fresh colours and rich tastes to your kitchen, and big smiles to the faces of the friends and family you share them with.

THE STORY OF THE SHED

We were brought up on a vineyard farm in an idyllic place in West Sussex called Nutbourne. Our childhoods were intimately entwined with the seasons, from the bursting of the buds in the spring to the ripening of fruits in the summer, harvesting in the autumn and winemaking and bottling in the winter. When school was over, our lives were all about driving tractors, adventures in the woods, digging in the veg patch, animal husbandry, Mum baking delicious things for tea and a constant stream of friends coming and going. To find the roots of The Shed, the restaurant we run in London's Notting Hill, you need look no further than our home in Nutbourne.

With hindsight, our career choices look like some sinister genetic plan by our parents. Gregory, the youngest brother, chose farming; Oliver, the 'middlest', became a chef, and Richard, the eldest, went into the hospitality business. Even we couldn't help noticing that these professions make a perfect food cycle, so we decided to go into business together.

Gregs is a countryman through and through. He's devoted to his Sussex lambs, free-range pigs, organic beef herd and getting the very best from the land. Oliver, the chef, is dedicated to seasonal, sustainable cooking and using every part of an animal to make something delicious. He's self-sufficient in his kitchen, butchering, curing, baking bread, preserving and plenty more besides. Richard is the ideas man, dreaming up some new scheme every few minutes. His passions include winemaking, foraging, growing vegetables and above all running the most hospitable and environmentally sustainable restaurant in town.

Naturally we like to balance all this hard work with the good stuff in life: using a tractor bonnet as a sledge, throwing mud at one another in a turnip field or drinking in The Rising Sun, or 'Riser', our local pub down in Sussex. Being siblings, it's inevitable that we squabble from time to time, but we genuinely are great friends, and work and play often merge into one another.

Our vision for The Shed was for Richard to generate a relaxed, vibrant and fun atmosphere, for Oliver to have free reign in the kitchen and cook in front of the guests, and for Gregory to provide delicious produce and wine from the family farm. Then, by serving small sharing plates, we would move away from traditional restaurant dining towards a more communal experience.

Our restaurant is the embodiment of a philosophy of eating based on local sourcing, seasonality and sustainability. With this book, we aim to bring the spirit of The Shed into your kitchen.

Oliver   Richard   Gregory

RICHARD
THE BIG IDEA

People are always asking me how The Shed came about. I just tell them it happened naturally.

When we were kids, our dad, who has been a caterer/restaurateur for a thousand years, used to sometimes take us to help at special events. Meanwhile, thanks to Mum's example, growing our own food and eating from our garden came as naturally to us as breathing.

When I was about ten, someone asked me what I wanted to be when I grew up. I said, 'A secret agent'. It wasn't long, though, before my future career path became clear. A couple of years later, a school friend and I went on a day's expedition to London and discussed our future professions. Tom said he was going to be a City property developer, which he now is. I said I was going to be a restaurant man (I didn't know the word 'restaurateur' at that stage).

Apart from a stint as a winemaker, which I loved but found too slow-paced to do full time, I have been on that track ever since. From waiting tables in the local bistro during school holidays to working at Soho House, Brawn and Bunga Bunga, I have learnt from a lot of amazing people in the restaurant trade. But I always knew my own place would be a bit different.

While I was doing all this, my brothers were growing up too. Oliver was almost completely uninterested in school, always preferring life in the kitchen. He got his first ice-cream maker for his thirteenth birthday and lives to cook, with occasional interruptions for beer drinking. Gregory, meanwhile, had his first flock of sheep at an age at which I could barely ride a bicycle!

We all knew we were going to work together when the time was right and over Christmas 2011 we hatched a plan. Gregs would supply the food; Mowgli (which is what we call Oliver) would be head chef and I would find suitable premises and manage the restaurant.

Two weeks later, Oliver and I found ourselves on a ski lift in the Alps brainstorming our informal dining concept in the midst of a blizzard. The core principles, we agreed, should be nose-to-tail cooking, sharing plates and local sourcing. We have stuck to these fundamentals ever since.

The search for the right premises was pretty stressful. I was still managing at Bunga Bunga, Oliver was working with Hugh Fearnley-Whittingstall down in Dorset and Gregory was based in Sussex. I viewed countless rundown, dreary sites of restaurants which had gone out of business and were looking for a new owner. But when I walked into The Ark in Notting Hill it was love at first sight. I didn't know then that the place had a famous history dating back to the early 1960s. It was just somewhere a bit quirky and fun, in a rustic wooden building which immediately lent itself to becoming the 'little bit of the countryside in the middle of London' that we were looking for. The Shed was born at that moment.

OLIVER
THE FOOD

Good food is all about great ingredients prepared with care, understanding and love. I'm not the first person to say this, but if you pull your own carrots out of the ground, intimately know the hand-reared animal you send to slaughter, and forage for your own wild herbs and fruits, the ingredients really do taste better.

When my brothers and I decided to set up a restaurant together, I was working at the River Cottage Cookery School in Dorset. I had done a few years in some of the big London restaurants, sweating in basement kitchens, being shouted at by head chefs and cooking menus that didn't vary for weeks on end. Things at River Cottage were different. The people there were wonderful to work with, fantastically creative and accustomed to using lovely produce in an incredibly relaxed atmosphere. I needed more, though.

Working with my brothers gives me the opportunity to do my own thing. I find creating my own menus and recipes from scratch utterly irresistible.

FLAIR COOKING

I firmly believe in selecting what dishes to prepare on the basis of the best ingredients available on that particular day, not the other way around. Our dishes at The Shed change every day. This demands an adaptable, inspiration-led approach, which I call 'flair cooking'.

I try to teach my whole brigade of chefs to think in this way. A ripe, soft courgette, for example, needs different treatment from a young, firm one, but both can be delicious if judiciously handled.

Flair cooking demands versatility. When wild cherries are in season, they will appear in two or three different dishes on The Shed's menu. A bountiful catch of fresh pollock from the South Coast may be grilled, stuffed or baked, or alternatively prepared as ceviche. And the dispatching of one of our prized free-range pigs will call for an intensive week of curing, smoking, mincing, sausage-making and roasting.

SLOW & FAST COOKING

I describe a lot of dishes as 'slow' or 'fast'. 'Slow' recipes are generally cooked at low temperature over a long period of time, allowing their ingredients to mature, tenderise and develop in flavour. 'Fast' dishes, on the other hand, are seared, grilled, rare or even raw. Such techniques are used whenever too long a cooking time would cause the food to lose its essential character. To fulfil The Shed's aim of using every part of an animal, mastery of both approaches is essential in my kitchen.

WHY SHARING PLATES?

We serve all the dishes on The Shed menu as sharing plates. The rationale is simple: don't you want to try everything on offer when you go to a restaurant? Small sharing plates give me the opportunity to present a spectrum of comparatively simple vegetable-, fish- and meat-based dishes that work individually or in combination. When following the recipes at home you may wish to prepare them one at a time, but don't be afraid of the sharing style. Food has been a communal experience since time began and half the fun of eating is discussion, passing, comparing and sharing.

GREGORY
THE FARM

Richard and Oliver may have come up with many of the big ideas – 'countryside in the city', flair cooking in front of the customers and rustic farmyard interior design – but it was down to me and Dad to make it happen.

My brothers wanted to create the interior of a farmyard shed in the centre of London. This involved countless trips up from Sussex with trailer loads of oak offcuts to panel the walls; laying sleepers on the floors, building a central chef station out of corrugated tin and hanging an old John Deere Tractor bonnet over the bar. Not to mention supplying the hand-built table tops mounted on old barrels, the wooden stools and benches, or the countless rusty old farm machinery signs, cart wheels and other bits and pieces displayed on the walls and ceiling. While all this was going on, the grape harvest was approaching, two new litters of piglets arrived and we had to cut, turn, rake and bail hay for winter feed.

THE VINEYARD AT NUTBOURNE

They say a farmer's work is never done, and that's without having a vineyard plus two brothers who are always asking you to help with other things as well! The vineyard is extraordinarily demanding. The vines only display signs of life for six months of the year but the activities involved in caring for them go on for the whole of it. Grapes seem to require more attention than anything I know, from nurturing, trimming and pruning to pressing, filtering and bottling. Livestock can at least look after itself some of the time!

FORAGING

We enjoy the countryside for what it produces spontaneously as much as for the crops and animals we farm. It is amazing what can be found growing wild on our land at almost any time of year – wild herbs, mosses, roots, salads, hedgerow fruits, mushrooms, not to mention the odd shot pheasant, wood pigeon or rabbit. And a quick trip down to the South Coast can yield samphire, purslane, sea spinach and wild shellfish. The next day it is all on the menu at The Shed.

FARMING

For me, what makes farming so fulfilling is experiencing the full circle of life while meeting the challenges of the different seasons. Battling it out through the foul winter weather is followed by the joy of new life in the spring with the calving and lambing seasons, then the long, long hours wearing just shorts in the summer give way to the fruition of the land in the autumn.

THE SPRING

GREGORY
SPRINGTIME ON THE FARM

I always think the year should start in the spring. After all, a damp, muddy day in December is much the same as a damp, muddy day in January. Either way, it gets dark by 4.30pm and being outdoors is not for the faint-hearted. But when spring arrives, everything suddenly changes. Without notice the forces of nature kick in and new life begins to appear. Shoots poke out of the ground, a light green tinge appears in the hedgerows, and the calving and lambing season gets underway. For me, this is the most exciting time of year.

Milk-fed spring lamb is a well-known delicacy but we don't produce it at Nutbourne. We would rather let our lambs grow to a decent size than rush them off to the abattoir when they are barely big enough to furnish a single portion. They therefore spend six to twelve months on the meadow, growing slowly and developing flavour.

Unless there has been a little accident with the ram getting into the wrong field at the wrong time, lambing kicks off sometime in March. Sheep are generally quite capable of giving birth on their own. The farmer's job is just to be on the lookout for any problems and make sure that the ewes quickly bond with their new lambs. Lambing can be a highly emotional process, veering from the triumph of the safe delivery of a pair of healthy twins to the tragedy of losing a mother. We inevitably end up with a few orphans every year. It is usually possible to attach them to other ewes but when that fails we acquire a new family pet. Poppy the lamb was convinced that our mum was her mum and wouldn't see it any other way. She slept in the kitchen, waited by the door if she was put out and trailed round the vineyard just one step behind mum, demanding her bottle whenever she felt like it.

Calving is a much bigger challenge. I have to be on duty right through the night to make sure our thoroughbred Simmentals deliver without any complications. I do a midnight check, grab a brief kip, get up at 3am to see if there is any action, then grab an even briefer kip before rising for good at 5am. The next three hours are the peak time for new calves to arrive. The cows are used to being in the barns, where they are cared for and fed through the worst of the winter, but I sense that they know the reward for calving successfully will be a speedy

return to the spring pasture with their young 'at foot'.

Some people think that cows are aggressive and scary animals. Some of them are certainly extremely protective of their calves and personal space. But through working with them every day, you develop relationships based on mutual respect. They seem to understand I am trying to help them but there is a definite line that neither I nor the vet nor anyone else must cross. If it comes to a showdown, the odds are overwhelmingly on a cow's side because of her bulk.

My brothers regularly come down to the farm from London to pick up produce, do a spot of foraging and help out with livestock movement. They enjoy the contrast with the city. I quickly rope them into action, be it putting cows through the crush to be vaccinated or mucking out their sheds with hay forks. It's good for them have a dose of reality.

MAKING THE BBQ BENCH

Once a tree, now a bench. With the right tools this is an easy half an hour for a farmer.

RICHARD
GROWING SPRING VEGETABLES & VINEYARD ACTION

Sustainable food is much discussed, but few people understand just how simple it is to embrace. If you eat what grows plentifully, naturally and locally at each time of year and take care to avoid wastage, you are already doing your bit.

I believe there is a vegetable grower somewhere inside most of us. These days I'm a bit of a Rurbanite (a person living the rural dream in the city), so for the time being my own garden exists only in my head. The Shed has to get most of its vegetables from a network of local suppliers, supplemented by some special items grown by Mum down at Nutbourne such as edible flowers and herbs - marigolds, chives and purple wood sorrel - and plentiful foraged delicacies found growing in the wild.

I do, however, have a wonderful 'virtual' vegetable patch inside my head. It is a source of great inspiration, not least because everything in it works perfectly. It digs, seeds, hoes, weeds and waters itself, and in the springtime all manner of seasonal wonders suddenly sprout from the ground, like cabbages, sorrel , young spinach, curly kale, Welsh and spring onions, radishes and purple sprouting broccoli. Then later in the season it yields asparagus, new season lettuces, rocket and much more besides. Meanwhile, in the herb bed, young seedlings of mint, parsley, chives, lovage and marjoram are flourishing, along with tiny edible viola pansies and marigolds. They have nothing to fear from frost or slugs because the whole thing is in my imagination.

Moving back to reality, there is no sign of life in the vineyard early in the season. The vine buds burst late in the spring. Once this happens, frost can do terrible damage to the crop. From April onwards we watch out for cold nights with trepidation.

In the winery, on the other hand, things are really happening in early spring. Each time I go down to Nutbourne, I sample last year's wines direct from the tanks to see how they are developing. It is amazing how a wine can change in just a couple of weeks. We have Pinot Noir maturing in oak barrels, Chardonnay still sitting on its lees (natural sediment) and the base for our Traditional Method sparkling wine, appropriately named Nutty, waiting to be bottled. If there is a free day, we are all seconded into helping with the bottling line. This may sound like boring factory work but there is something extremely satisfying about watching thousands upon thousands of bottles coming off the bottler/corker. Our average production is 40-50,000 bottles per year.

Our family's range of English wine is a hugely important aspect of The Shed. London is a cosmopolitan city and half our customers come to us unaware that England is now a serious wine producing

country. They can be a bit sceptical at first but once I have forced a little sample on them I usually manage to convert them - or at least they are polite enough to say nice things.

We are great believers in the old adage that 'what grows together goes together'. Our Sussex fare is a great example - our aromatic and fruity Nutbourne wines really suit our Shed cuisine.

OLIVER
ADVENTURES ON THE WATER

Spring always makes me think of the two small lakes to the south of our vineyard at Nutbourne. As children, we couldn't wait for the weather to start warming up so that water based activities were back on the agenda. Mum would take a picnic down to the waterside on the first sunny spring day. Then we would start mucking about in an old rowing boat with only one oar that lived in a wooden hut built by Dad and known for some reason as Antigua.

As we got older, the adventures got bolder. For one birthday party we built a huge ramp out of pallets and plywood. The idea was to use it as a launching pad for a bike, ridden towards it at top speed and jettisoned in mid-air. After a mighty splash the rider would swim back and the bike would be dredged from the bottom of the lake and presented to the next daredevil. It worked amazingly well, though the bike was never quite the same again.

Our attempt at water skiing was less successful. We had found a discarded pair of wooden water skis somewhere but we didn't have a speedboat. What we did have was Richard's first car. He devised a system involving a very long rope and a series of pulleys attached to the large tree at the far end of the lake. By hooking the rope up to his old Skoda and driving parallel to the lake across the field, he reckoned he could tow a waterskier. This was not a successful plan! After several attempts and considerable damage to our good friend Philly Winser (who has gone on to become one of the most successful restaurateurs in New York, with a stable including The Fat Radish and The Ledbelly) the idea was abandoned.

Back in the kitchen, the joy of the arrival of spring is the chance to prepare lighter vegetable dishes, marinate fish and cook more delicate meat dishes. There is a sudden abundance of new ingredients to forage for in the countryside, including wild garlic, three-cornered wild leeks, chervil and alexander. Further into the spring, English asparagus starts its short season. At this time of year I like to start serving rabbit, quail and guinea fowl dishes. There is also a wonderful range of fresh green herbs sprouting in the vegetable garden. Home-grown fruits are in short supply though. We tend to focus puddings on the myriad of different things that can done with rhubarb, supplemented by a few essentials like last year's apples and imported citrus.

FORAGING IN SPRING

IN THE WOODS

Wild chervil/cow parsley	Fresh, slight aniseed finish	Sea Trout Tartare with Pickled Cucumber (page 23)
Lesser celandine	Sweet, green, delicate flowers	Bulls Blood Beetroot and Blue Cheese Tartlets (page 133)
Ground elder	Strong with raw hardy leaves	Serve in pasta, risotto or as a side of greens
Nettles	Fragrant, very distinctive	Spring Stinger (page 65)

ON A LEAFY LANE

Wild garlic/ransoms	Powerful, abundant, green	Wild Garlic Yogurt (page 67)
Three-cornered leek	Oniony, fresh	Red Gurnard Fillets with Radishes and Wild Leek Butter (page 37)
Pansies	Grassy, sweet, special	Use to garnish salads, desserts or cakes

BY A STREAM

Watercress	Burst of citrus, zingy	Wild Watercress and Almond Soup (page 26)
Wild sorrel	Peppery, strong, stalky	Chorizo, Labneh and Crispbread (page 22)

IN THE MEADOWS

Young dandelion	Bold, slightly bitter	Mackerel, Peach and Dandelion Salad (page 88)
St George's mushrooms	Buttery, orangey	The Mushroom Forager's Ragù with Celeriac Purée (page 136)
Morels	Rich, meaty strength	Serve with red meat, such as beef fillet

BY THE SEA

Sea spinach	Hardy, wild strength	Pollock Soufflé with Cockles and Sea Rosemary (page 142)
Sea lettuce	Slimy, chewy, salty	Use in salads, soups or dry into crisps
Mussels, cockles and whelks	Fresh, salty	Mussel and Nettle Soup (page 34)
Alexander	Lemony, perfumed, celery-ish	Kohlrabi, Alexander and Rock Samphire Salad (pages 84-85)

SPRING MOUTHFULS

SWEET POTATO ROSTI WITH SMOKED BACON

The Shed is a bit too bohemian and rustic to use a word like 'canapé' so we coined our own term 'mouthful' to describe a healthy-sized single bite which will always be an explosion of taste and texture in your mouth. For each season we have compiled a selection of these dishes which are presented as the lead in to a well-balanced Shed meal.

Rösti makes for a great moreish mouthful. This recipe uses a mixture of sweet and ordinary potatoes but you could use just one or the other. Perfect for pre-dinner but you might also make them for brunch, as a snack, or for a midnight feast. Makes 24 mouthfuls

2 medium sweet potatoes, peeled
2 medium waxy potatoes (such as Maris Piper or Désirée), peeled
200g smoked bacon, finely diced
salt and freshly ground black pepper
80g unsalted butter

Grate the potatoes by hand on a box grater and drain well on a thick tea-towel to absorb as much moisture as possible.

Put a frying pan over a moderate heat and dry-fry the bacon until crisp, approx. 5 minutes. Combine the bacon with the grated potato in a large mixing bowl and season well with salt and pepper.

Heat some of the butter in a large frying pan over a moderate heat. Shape the potato mixture into approx. 24 little balls, about the size of a ping-pong ball, and fry them in batches in the hot butter until golden on all sides, approx. 2–3 minutes. Remove from the pan and drain on kitchen paper while you fry the rest in the remaining butter.

Serve immediately or reheat when required in a moderate oven (180°C/gas mark 4) for approx. 5 minutes. They are a delicious mouthful just as they are, or you can serve them with a little soured cream dip alongside.

1.

2.

3.

4.

5.

6.

ROSEMARY CHEESE SCONES

Our grandmother, Margaret Lawson, was apparently a great scone-maker. She taught my mum and then Mum taught me. A freshly baked homemade savoury scone is a wonderful thing that can lift a salad or soup course to another level. As with a lot of our baking and pastry advice, the important thing with scone-making is a light touch so that you do not overwork the dough and make it chewy. Makes a baker's dozen - 12 to serve, plus a sneaky one for the cook

225g plain flour, plus extra
 for dusting
2 teaspoons baking powder
1 teaspoon salt
55g unsalted butter, chilled
150g Cheddar cheese, grated
150ml whole milk, plus extra
 for brushing
1 sprig of rosemary, leaves
 removed and finely chopped

Preheat the oven to 190°C/gas mark 5 and line a baking tray with baking parchment.

Sift the flour, baking powder and salt into a mixing bowl. Cut the butter into small knobs, add it to the flour and rub it in with your fingertips until the mixture resembles breadcrumbs. Mix in the grated cheese.

Using a small palette knife, make a well in the centre of the mixture and pour in the milk. 'Chop' the mixture using a knife to blend it until it comes together in a ball. Turn the dough out onto a floured surface, knead lightly, and then roll it out to a thickness of 3cm. Then stamp out 6cm rounds using a pastry cutter.

Place the scones slightly apart from one another on the lined baking tray, brush the tops with a dash of milk and sprinkle over some chopped rosemary. Bake for 12–15 minutes until risen and golden.

Serve just as they are or reheat in a moderate oven (180°C/gas mark 4) for 5 minutes.

CHORIZO, LABNEH & CRISPBREAD

This recipe brings together three separate elements as a Shed mouthful, but the different components are very versatile and can be adapted for many different recipes. If you can get hold of some sausage skins, the chorizo (paprika-flavoured sausagemeat) makes a delicious spicy filling, served up with salad and roasted vegetables. At The Shed we air-dry these to make salamis.

Labneh is made from full-fat yogurt, which has been strained to remove the whey. In this recipe we flavour it with wild sorrel to complement the chorizo, but you could flavour it with a whole variety of spices such as sumac or fennel seed. Alternatively, mix it with dried fruits such as chopped apricots, cranberries or figs, and sweeten it with honey or sugar to serve as a dessert.

One of the huge number of benefits of setting up and maintaining your own sourdough starter (see page 62) is making your own crispbread. Here, the sourdough starter is quite simply fried off in a pan to form large pancakes. These make great bases for all sorts of dips as well as well as adding crunchy texture to dishes such as a feta, tomato and Cos lettuce salad. Makes 24 mouthfuls

FOR THE CHORIZO
400g minced pork
1 heaped tablespoon sweet paprika
1 tablespoon smoked paprika
1 teaspoon chilli flakes
2 garlic cloves, finely diced
1 heaped teaspoon salt (or more precisely 2 per cent salt of the weight of the minced pork)
1 tablespoon fennel seeds, toasted
25ml red wine

FOR THE LABNEH
300g full-fat plain yogurt
30g wild sorrel, washed and finely shredded
1 teaspoon freshly ground black pepper

FOR THE CRISPBREAD
30ml rapeseed oil
200ml sourdough starter (see page 62)

To prepare the chorizo, put all the ingredients in a large bowl and mix well using a wooden spoon. Transfer the mixture into a 1-litre plastic container, packing it down tightly, and cover with a lid. Transfer to the fridge to marinate for at least 24 hours.

Meanwhile, prepare the labneh. Put the yogurt, sorrel and black pepper in a mixing bowl and mix well with a wooden spoon. Cut out a 30cm square of cheesecloth or muslin and put it in a colander. Set the colander over a bowl and spoon the yogurt mixture into the centre of the cloth. Gather up the edges and tie in a tight bundle. Put a saucer on top of the bundle to weigh it down and transfer to the fridge for 24 hours to allow all the whey to drain out and collect in the bowl underneath.

To make the crispbread, use a piece of kitchen paper to lightly oil a large, heavy-based, non-stick frying pan. Put it over a moderate heat and add a ladleful of the sourdough starter. Tilt the pan so the batter spreads out in a thin layer, rather like a pancake, and cook for approx. 1 minute until crisp. Flip the crispbread over and cook briefly on the other side until crisp. Remove the crispbread from the pan and set aside on a plate while you cook the rest.

To cook the chorizo mixture, heat 1 tablespoon of rapeseed oil in a medium, heavy-based saucepan over a moderate heat. Add the chorizo mixture and cook for 10 minutes, stirring to ensure it does not catch on the bottom of the pan.

Meanwhile, remove the labneh from the fridge and turn it out of its muslin into a serving dish.

To serve, spoon the steaming chorizo onto a serving dish and accompany with the labneh and the pile of crispbreads to scoop with and share.

POTTED BROWN SHRIMP ON MELBA TOAST

Such a delicious traditional mouthful, I don't know why potted shrimp has gone out of fashion. Small cool-water brown shrimps are one of our great shellfish delicacies. Like so many of our coastal specialities, the continent gets the majority but we should celebrate and use them during the summer season. Our recipe also uses anchovy, which adds to the savoury tang.

James Bond used to order Potted Shrimps with his Bollinger champagne and that is enough for us Gladwin boys to think of it as a must-have on The Shed menu.

Makes 20 mouthfuls

120g unsalted butter
1 teaspoon lemon juice
1 bay leaf
pinch of cayenne pepper
pinch of grated nutmeg
200g brown shrimps
2 salted anchovy fillets, finely chopped
2 teaspoons finely chopped chives

FOR THE MELBA TOAST
6 slices of white or brown bread

Melt the butter in a small saucepan over a low heat. Add the lemon juice, bay leaf, cayenne and nutmeg and simmer gently for 5 minutes. Add the brown shrimps and anchovies and cook for a further 4 minutes. Remove the pan from the heat and stir in the chopped chives. Discard the bay leaf.

Spoon the shrimps into a 5cm deep china dish and pour over the melted butter from the pan to seal the top. Transfer the potted shrimps to the fridge to set for a minimum of 2 hours. (If necessary, the potted shrimps can be stored in the fridge for up to 5 days.)

There is something very satisfying about making melba toast. Simply toast the bread under the grill on both sides. Then remove the crusts and, using a sharp, thin-bladed knife, slice the toast laterally into two pieces. (This is surprisingly easy.) Then grill the uncooked sides and the melba will crisp and curl.

Remove the potted shrimps from the fridge and allow them to come up to room temperature for 30 minutes before serving. To serve, spoon a generous dollop of potted shrimp onto small triangles of melba toast. Sublime, Mr Bond…

SEA TROUT TARTARE WITH PICKLED CUCUMBER

These days tartare basically means chopped and raw, although the original dish was raw steak served with a tartare sauce. The great thing about raw is that you are letting the ingredients speak for themselves and enjoying the full natural flavour without any interference. Sea trout is a lovely fish and here we serve it very simply, presented on a base of lightly pickled cucumber. Makes 20 mouthfuls

240g skinless sea trout fillet
1 cucumber, washed
1 tablespoon white wine vinegar
1 tablespoon freshly squeezed orange juice (optional)
1 tablespoon water
1 teaspoon caster sugar
3 drops Tabasco sauce
pinch of salt
a few wild chervil leaves, to garnish

For best results dice, rather than mince, the sea trout. The easiest way to do this is to put the fish on a chopping board and slice it one way, then the other, repeatedly, so you get really tiny squares.

Slice the cucumber into 5mm discs and lay them out in a single layer on a large serving tray. Mix the vinegar, orange juice (if using), water, sugar, Tabasco and salt together in a cup and drip a few drops onto each slice of cucumber.

To serve, spoon a good mound of the chopped fish on top of each piece of cucumber and finish with some wild chervil leaves.

MUM'S NUTBOURNE FETA & SPINACH PARCELS

Our mum, Bridget, decided quite out of the blue one day that we should be making our own cheeses. She went on a cheesemaking course, bought all sorts of paraphernalia and overnight our kitchen at Nutbourne was converted into a smelly cheesemaking factory. I won't go into how the cheese is made here because it is a very precise and refined art requiring raw milk straight from the cow, bacteria culture, rennet and a lot of dedication and patience. The results, however, are terrific and now we are able to offer homemade feta, Sussex Camembert and ricotta. Serves 6 as a starter (Makes 12 parcels)

30g unsalted butter
2 small onions, thinly sliced
300g spinach, washed, picked and
    roughly chopped
200g feta cheese
2 tablespoons finely chopped
    fresh coriander stalks
2 tablespoons toasted sunflower
    seeds
salt and freshly ground black
    pepper
1/2 teaspoon ground nutmeg
juice of 1/2 lemon
220g filo pastry
Wild Garlic Yogurt (see
    page 67), to serve

Preheat the oven to 200°C/gas mark 6 and line a baking tray with baking parchment.

Melt 20g of the butter in a small saucepan over a moderate heat, add the onions and cook until soft and caramelised, approx. 15 minutes.

Meanwhile, wilt the spinach in a dry pan over a low heat for 2–3 minutes. Drain well through a sieve, squeezing out all the water.

Crumble the feta into a bowl and mix in the cooked onion, wilted spinach, coriander stalks and sunflower seeds. Season to taste with salt, pepper, nutmeg and lemon juice.

Melt the remaining butter in a small saucepan and set aside. Lay out three sheets of filo pastry and cut them into six 12cm squares. To assemble the parcels, arrange three squares of filo pastry on top of one another at different angles to form a star. Dab a little water between the layers of pastry to stick them together. Put a dessertspoon of the feta mixture into the centre of each pastry star, gather up the edges and squeeze the top to form a small money bag shape. Again dab with a little water to help the layers of pastry stick together.

Transfer the parcels to the baking tray and brush them all over with the melted butter. Bake for 8–10 minutes until golden brown.

Serve warm with Wild Garlic Yogurt.

1.

2.

3.

4.

5.

6.

WILD WATERCRESS & ALMOND SOUP

When we were three small boys growing up in Nutbourne, one of the great adventures was to take our beaten up old rowing boat on a voyage of discovery along the marshy course of the river Nut. Hence the name of our village Nutbourne. What made this especially intrepid was that part of the stream strayed over the boundary into the gruff Farmer Lawson's property next door. I remember when, as brave sailors together with our friend, Christopher White, with far too many of us in the boat, we had to punt with a broken oar, pull from the reeds and in the end simply get out to wade and push our craft over the shallow bits. Little did we know then that we were journeying along the old Nutbourne wild watercress beds.

Watercress grows naturally along shallow streams and the edges of small rivers. It is a lovely thing to discover and forage - full of vitamins and nourishment - but unfortunately it can carry a nasty disease called liver fluke. If you are going to eat it raw I recommend soaking it in a solution of Milton (or other sterilising solution) before you do so. However, cooking it kills all the bugs and it makes for a wonderful soup. Serves 6

15g unsalted butter

1 medium onion, chopped

2 large bunches of watercress, washed and picked - 1 bunch roughly chopped and 1 bunch puréed in a blender

200g 'old' potatoes, peeled and diced

1 litre hot vegetable stock

salt and freshly ground black pepper

juice of 1 lemon

100g ground almonds

100ml double cream

In a large saucepan, melt the butter over a moderate heat. Add the onion, the bunch of chopped watercress and the potatoes and cook for 2 minutes, stirring occasionally.

Pour in the stock, season well with salt and pepper and bring to the boil. Reduce the heat and simmer for 25 minutes, or until the potatoes are cooked. Stir in the lemon juice and ground almonds.

Liquidise the soup in a food processor or using a hand-held immersion blender and set aside until ready to serve.

To serve, reheat the soup over a gentle heat, stirring occasionally. Add the cream and the puréed watercress at the last moment and stir to combine.

ASPARAGUS & QUAIL EGG SALAD

Asparagus has been a delicacy for thousands of years - originally, like all primary ingredients it started off as a wild seashore plant and then, in Roman times, it was bred into a cultivated vegetable product. You can see why it is considered to be so special. Suddenly in the middle of spring, it sprouts out of the ground as a single, wholly edible spear. It is tender and delicious so that you can eat it raw, lightly boiled, steamed or chargrilled. It is one of the greatest seasonal treats.

There used to be a lot of asparagus farming around us in Sussex and as children we would go with Mum to 'pick your own'. The problem was that if it had been raining, the asparagus fields became quite muddy and I think the mud and a chance to throw some at my brothers tended to take over. Once back home (and washed) the asparagus would be served with melted butter, salt and pepper and the best bit was that we were allowed to eat with our fingers. Serves 6 as a starter or more to share

```
sea salt and freshly ground
   black pepper 1kg green
asparagus spears,
   trimmed
12 quail eggs
1 bunch of breakfast radishes,
   washed and trimmed
50ml rapeseed oil
juice of 1 lemon
```

If the asparagus is young and fresh, it should not need peeling. If you do need to peel it, use a wide-mouthed peeler and cut away from the tip, removing the outside of the lower half only.

Put a large pan of lightly salted water over a moderate heat and bring to the boil. Add the asparagus and boil for 4–5 minutes. Remove the asparagus with a slotted spoon and immediately dunk them in cold water to cool down and retain the green colour.

Carefully lower the quail eggs into the same water and cook for precisely 2½ minutes. Plunge into cold water immediately and delicately peel them under cold running water while they are still warm.

Arrange the asparagus on a serving platter. Halve the quail eggs and radishes and dot them among the spears. Drizzle with the rapeseed oil and lemon juice and season with salt and pepper.

RHUBARB & WHITE SESAME FOCACCIA

Focaccia is a great bread to develop your baking skills and hugely enjoyable to make. As with all bread-making, the very first advice I can offer is to handle your dough with gentleness and show it some love. Focaccia is an enriched oily bread that is proved in the tin it's baked in. Traditionally it has lots of garlic, rosemary and olive oil. In this recipe I mix it up a little and use the lovely tartness of rhubarb, the crunch of sesame and linseed oil to enrich the bread. Served warm from the oven with a pâté or cured meats, it is a taste sensation. Serves 8-12

50ml linseed oil or extra virgin olive oil, plus extra for greasing
500g strong bread flour, plus extra for dusting
2 teaspoons salt
1 teaspoon fast-action dried yeast
350ml warm water
150g rhubarb, cut into 2cm lengths
50g caster sugar
50g white sesame seeds
100g honey

(You will need a 20 x 30cm baking tray)

Grease the baking tray lightly with oil. Sift the flour and salt into a large mixing bowl. In a separate small bowl, mix the yeast with 30ml of the warm water. Add the yeast to the flour and begin to work the mixture with your hands. Add half the oil and slowly incorporate the remaining water, mixing to a pliable dough.

Turn out the dough onto a floured work surface and knead it vigorously for 5–10 minutes to release the gluten in the flour and create elasticity. Once the dough is smooth, roll it out to a rectangle the same size as the prepared baking tray. Lift the dough onto the tray and use your fingertips to gently push it into the corners. Brush the surface with the remaining oil. Set aside to prove at room temperature for 30 minutes

After the first prove, push your fingers into the dough at 5cm intervals. This creates little pockets of air and oil within the loaf. Set aside to prove for a further hour.

Meanwhile, put the rhubarb in a bowl, sprinkle over the sugar and set aside to macerate at room temperature while the dough is proving.

After the second proving, poke the pieces of rhubarb into the dough at regular intervals, sprinkle the surface evenly with sesame seeds and set aside for a further 15 minutes.

Preheat the oven to 190°C/gas mark 5.

Bake for 25 minutes until golden on top. Turn out onto a wire rack to cool before glazing with the honey. Tear the bread into chunks and serve with Potted Goose (see page 155) or coppa.

PURPLE SPROUTING BROCCOLI WITH PANCETTA

500g purple sprouting broccoli
12 thin slices of pancetta
salt and freshly ground black
    pepper
a little rapeseed oil
Tarragon Mayonnaise (see
    page 66) or Béarnaise Sauce
    (see page 116), to serve

This is a lovely vegetable to grow yourself because it's particularly easy to grow, abundant and so versatile as an ingredient. Failing that, it is usually available in spring to buy from local, organic farm shops and markets. It is full of nutrients, including vitamins and protein, and packed with flavour, so can be used in all sorts of recipes including fish pies, risottos and salads. At The Shed I wrap it in our own cured pancetta bacon to turn it into an interesting brunch-style sharing dish.

Serves 6 as a sharing dish

Cut the broccoli carefully into individual stems, complete with florets and leaves. (Split any large stem sections into two lengthways.)

Wrap a spiral of pancetta around each stem of broccoli and tuck the top into the floret. Season with salt and pepper. Brush with a little rapeseed oil.

Heat a griddle pan over a moderate heat until very hot. Add the wrapped broccoli to the pan and cook for 6–8 minutes, turning it several times until the pancetta is evenly cooked and crisp. During this time, the broccoli will have cooked and softened inside the pancetta.

Serve immediately with Tarragon Mayonnaise or Béarnaise Sauce.

MUSSEL & NETTLE SOUP

MUSSEL & NETTLE SOUP

The perfect field and coast combo - and both are free for the intrepid forager. Gathering mussels off a rocky coastline is something everyone should do at least once in their life. Richard is a great seaside forager, the worse the weather and the steeper the cliff or rocks to climb down, the happier he is with his haul. Picking stinging nettles is rather less adventurous, but onerous in a different way. Use gloves to protect your hands when picking and only select the delicate young tops, which have the best sweet and fragrant flavour and are full of iron and nutrition. They used to be eaten for health reasons, to ease joint pain, reduce cholesterol and apparently even fight hair loss. The combination of these two ingredients makes a great wholesome soup with the satisfaction of very little expense. Serves 6

1kg mussels, shell on
30ml rapeseed oil
1 large onion, finely chopped
2 garlic cloves, thinly sliced
125ml dry white wine
100ml water
sea salt and freshly ground
   black pepper
8-10 nettle tops
100ml full-fat natural yogurt
homemade sourdough bread
   (see pages 62-63), to serve

Give the mussels a good wash in a sink of cold water, discarding any that are broken or do not close when tapped. Pull off any beards and scrape off any barnacles.

Heat the oil in a large, heavy-based saucepan over a moderate heat. Fry off the onion and garlic until lightly coloured, approx. 2 minutes. Add the mussels and white wine. Put a lid on the pan and simmer for approx. 4 minutes until all the mussels have opened, giving the pan an occasional shake. Using a slotted spoon, scoop out the mussels onto a tray, reserving the cooking liquor in the pan.

Open the mussels over the tray. Save all the juice and the meat, but discard the shells. (Sprinkle the shells on your garden – they are good for your plants.)

Return the pan to a moderate heat, add the water and bring to the boil. Season well with salt and pepper, stir in the nettles and simmer for 4 minutes. Remove the pan from the heat and blitz the soup with a hand-held immersion blender. Check the seasoning.

To finish, stir in the yogurt, mussels and the reserved cooking juices from the tray and reheat over a gentle heat. Accompany with some freshly baked sourdough bread.

RED GURNARD FILLETS
WITH RADISHES & WILD LEEK BUTTER

Red gurnard used to be rejected from fishermen's catches because of its ugly appearance and off-putting bright colours, but now it has become rather fashionable as a full-flavoured, dense-fleshed sustainable fish. If you can't find gurnard, whiting would be a good alternative. Red gurnard does need careful filleting and then pin-boning afterwards with a pair of tweezers. Ask your fishmonger to cut the fillets for you, but when you lay them out in your kitchen feel along the middle for a sharp row of tiny bones. These need pulling out one by one before cooking. This recipe pairs red gurnard with some lovely spring radishes and foraged wild leeks, also known as three-cornered leeks. In early spring wild leeks are easy to find along the side of leafy pathways - they look like little spring onions with pretty white flowers. Pull them gently from the ground to ensure you gather the bulb as well.

Serves 4 as a starter

        salt and freshly ground black pepper
        1 bunch of radishes, trimmed and halved
        12 wild leeks (or spring onions if you can't find them),
            tops shredded and bulbs trimmed to approx. 10cm
        100ml crème fraîche
        1 tablespoon white wine vinegar
        zest and juice of 1/2 lemon
        1 teaspoon Tabasco sauce
        1 teaspoon caster sugar
        100g unsalted butter
        1-2 tablespoons rapeseed oil
        2 x 700g red gurnards, filleted and pin-boned

Put a small pan of lightly salted water over a moderate heat and bring to the boil. Put the radishes and trimmed wild leek bulbs (or spring onions) in the water and blanch briefly for a few seconds; drain and refresh under cold running water.

Warm the crème fraîche, vinegar and lemon zest and juice in a small pan over a low heat. Add the shredded wild leek tops and season with the Tabasco, salt and sugar. Remove the pan from the heat just before the sauce comes to the boil and stir in the butter. Keep warm, ready to serve with the fish.

Heat the oil in a heavy-based frying pan over a high heat. Put the gurnard fillets skin-side down into the hot oil and cook for 3 minutes without disturbing them, so the skin becomes crisp. Flick the fillets over and cook for 1 minute on the other side. Carefully lift the fish out of the pan, season with salt and pepper and set aside on a plate while you finish the dish.

Return the frying pan to the heat, drop in the blanched leeks and radishes and heat through for 1 minute.

To serve, arrange a bed of vegetables on each serving plate, top with a gurnard fillet and spoon over the butter sauce.

1.

2.

3.

FENNEL-CURED POLLOCK WITH PICKLED CUCUMBER

From the same family as cod and haddock, pollock is a sustainable fish (for the time being), especially when caught by small, independent, inshore fishermen. We used to buy it down on the quayside in Lyme Regis when I was working at River Cottage with Gill Meller and Hugh Fearnley-Whittingstall. We would then use pollock as part of the Fish Skills masterclasses to teach the values of sustainable, locally caught products.

Curing the fish is a process that draws out moisture from the flesh, leaving it firmer, full of flavour and with a much longer shelf life. In this recipe I cure the pollock with fennel seeds and serve it with a crunchy fennel bulb salad for a full-on aniseedy tang that beautifully complements the delicate flavour and texture of the pollock. Serves 6 as a starter

60g fennel seeds
75g salt
150g caster sugar
400g pollock fillet, skin on

FOR THE PICKLED CUCUMBER
50ml white wine vinegar
50ml water
100g caster sugar
¹/₂ teaspoon rock salt
1 teaspoon pink or black
   peppercorns
2 large sprigs of fresh dill,
   chopped
1 garlic clove, crushed
1 fennel bulb, cored and very
   finely sliced
¹/₂ cucumber, cut lengthways
   into long ribbons using a
   wide-mouthed peeler
a few wild chervil leaves,
   to garnish

Mix the fennel seeds, salt and sugar together in a bowl. Put the pollock on a large piece of foil and spread the flavoured salt mixture all over the flesh in an even layer. Wrap the fish up tightly and transfer it to the fridge to cure for 24 hours.

Check your cure has taken by sampling a little slice of fish off the tail end – it should be opaque and firm. If it is ready, wash off the cure, pat the fish dry on kitchen paper and set aside until ready to carve. If the cure hasn't completely taken, rework the dry mix onto the flesh and put back for another couple of hours or so.

To prepare the vegetable pickling liquor, put the vinegar, water and sugar in a small saucepan over a moderate heat and bring to the boil, stirring to dissolve the sugar. Add the salt, pink or black peppercorns, dill and garlic.

Drop the fennel slices into the boiling liquid and blanch for 3 minutes. Remove the pan from the heat and set aside to cool slightly before stirring in the strips of cucumber. Set aside for a further hour to allow the vegetables to pickle.

Carefully pin-bone the pollock using a pair of tweezers. This should be much easier now the fish is cured. Once you are sure you have removed all the bones, carve the fish crossways into even 3cm slices, discarding the skin.

To serve, arrange the cured fish slices on serving plates, spoon a pile of the pickled fennel and cucumber into the centre, spoon over some of the pickling liquor and garnish with a few wild chervil leaves.

DEVILLED CRAB CAKES

These are our dad's favourite, so we had to include them in this book. There are two key elements to a good crab cake: one, not to be too stingy with the crabmeat - it is too easy to end up with a potato cake - and two, to balance the seasoning carefully. Crab benefits from a bit of spice but not so much that you drown its own flavour.

We source our crab from the Dorset coast but there are many good suppliers around the British Isles and indeed many other parts of the world.

Serves 6 (Makes 6 or 12 as a main course or 20 small mouthfuls)

250g cooked brown and white
    crabmeat
250g mashed potato
3 spring onions, finely chopped
1 teaspoon Worcestershire sauce
1 teaspoon English mustard
1 teaspoon ground ginger
pinch or two of cayenne
    pepper
zest and juice of 1 lemon
salt
50g unsalted butter
seasoned plain flour, to coat
1 large egg, beaten
100g fresh white breadcrumbs
50ml rapeseed oil
green salad and Wild Garlic
    Yogurt (see page 67),
    to serve

In a large mixing bowl, combine the crabmeat, mashed potato, spring onions, Worcestershire sauce, mustard, ginger, cayenne pepper, lemon zest and juice and a couple of pinches of salt.

Melt the butter in a small saucepan over a low heat and pour it over the crab mixture. Gently mix everything together with a wooden spoon and taste to check the seasoning.

Mould the crab mixture by hand into even-sized cakes (you can choose the size from 6 large cakes, 12 medium-sized or approx. 20 little ones to serve as mouthfuls).

Put the flour, beaten egg and breadcrumbs in 3 separate bowls ready for coating the crab cakes. First dip the cakes into the flour, then into the egg and finally into the breadcrumbs, making sure they are evenly coated on both sides. Transfer the cakes to a plate, cover with clingfilm and set aside in the fridge to firm up until you are ready to cook them.

Heat the oil in a heavy-based frying pan over a moderate heat. Fry the cakes evenly on both sides for approx. 5 minutes for the small ones and a bit longer (approx. 8 minutes) for the large ones, until golden brown. Serve with a crisp green salad and a blob of Wild Garlic Yogurt.

SMOKED TROUT & HORSERADISH MOUSSE

Our ethos at The Shed is that food does not have to be complex or sophisticated to be good. On the contrary, some of the simplest things to make and present can be the most popular. The test is: would Gregory make it for himself at the farm? If there are more than three base ingredients and more than two steps to the recipe, he probably wouldn't bother.

We do hot smoke our own trout, but for this quick mousse recipe we are going to cheat a bit and use a couple of ready-smoked trout fillets.

Serves 6 as a sharing starter

400g skinless smoked trout
   fillets
60ml mayonnaise
2 teaspoons freshly grated
   horseradish
2 teaspoons finely chopped
   chives
Juice of 1 lemon
1 teaspoon freshly ground black
   pepper
60ml double cream
a few chive flowers, to garnish
wholemeal toast or crackers,
   or sourdough crispbread (see
   page 22), to serve

Break the trout into flakes and put it in a mixing bowl with the mayonnaise, horseradish, chives, lemon juice and black pepper. Using a wooden spoon, carefully mix everything together.

In a separate bowl, lightly whip the double cream to a thick but still flowing consistency. Fold the cream into the fish mixture.

Transfer the fish mousse to a serving dish and garnish with chive flowers. Cover with clingfilm and chill in the fridge until ready to serve.

Serve the trout mousse with wholemeal toast, crackers or sourdough crispbread.

VENISON CARPACCIO WITH FENNEL, ORANGE & TARRAGON SALAD

A key part of what we do at The Shed is finding the best possible use for every single part of an animal. When one of your brothers is a farmer and another writes the cheques, as a cook, you make sure you are achieving the best possible value! But more importantly, for me, there is something incredibly satisfying about not wasting any part of an animal and working out the right recipe and dish for each bit of it.

For many, the fillet of an animal is the most prized cut (and certainly the most expensive if you buy it on its own). Here it is served very sparingly as wafer-thin carpaccio, accompanied by a tangy, crunchy salad.

Serves 6 as a starter or more for sharing

400g venison fillet, fully trimmed
1 tablespoon sweet paprika
1/2 teaspoon coarsely ground black pepper
1 large fennel bulb, cored and finely shredded
2 oranges, peel and pith removed, cut into segments
1 teaspoon mustard seeds
1 teaspoon finely chopped fresh tarragon
sea salt and freshly ground black pepper
a drizzle of rapeseed oil

Heat a cast-iron griddle pan or non-stick frying pan over a high heat. Roll the venison fillet in the paprika and black pepper, and then quickly sear it on the hot griddle for just a few seconds on each side; the idea is to create a seasoned crisp edge, not to cook it. Immediately remove the meat from the heat and set aside on a plate to cool.

Unroll a large sheet of clingfilm onto your work surface and put the venison in the centre. Roll up the venison very tightly in lots of layers of clingfilm to form a perfect round log. Cut the clingfilm and twist each end to further seal and shape the meat. Transfer the rolled meat to the freezer for at least 2 hours until it begins to freeze.

Meanwhile, prepare the salad garnish. Toss the fennel, orange segments, mustard seeds and tarragon together in a bowl and season with salt and pepper.

Now for the skilled part: removing the semi-frozen venison fillet from the clingfilm. (If you have allowed it to freeze fully, make sure you defrost it for an hour before attempting to unravel it and slice while still semi-frozen.)

Using a very sharp knife, slice the semi-frozen meat into wafer-thin slices and lay them out on individual plates. They will defrost in moments. Arrange a little 'bonfire' pile of fennel salad in the centre of each plate and drizzle with rapeseed oil to finish.

WOOD PIGEON SALTIMBOCCA

Saltimbocca is a traditional Italian recipe in which cooked meat is wrapped with sage and prosciutto. However, I think we can get away with including it in our cookbook because we shoot our own pigeons in Sussex (to stop them nicking the grapes in the vineyard), cure our own ham and grow our own sage.

Traditional dishes such as this have survived the centuries for good reason - the simple idea of lightly sautéing tender veal (or in our case pigeon), infusing it with sage and encasing the whole thing in pork to encapsulate all the flavours must have been someone's moment of brilliance. We serve it very simply as a sharing plate with some tender salad leaves and the cooking juices. This recipe may be for sharing but don't be surprised if someone wants one all to themselves. Serves 2 as a starter or 6 as a sharing plate

2 wood pigeon breasts
2 sage leaves
2 thin slices of lemon
2 long slices of cured ham (such as Cumbrian or Parma ham)
salt and freshly ground black pepper
40g unsalted butter
a handful of mixed salad leaves
20ml red wine
1 teaspoon balsamic vinegar

Put the pigeon breasts on a chopping board and lay a sage leaf and a slice of lemon on top of each one. Wrap a slice of ham around each pigeon breast to form a parcel and season all over with salt and pepper.

Heat a heavy-based frying pan over a moderate heat, melt the butter and fry the pigeon breasts for 2–3 minutes on each side. Meanwhile, scatter some colourful salad leaves over a large platter ready for serving. Transfer the breasts to a carving board, slice each one into three and arrange on the bed of salad leaves.

Return the frying pan to a high heat and add the red wine and balsamic vinegar. Let it sizzle and deglaze (that's a cheffy term that means to capture the flavours and juices), then pour over the pigeon and serve.

WILD RABBIT & CABBAGE BURGERS

Rabbit is such a great meat - lean, flavoursome
and low in cholesterol; I don't know why it is so
underused and underrated. We have to keep the rabbit
population down at the vineyard or they chew the
bark off the young vines, so there is often an ample
supply. When I came up with this unusual burger
recipe we were cutting a huge fallen oak tree into
a bench to face the view at the top of the farm.
I had already prepared some slow-braised rabbit meat
but then I had the idea of shaping it into patties,
wrapping them in cabbage leaves and cooking them over
a smoky barbecue. You will need caul fat to wrap the
burgers in, which protects, seals and moistens the
meat. Caul fat, also known as crépine, is the very
thin layer of fat that separates a pig's stomach and
diaphragm - it can be bought from any traditional
butcher. Serves 6

1kg rabbit, skinned and jointed
1 medium onion, chopped
1 medium carrot, sliced
1 lemon, halved
2 bay leaves
1 teaspoon black peppercorns
salt
100ml water
1 Savoy cabbage, 6 good leaves
  peeled off
200g caul fat, cut into 6
pieces
6 ciabatta rolls, to serve
Wild Garlic Yogurt (see
  page 67), to serve

Preheat the oven to 160°C/gas mark 3.

Put the rabbit pieces in an ovenproof
casserole along with the onion, carrot,
lemon and bay leaves. Sprinkle in the
peppercorns and salt. Add the water, cover
with a tight-fitting lid, and put the casserole
dish over a moderate heat to bring the
liquid to the boil. Then transfer to the oven
and braise for 1 hour.

Meanwhile, blanch the Savoy cabbage leaves
in boiling water for 2 minutes; drain under
cold running water and set aside to cool.

Remove the braised rabbit from the oven
and allow it to cool slightly before picking
off the meat, discarding any sinew or bones.
Put the meat in a mixing bowl with the
onion and carrot and moisten with some of the cooking juices.

Divide the meat mixture into six portions and squeeze into
even-sized patties. Then wrap each one in a cabbage leaf
followed by a piece of caul fat.

Light the barbecue or preheat a griddle pan until smoking
hot. Grill the rabbit burgers on the barbecue or griddle for
3 minutes on each side. Meanwhile, lightly toast the rolls.

Serve the burgers inside the rolls with a generous dollop of
Wild Garlic Yogurt.

SHED SAUSAGE ROLL

A lot of people in the City take manic exercise in order to lose weight. You see them running around West London of an evening - good luck to them I say, because the tendency is to get so worn out that they then go and eat some hugely fattening treat that they think they deserve and then their efforts are wasted. Shed Sausage Roll is the perfect replacement and you don't even have to put your jogging kit on! Making rough puff pastry is great physical exercise and at the end of it you will have some simply wonderful freshly baked sausage rolls to gorge on - what could be better? Serves 8-10 as a snack

FOR THE ROUGH PUFF PASTRY
250g strong flour, plus extra
  for dusting
1/2 teaspoon salt
200g unsalted butter, at room
  temperature, cut into small
  cubes
140ml water

FOR THE SAUSAGE FILLING
400g good-quality minced pork
80g yellow sultanas
1 tablespoon finely shredded
  fresh sage
salt and coarsely ground black
  pepper
1 beaten egg, to glaze
1 teaspoon sesame seeds,
  to garnish
Romesco Sauce (see page 169),
  to serve

Sift the flour and salt into a large mixing bowl and add the butter. Rub the mixture together with your fingertips – making sure that you don't overwork it – until it resembles breadcrumbs. Make a well in the centre, pour in the water and work it together to form a rough, mottled dough.

Turn the dough out onto a floured surface and roll it into an even rectangle, approx. 40 x 20cm. Turn the pastry over so the flour is on both sides and fold into three, as you would fold a business letter. Wrap the pastry in clingfilm and transfer it to the fridge to chill for 30 minutes.

Put the chilled pastry on a floured surface and roll it out again into a 40 x 20cm rectangle. Fold the rectangle into three again. Flip the pastry over, turn through 90 degrees and roll it out again, sprinkling with a little extra flour. Fold, turn, roll again, and keep repeating until you are exhausted, approx. 7 times. This process disperses the butter and builds up layers in the pastry that will expand and puff up during cooking. Wrap the folded pastry in clingfilm and transfer it to the fridge for at least 20 minutes or until you are ready to use it.

Meanwhile, prepare the sausage filling by mixing together the minced pork, sultanas and sage with a pinch or two of salt and plenty of freshly ground black pepper.

Remove the pastry from the fridge and roll it out again to form a large rectangle, approx. 30 x 40cm, as thin as you can get it. Arrange the sausage filling across one long side and roll tightly into a cylinder with a small overlap. Slash the top for decoration, paint with the beaten egg and sprinkle evenly with sesame seeds.

Carefully lift the sausage roll onto a baking tray and transfer it to the fridge to firm up while you preheat the oven to 200°C/ gas mark 6.

Remove the chilled sausage roll from the fridge and bake for 25 minutes until golden and crisp.

Cut into 4cm sections and serve while still warm with Romesco sauce.

LAMB SWEETBREADS WITH HERITAGE CARROTS, SWEET ONIONS & MUSTARD SEEDS

Sweetbreads are the glands from a sheep's throat and pancreas, and very delicious they are too. Lots of sweetbread recipes will tell you to blanch them before peeling and sautéing. I tend not to do this because at the time of the year we have them on the menu the new season lambs provide sweetbreads that are small and tender with very little outer casing. Also, the mustard-flour crust allows the sweetbread to properly caramelise so the skin is broken down and just becomes crispy. Serves 6 as a main course or more for sharing

500g lamb sweetbreads
2 tablespoons plain flour
120g unsalted butter
1 curly endive lettuce, leaves torn into pieces
2 colourful heritage carrots, peeled, cut lengthways and then into matchsticks

FOR THE MUSTARD SEED EMULSION
60g black mustard seeds
60g yellow mustard seeds
1 tablespoon Dijon mustard
1 tablespoon honey
1 tablespoon English mustard powder
1 tablespoon sherry vinegar
200ml rapeseed oil
salt and freshly ground black pepper

Begin by making the mustard seed emulsion. Blanch the black and yellow mustard seeds in a small pan of boiling water for 5 minutes. Drain through a sieve, discarding the bitter water. Put the blanched mustard seeds in a bowl with the Dijon mustard, honey and English mustard powder. Add the vinegar and then slowly drizzle in the oil, whisking constantly to form a thick emulsion. Season with salt and pepper.

Heat a large, heavy-based frying pan over a moderate heat. Put the flour in a bowl and season with salt and pepper. Dip the sweetbreads in the seasoned flour, coating them on all sides. Then add the sweetbreads to the pan and cook for 4 minutes, adding a few knobs of butter as they cook and basting the sweetbreads while turning them to create an even colour on all sides.

To serve, arrange the endive leaves and raw carrots on a plate, spoon over the hot sweetbreads, and drizzle with the mustard seed emulsion.

HONEYCOMB DIPPED IN DARK CHOCOLATE WITH TARRAGON & VANILLA MASCARPONE

Those of you who know The Shed restaurant will be aware that our premises are very small. Cosy, intimate, atmospheric maybe but spacious - certainly not! Because of this there is always competition for space. We have one large table at the far end of the dining room, The Butcher's Table as we call it, used for bigger parties in the evenings and as Richard's desk in the day. Then, sometime late morning it becomes the pouring table for our honeycomb making. This provides great entertainment for any early lunch customers and a degree of annoyance to Richard when trays of bubbling sugar, which spread like lava from a volcano, invade his piles of invoices and schedules.

This recipe is exciting, dangerous and skilled, but don't let that put you off - it only takes 10 minutes to have a go and is well worth the effort when your family and friends are wowed by your expertise. You will need a sugar thermometer to make honeycomb. Caramel boils at a higher temperature than water and could spatter onto your skin - so please be careful or wear a thin glove for your first attempt. Serves 10

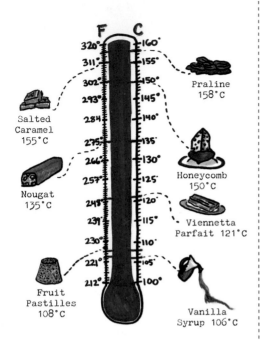

F   C

320° — 160°
311° — 155°
302° — 150°   Praline 158°C
293° — 145°
284° — 140°
275° — 135°
266° — 130°   Honeycomb 150°C
257° — 125°
248° — 120°
239° — 115°   Viennetta Parfait 121°C
230° — 110°
221° — 105°
212° — 100°   Vanilla Syrup 106°C

Salted Caramel 155°C

Nougat 135°C

Fruit Pastilles 108°C

FOR THE HONEYCOMB
rapeseed oil, for greasing
100ml water
250g caster sugar
100g liquid glucose
2 tablespoons honey
1½ teaspoons bicarbonate of soda, sifted

TO SERVE
400g dark chocolate (approx. 70 per cent cocoa solids), broken into small pieces
1 vanilla pod
250g mascarpone
12 tarragon leaves, 6 finely chopped and 6 to garnish

(You will need a 20 x 30cm baking tray)

Line a 20 x 30cm baking tray with baking parchment, sticking it down with a little oil.

Put the water, sugar, glucose and honey in a large, heavy-based saucepan and set over a low heat to dissolve the sugar. Do not stir. Once the sugar has dissolved, increase the heat to moderate/high and, using a sugar thermometer, carefully monitor the temperature as it steadily rises. Have a whisk and the bicarbonate of soda at the ready.

Once the temperature reaches 150°C, remove the pan from the heat, add the bicarbonate of soda and whisk gently for 10 seconds. The mixture will react like a volcano; it will increase in volume by eight times and bubble up in the pan. Wait for 10 seconds and then, once the bubbling is less aggressive, carefully pour the mixture onto the lined baking tray. Set aside to cool for approx. 1 hour to room temperature, and then turn out the honeycomb and cut into exciting shapes and shards.

Prepare a bain-marie by setting a heatproof bowl over a pan of gently simmering water. Put the dark chocolate in the bowl and stir until it has fully melted – it should be shiny and smooth. Dip one half of each honeycomb piece into the melted chocolate, and then transfer it to a clean sheet of greaseproof paper to set.

To make the vanilla mascarpone, scrape out the seeds from the vanilla pod and combine them with the mascarpone and chopped tarragon in a bowl. Serve this as a base for your triumphant dark chocolate honeycomb, garnished with some extra tarragon leaves.

SWEET BASIL PANNA COTTA

We were brought up with the rule that puddings were the treat at the end of a meal, which you only got when you finished your main course. These days it is for some reason fashionable in London restaurants to say 'I couldn't possibly' then skip dessert and just have a coffee. To me they are all missing out on the treat and at The Shed we make a big deal of encouraging our guests to have something sweet at the end of their dinner.

This is a lovely spring or summertime dessert, perfect with rhubarb compote or mixed berries. The pungent, herby flavour of basil beautifully complements the richness of the panna cotta to create an unusual but harmonious eating sensation. Serves 6

2 sheets of bronze leaf
   gelatine
600ml double cream
60g caster sugar
4 large sprigs of basil,
   plus 6 individual leaves
   to garnish

(You will need 6 small glasses
or 100ml dariole moulds)

Put the gelatine in a small dish, cover with cold water and set aside to soak.

Meanwhile, put the cream, sugar and basil sprigs in a small, heavy-based saucepan over a moderate heat. Just before the mixture comes to the boil, remove the pan from the heat and set aside for 30 minutes to allow the flavours to infuse.

Return the pan to the heat, bring the infused cream back up to the boil, and then strain it through a sieve into a clean bowl. Squeeze the basil sprigs with the back of a wooden spoon to extract as much of the flavour as possible before discarding them.

Gently squeeze out any excess water from the gelatine, add to the hot infused cream and stir until fully dissolved. Pour the mixture into individual glasses or dariole moulds and transfer them to the fridge to set for 2–3 hours or preferably overnight.

To serve, turn out of the moulds and garnish with basil leaves. Accompany with some fresh fruit, if you wish.

EVER-SO-EASY TANGY LEMON ICE CREAM

No ice-cream maker, no churning, and totally indulgent and bad for you – just what ice cream should be. This simple tangy ice cream is a great companion for really sticky puddings. We serve it alongside my special treacle sponge, but its moreish character makes it equally good with all sorts of fruits and compotes.

This is a great base recipe and will adapt very well to different ingredients so you can use whatever takes your fancy on the day. Try replacing the lemon with passion fruit or a raspberry purée. Or experiment with reducing the sugar quantity and use fresh mint, lemon verbena or tarragon to make a herby ice cream. Serves 6-8

6 large egg yolks
225g caster sugar
100ml whole milk
150ml double cream
150ml thick natural yogurt
zest and juice of 3 lemons

Using an electric whisk, beat the egg yolks and sugar together in a large mixing bowl until the mixture becomes pale and doubles in volume.

Heat the milk in a small saucepan over a moderate heat. Just before it comes to the boil, pour the milk slowly over the egg mixture, beating constantly. Continue beating for a further 5 minutes.

In a separate bowl, whip the cream until stiff peaks form, and then beat in the yogurt. Fold the whipped cream mixture into the egg mixture along with the lemon juice and zest.

Spoon into a suitable container (this could be a plastic tub or a much more exciting ice-cream mould) and transfer to the freezer to set overnight. The ice cream will be ready to serve the following day or you can store it in a sealed container in the freezer for up to 2 weeks.

RHUBARB & GINGER FOOL
WITH BLOOD ORANGE SALAD

Rhubarb is really a vegetable but from a cook's perspective we treat it as a fruit. In Nutbourne there is always a big patch in the vegetable garden and we need to be quite imaginative in finding different ways to prepare and present it. Crumbles, pies, stewed and jellied, but there is nothing quite as good as a good old-fashioned fool. You can, of course, use almost any fruit for a fool throughout the year, but the classics are rhubarb in spring, gooseberry in summer and plum in autumn. Serves 6

450g rhubarb, chopped into
  3cm lengths
2 knobs of stem ginger in
  syrup, cut into small strips,
  plus extra to garnish
2 tablespoons ginger syrup from
  the jar of stem ginger
2 tablespoons caster sugar
  (optional), to taste
300ml double cream
2 blood oranges, peel and pith
  removed, cut into individual
  segments

FOR THE CUSTARD
600ml whole milk
4 large egg yolks
1 heaped tablespoon cornflour
3 tablespoons caster sugar

First make the custard. Heat the milk in a heavy-based saucepan over a moderate heat and bring it almost up to boil.

In a separate bowl, whisk the egg yolks, cornflour and sugar together to form a smooth paste. Pour this mixture into the hot milk, whisking constantly until the custard thickens. Immediately pour the custard from the pan back into the mixing bowl and set aside to cool, then chill in the fridge.

Put the rhubarb, ginger strips and ginger syrup in a saucepan and simmer over a low heat for 5–10 minutes until the rhubarb is soft. Set aside to cool, then chill in the fridge. Check the rhubarb for tartness – it doesn't need to be sweet, but if it is very tart it might need a little more ginger syrup or sugar to taste.

Whip the double cream to a thick, folding consistency so it heaps on a spoon but is not stiff, and then gently combine it with the chilled rhubarb and custard by spooning the different layers into individual glass dishes. Garnish with a few strips of stem ginger and some segments of blood orange.

APPLE & MARMALADE BAKEWELL TART

Cooking with the seasons is a year-round activity and involves preserving, bottling, pickling and storing the best fruits and vegetables of each time of year for use later on. Once you have a bountiful supply of homemade marmalade made in midwinter (see page 218) there are 101 different uses for it. This delicious Bakewell tart uses orange marmalade and apples that have been stored since last autumn. With the exception of rhubarb, there are no British-grown spring fruits, so now is the perfect time to delve into your hoarded stash of delicacies. The traditional way of storing orchard fruits is to lay out apples and pears on newspaper in a cool, dark outbuilding or garden shed, making sure they don't touch one another. Stored carefully like this they should last for several months. Serves 12 (or 6 if everyone wants second helpings!)

FOR THE PASTRY
225g plain flour, plus extra for dusting
80g caster sugar
110g unsalted butter, cut into small knobs, plus extra for greasing
1 large egg

FOR THE FILLING
2 large Cox's apples, peeled, cored and cut into chunks
225g unsalted butter, softened
225g caster sugar
2 large eggs
110g plain flour
1 teaspoon baking powder
225g ground almonds
2 tablespoons whole milk
400g homemade marmalade (see page 218)
3 tablespoons flaked almonds
whipped cream, to serve

(You will need a 25cm loose-bottomed tart tin)

First make the pastry. Put the flour and sugar in a large mixing bowl and rub in the butter with your fingertips until the mixture resembles breadcrumbs. Make a well in the centre, break in the egg and mix to a firm dough. Turn the pastry out onto a floured surface and gently bring together into a small ball. Wrap in clingfilm and transfer to the fridge to rest for 30 minutes.

Preheat the oven to 200°C/gas mark 6. Line the base of a 25cm loose-bottomed tart tin with baking parchment and grease the sides. Roll the pastry out into a 30cm circle, carefully lift it into the tin and pinch it gently around the edges, using two fingers and your thumb. If the pastry is thin enough I prefer not to prick the base.

Crumple up a sheet of greaseproof paper, flatten it out again and use it to line the base and sides of the pastry case. Fill the centre with dried beans or uncooked rice; this is called baking blind. Bake the pastry case for 10 minutes, and then carefully remove the beans and paper and cook for a further 10 minutes. Remove from the oven and set aside on a wire rack.

Put the apples in a medium saucepan with 25g butter and 25g sugar. Put the pan over a low heat and cook gently until the apples soften, approx. 10 minutes.

Meanwhile, prepare the filling. Put the remaining butter and sugar in a large mixing bowl and beat well with a wooden spoon until light and fluffy. Stir in the eggs, flour, baking powder and ground almonds, and then mix in the milk to form a firm dropping consistency.

To assemble the tart, spread an even layer of marmalade over the cooked pastry case and top with the apple mixture. Carefully spoon the filling evenly over the apple mixture and finish with a generous sprinkling of flaked almonds.

Bake for 10 minutes until risen and golden. Serve warm with whipped cream.

SOURDOUGH: NATURE'S BREAD

When making sourdough, you have to make a starter (also known as a mother), which is a mixture of equal quantities of water and strong bread flour and looks like a smooth batter. This creates a fantastic environment for yeast to feed and grow. The natural sugars in the flour feed and attract the wild yeasts in the atmosphere, causing the yeasts to breed. This causes a chemical reaction creating carbon dioxide. The reason we knead bread is to stretch the gluten, which makes the dough elastic. It then fills itself with air when it proves and can expand and hold its shape, which is why sourdough bread is light and hole-y.

If you are very strict with your starter you will see it change throughout the seasons. Flour is seasonal and wild yeasts can change just because of a tree blossoming next to your kitchen. Even the water you use changes depending on where and when you make and feed your starter.

There are many ways of making bread; you can make a sourdough focaccia by making an elastic dough with the starter, putting it in a baking tray until it doubles in size, then putting a topping on it and baking it. This is known as a first prove bake and the finished loaf will have uniform air pockets. The process of proving bread and then knocking it back is done to create random-sized air pockets in the loaf, such as those you see in sourdough.

Real bread should only need water, flour and the yeast for the starter, and four ingredients in total – the starter, flour, water and salt. So I would love to know why mass-produced bread has over 15 softeners, preservatives and whatever else? I believe this has strong links to dietary issues, such as allergies to wheat, because commercial factories create and bake their bread within an hour. Due to the speed of production the bread dough is filled with softeners, sugars and more yeast than is needed. The yeast in the bought loaf is often rehydrated in your stomach, becoming active and hard for the body to deal with. Natural bread is good for you, and the slower it's produced, the better the flavour.

THE SHED SOURDOUGH

I make bread as a percentage because the only real change in dough is how hydrated it is. So for 100 per cent flour I add 65 per cent water and 1 per cent salt for 10 per cent starter. So this means for every 1kg flour, I use 650ml water and 10g salt for every 100ml starter. I can therefore make any quantity of dough using this ratio, scaling it up for the restaurant and down for making bread at home.

The flour you use is just as important as how strong and active your starter is. I use Shipton Mill organic flour. Every sack is different and gives an individual flavour; this is one of the joys of artisan baking. This flour also contains 12 per cent gluten, which means that the resulting dough is very elastic. It is important to use organic flour as this helps the yeasts in the starter to grow, uninhibited by any chemicals. Rye flour is the best type of flour to feed your starter because it holds a lot of natural sweetness. I like to use the same flour for the starter and the bread to keep the flavour consistent.

FOR THE STARTER
Makes approx. 1 litre

1.5 litres water (I use water
   from our spring in Nutbourne,
   but tap water is fine)
1.5kg organic strong bread flour
1 small stick of rhubarb, or
   1 wild crab apple (anything
   that has natural yeast on it)

Mix 500ml water and 500g flour together in a bowl until they form a smooth batter. Add the whole fruit and cover the bowl with clingfilm. Pierce a few holes in the clingfilm so the yeasts can breathe and set aside at room temperature out of direct sunlight.

The following day, add 250g flour and 250ml water to the starter and stir through. Cover with the pierced clingfilm and set aside at room temperature out of direct sunlight. Repeat this process every day for three days (four times in total) and you will see the yeasts sporing (breeding), eating the sugar and creating carbon dioxide.

Taste your starter; it should taste a little sour and resemble a batter with air bubbles. Feed your starter twice a week to keep it active and 2–3 times 24 hours before baking. (If you use your starter to make bread every day it will stay active – it needs constant love!)

1.

2.

3.

4.

5.

6.

FOR THE BREAD
Makes 1 large 2.5kg loaf

1.5kg strong bread flour, plus
  extra for dusting
250ml active starter
  (see opposite)
15g salt
750ml water (use cold water
  if you ferment the bread for
  24 hours but if you need it
  sooner then use warm water)
oil, for greasing
2 tablespoons coating for the
  crust (such as poppy seeds,
  coriander seeds or semolina)
  (optional)

Add the flour, starter and salt to the bowl of a food mixer. Then, with the dough hook attachment fitted, turn the mixer on to slow speed and slowly add three-quarters of the water. Bread kneads better when at 55–60 per cent hydration, so leave it to knead for 5 minutes, then slowly add the remaining water. You should now have a very sticky dough in the bottom of a very clean bowl.

Take a handful of the dough and pull it apart so if you hold it on two fingers and two thumbs you can stretch it really thin. I call this 'the stained-glass window test'; you should be able to see the light through the dough as your hands separate and the dough stretches. It means that the gluten has been worked so much that the dough holds its shape but is still elastic. It's sticky but workable.

Cover the bowl and transfer the dough to the fridge for 12 hours to gain strength in flavour and body. When you are ready (it could be up to 24 hours later, as long as your starter is active enough), shape the dough. It's best to have a bread-proving basket, but if you don't you can just rub the inside of a large bowl with a thin layer of cooking oil. Dust the bowl with your chosen crust topping, which will then stick to the oil. Repeat with a little flour to fill in any of the small edges. Tap out the excess flour. This

is great as you don't need another bowl in your kitchen and you gain a great crust on your loaf. If you have a proving basket, lightly flour the proving basket and dust with your chosen crust topping.

To shape the dough, dust a work surface with flour and begin by rolling the dough into a thick pizza, approx. 12.5cm in diameter and 5cm thick, then lift the sides in; this creates large, random baker's air pockets. Keep pulling in until the dough ball feels tight, then start to push the dough into the work surface so it forms a very proud ball. If it's saggy and not holding its shape, repeat the process again; the more you practise the easier it gets.

Then put the shaped loaf, belly-side down, into the lined bowl or bread-proving basket. Leave to prove at room temperature until doubled in size, approx. 4–8 hours. Preheat the oven to 240°C/gas mark 9 and heat two baking trays, one at the top and one at the bottom of the oven.

To test if the dough is ready, poke your finger into the dough; if it bounces back, it needs to prove for longer, but if your incision stays, then you are ready to bake.

Turn out the proved dough onto a hot baking tray and transfer to the oven. Then pour a glass of hot water in the hot tray at the bottom of the oven so steam hits the crust of the loaf. Bake for 15 minutes and you will see the bread 'jump' and lift itself off the hot baking tray. Reduce the oven temperature to 180°C/gas mark 4 and bake for a further 30 minutes to cook through completely.

Remove the bread from the oven and transfer it to a wire rack to help the loaf hold its crust. Don't cut into it until it has reached room temperature, which will take approx. 45 minutes.

If cooked with a great crust, sourdough will last longer than normal bread because of the acidity that the starter gives. I make lardo soldiers (see page 99) with my sourdough 4–5 days after baking.

SPRING LARDER

ELDERFLOWER CHAMPAGNE

Foraging for elderflowers is an irresistible prelude
to summer and you can find elder trees flowering all
over the place. A lady called Vicky, who works with
our dad, was once caught picking the lovely-looking
white blooms in a well-known London park. She would
have got away with it had there not been a team of
15 people armed with large white storage buckets
preparing for some mass-production! Stick to the
countryside where elders are plentiful and no one will
mind a little harvesting for domestic use.

   Elder trees provide our kitchen with lots of
different produce through the season. After the
flowers turn into little green berries before ripening
this is a great moment to pick the berries and
preserve them in sweet brine for summer salad acidity.
Then when the berries ripen and turn dark purple,
harvest them as a delicate fruit or make elderberry
vinegar.

   The elderflower juice will lightly ferment creating
a small amount of alcohol and lots of fizz. You will
need some traditional flip-top glass bottles to store
your champagne, which might involve drinking a few
lagers first! Note: If the rubber seals are damaged
you may need to replace them with new ones from a
hardware or home-brew store. Makes 5 litres

20 elderflower heads
juice and zest of 2 lemons
500g granulated sugar
2 tablespoons white wine vinegar
5 litres water

(You will need 5 x 1-litre
sterilised flip-top glass
bottles)

Put all the ingredients in a large preserving
pan over a high heat and bring to the boil,
stirring occasionally to dissolve the sugar.
Once the liquid is boiling, remove the pan
from the heat and set aside to steep for
24 hours in a cool place. Cover the pan
with a piece of muslin to keep flies out
but do not seal.

Strain out the flowers, decant the liquid
into sterilised flip-top bottles and fasten
the lids.

Lie the bottles on their side in a cool,
dark place and set aside to ferment for
2–3 weeks. During this time the champagne
will become fizzy and start to develop a
very low degree of alcohol.

Serve chilled and use the whole bottle
once opened. Unopened bottles can be
stored for up to 6 months.

RICHARD'S DAILY LOOSENER: SPRING STINGER

We create a cocktail every day in The Shed under the banner - The Daily Loosener. It is a collaboration between the bar and the kitchen where I act as judge, arbitrator and chief guinea pig. The only stipulation is that the drink must contain some strong alcohol to loosen up the recipient after a stressful day. Just like our food menu, the recipes change all the time according to the season, the weather and what we found out foraging on our most recent day in the countryside. Spring nettles are a classic ingredient - bountiful, and free, and they also provide a great name for the drink - even though they don't actually sting once they've been steeped in vodka! Makes approx. 1 litre

500g young nettle tops, washed and dried on kitchen paper
400ml vodka (50 per cent proof)
lots of ice
lemon slices
soda water

FOR THE SUGAR SYRUP
120ml caster sugar
120ml water

(You will need a 1-litre Kilner jar)

To prepare the sugar syrup, put the sugar and water in a small pan over a moderate heat. Keep stirring until the sugar has dissolved, and then boil for 4–6 minutes until the syrup thickens slightly.

Put the nettles in a 1-litre sterilised Kilner jar, add the vodka and then carefully pour in the hot sugar syrup. Stir together. Seal the jar and set aside for 1 week in a cool, dark place to steep.

After a week, open the jar and smell the fragrant 'spring nettles after the rain' aroma.

To build your drink, fill a tall glass with plenty of ice and a couple of lemon slices. Pour a good double measure of nettle vodka over the ice and top up the glass with soda water. The cocktail should be crisp and grassy with a good bite.

LEMON & LIME CURD

Fruit curds are another great preserve - any citrus fruits can be used, so why not try grapefruit, mandarin or clementine as well as the classic lemon. This curd recipe is very easy but also extremely satisfying to make. It keeps well in airtight jars in the fridge and can be used as a filling for cakes, tarts, desserts or scones and, of course, as a delicious tangy spread on toast. We add lime to give an extra little bite. Makes 2 x 250ml jars

zest and juice of 4 medium
  lemons
zest and juice of 2 large limes
220g caster sugar
120g unsalted butter
3 large eggs
2 large egg yolks
pinch of salt

(You will need 2 x 250ml
sterilised glass jars with lids)

Prepare a bain-marie by sitting a heatproof bowl over a saucepan of gently simmering water. Put the lemon and lime zest and juice in the bowl and stir in the sugar. Add the butter, a few small knobs at a time, and keep stirring until the butter has completely melted.

In a separate bowl, whisk the eggs and extra egg yolks together the salt. Add the egg mixture to the lemon and lime mixture and stir well to combine. Cook over the bain-marie for a further 10 minutes, stirring occasionally, until the curd thickens and becomes very smooth. Carefully remove the bowl from the heat and set aside to cool slightly.

Spoon the curd into sterilised glass jars, cover with waxed paper discs and put on the lids. The curd will last for 4–6 weeks in the fridge if the seal is not broken. Once opened, store in the fridge and consume within 2 weeks.

TARRAGON MAYONNAISE

We use tarragon mayonnaise with our bestselling Beef and Horseradish Cigars (see page 240), but it is also perfect with croquettes, fishcakes and more. The basic mayonnaise recipe can be adapted by omitting the tarragon and substituting other green herbs such as dill to serve with Plaice Straws (see page 96) or curried spices for chicken or citrus zest and chives for shrimps. Season your mayonnaise carefully and adjust the acidity if necessary by adding a little more or less vinegar. Makes 400ml

2 large egg yolks
2 teaspoons Dijon
  mustard
1 tablespoon wholegrain
  mustard
1 tablespoon cider
  vinegar
salt and freshly ground
  black pepper
300ml sunflower oil
1 heaped tablespoon
  finely chopped fresh
  tarragon leaves

Using an electric hand whisk (or balloon whisk if you wish), beat the egg yolks, mustards and vinegar together in a medium bowl. Season with salt and pepper. Whisking continuously, start to slowly add the oil, just a few drops at first and then a tablespoonful at a time. It will take approx. 5 minutes of whisking before all the oil is incorporated and the base mayonnaise is complete. Finally, stir in the tarragon. Cover the bowl with clingfilm and transfer the mayonnaise to the fridge for an hour or so to infuse. It will keep well in the fridge for 3–4 days.

WILD GARLIC YOGURT

Wild garlic is one of the delights of the countryside in early spring. It isn't grown commercially, but just suddenly appears along the banks of wooded lanes readily available for the eager forager! First, long green leaves shoot from the ground, and then a month or so later they blossom with lovely, delicate white flowers. The whole plant is edible and for us provides the wonderful aroma and flavour of garlic without any of the pungent harshness you sometimes get from a cultivated garlic bulb.

We use wild garlic for all sorts of things in our kitchen - including salads, salsas, pesto and sauces. This fragrant savoury yogurt is very versatile and makes a great dip to serve with breadsticks as well as a delicious accompaniment to crab cakes (see page 40) and burgers (see page 48). Makes 300ml

6 wild garlic leaves
300ml natural yogurt
juice and zest of $\frac{1}{2}$ lemon
$\frac{1}{2}$ teaspoon rock salt crystals
freshly ground black pepper

Lay the long wild garlic leaves on top of one another on a chopping board and use a really sharp knife to slice them as finely as possible – crossways into delicate shreds. Put them in a bowl and stir in the yogurt, lemon juice, zest and seasoning. Cover the bowl with clingfilm and set aside in the fridge for 1 hour to allow the flavours to infuse before serving.

Serve with breadsticks and new season salads. Wild garlic flowers make a lovely garnish. They can be picked a few days in advance and stored in the fridge in an airtight container.

THE
SUMMER

GREGORY
RAGWORT & RACING

Richard was always coming up with hair-brained schemes when we were growing up. Being the smallest I just had to go along with them and promise not to tell Mum. One summer he decided we needed a car to race around the vineyards.

To raise the money to buy one, we persuaded a neighbour to hire us to clear a paddock of ragwort. Ragwort is a nasty weed with a bright yellow flower that is prolific in the south of England. It is highly poisonous to horses and cattle. Although they generally know not to eat it when it is growing in a field they can easily ingest it when it has dried or gets chopped up and incorporated into hay. We therefore had to pull it out and then cart it away in a wheelbarrow to burn on the bonfire.

After a hard day's labour we had the cash we were after. Ragan, the publican at The Rising Sun, had a big old Peugeot he was waiting to scrap, and before Mum or Dad could say no we were the proud owners of our own racing car. We all piled in, Richard at the wheel and me consigned to the back. We hurtled down the farm tracks, producing clouds of dust and magnificent skids. Then Richard performed a daring chicane through the apple orchard and crashed slap bang into a tree that got in our way.

That was the end of our racing career, Dad said it was very lucky none of us were hurt and the car was towed away to the scrap merchant for three times the price we had paid for it.

Nowadays my summers are given over to more responsible pursuits. There is masses to do, so we have to make the most of the long days. The animals are all out in the big fields. For the most part they look after themselves: we put the bulls to the cows and heifers about mid-June and from then on it's a matter of checking on them twice a day to make sure everyone is behaving themselves. A more onerous task is making sure there is enough food to see the cattle and sheep through the winter. To produce this, we need to cut the meadows that are not being grazed twice. The wet juicy grass from the first cut is used to make silage. This is a nutritious cattle food consisting of fermented grass. We pile some 800 tonnes of the stuff into a mighty 'clamp', cover it over and leave it to ferment and mature. The second cut is for hay. We leave the grass to semi dry in the fields before bailing and wrapping it. There are also fields of maize to drill in and whole crop (a mixture of barley, beans and peas) to be harvested.

Another regular summer activity is taking on a batch of calves to rear for rose veal. This is hugely popular when we serve it at The Shed. We buy in the unwanted male calves from a local dairy herd. (Males are of no use to dairy farmers and until recently they were simply culled at birth.) We take them very young and initially feed them milk, before moving them to a meadow where they enjoy a pure grass diet until they are about eight months old. They have short lives but good ones, producing lovely rose coloured meat somewhere between traditional white veal and young beef.

RICHARD
DOWN AT THE VINEYARD & BACK OUTDOORS

It is early summer and the vines are covered in a lime green haze, with newly opened buds on every spur. Within a few short weeks these will shoot into canes, then delicate little white flowers will appear in early July. Then tiny bunches of grapes will form, which will need careful nurturing through the summer until they reach maturity in late September or October.

It's a challenge growing grapes in England. They don't like too much rain, they suffer from various mildews and pests, and ideally they need warm sunny days to maximise their sugar content and cooler nights to protect their acidity and flavour. Fortunately our vineyards at Nutbourne are ideally situated, on well-draining green sand soil which slopes gently to the south. They are protected from sea breezes by the ridge of the South Downs, which creates a warm microclimate.

Last year's still whites and rosé wines have all been bottled by now. The Sussex Reserve is our leading still white and our bestseller at The Shed. It positively zings with fruit and has a bouquet reminiscent of elderflower with citrus undertones. As a partner for asparagus it is impossible to beat.

We are about to embark on bottling the Nutty Sparkling. Our head winemaker, Owen, waits until the beginning of summer to ensure the temperature is high enough to get the ferment going. At this stage it is a still wine. It only becomes fizzy during a second fermentation process which takes place in the bottle. The wine is then laid down for 2-3 years for the flavour to mature and develop to its full potential. This is called establishing 'bottle age' - a procedure which all the great winemakers of Champagne are very proud of.

My imaginary vegetable patch is now augmented by real parsley, basil and tarragon, which I grow in window boxes on the sills of my London flat. I also have some chilli plants and a flourishing tomato grow-bag.

In the larger scale vegetable gardens which supply The Shed with produce the soft fruit bushes are now at their peak. Raspberries, both the regular English kind and the amazing Arctic yellow variety are in season, as are bilberries, loganberries and purple gooseberries, which we are particularly

fond of. Courgettes are in bloom,
yielding lovely delicate yellow flowers
for us to stuff or fry as well as young
vegetables to blanch or serve raw in
salads. There are also new potatoes,
peas, mangetouts, globe artichokes,
runner and broad beans, row upon row
of tender young lettuces and climbing
trellises of sweet peas for fragrance
and beauty.

The human components of The Shed also
flourish in the summer. Half our dining
tables move outdoors, the back door
of the kitchen is permanently open
and everyone is a little brighter and
smiles more. The team we have working
with us is a huge part of our success.
When we first opened we just recruited
our friends to help us. Doctor Piers
would operate behind the bar in between
his shifts at the hospital, with his
brother Charles taking over when he
really had to save lives. Jess welcomed
everyone who walked through the door
and big Dave, who was at school with
Oliver, helped out in the kitchen.
Then along came Theo. If we failed to

mention him and his family, the story
of The Shed would be incomplete: Our
landlords Colin and Sarah Harris opened
The Ark on site where The Shed now
stands back in 1961. In its day The
Ark was a famous celebrity haunt, with
regulars such as Ingrid Bergman and
Audrey Hepburn. Its biggest claim to
fame, though, was turning away a young
Prince Charles because there was no
table available. Mr Harris, who still
owns the freehold, came to The Shed
on our opening night to celebrate his
85th birthday. Mrs Harris introduced
us to her grandson, Theo, recommending
him for a part-time waiting job. Now
restaurant manager, Theo is well-known
to everyone who comes to The Shed. He
is always calm, charming, knowledgeable
and wonderfully efficient, just like
grandad, one imagines.

At this time of year the little outside
terrace buzzes with activity both day
and night. Even when it's raining
people are determined to sit outside,
making the most of the summer under the
semi-waterproof awning.

OLIVER
NATURAL & SUSTAINABLE

Summer cooking traditionally comprises light salads, marinated fish dishes, barbecued meats and fruity desserts. But if you are going to stick to the principles of utilising whole animals and foraging thecountryside for everything nature has on offer, there is a need to take a broader approach to cooking at this time of year. Of course we want lots of unadulterated fresh produce, but what about a tasty Rabbit and Wild Cherry Casserole (see page 100) or a tangy batch of Greengage Chutney (see page 116)?

At The Shed we make a point of offering a balance of fast- and slow-cooked dishes throughout the year. In the summer, items in the 'fast' category include the likes of salads, grilled sea bass, barbecued pork chops and pan-fried puffball mushrooms. Good examples of seasonal slow-cooked dishes are a delicious broth made from the remains of a chicken and our famous Lamb Chips (see page 102), made by gently braising the meat for several hours.

At this time of year nature is so bountiful that there is no excuse for not keeping your cooking local, natural and sustainable. Here are some of the ways in which you can do this:-

✳ Introduce a no wastage policy. Every vegetable peeling is good for the stockpot. Most joints or carcasses will yield a second meal in the form of a risotto or pasta dish, leftover vegetables can form the basis of your next salad and uneaten salad items can be the raw materials for your next salsa.

✳ Buy very locally from traditional small-scale suppliers.

✳ Check out the sustainable fishing charts online or visit the coast and find a supplier of line-caught fish.

✳ Use smaller quantities of fish and meat, offering a bigger range of vegetables, salads and breads to compensate.

✳ Set up a compost system, thus ensuring the nutrients in anything you don't eat go back into your veg patch.

✳ Forage the land and seashore for free food. In the summer the possibilities for foraging are endless. We use rose geraniums and lemon balm for dressings; nasturtiums, wild sorrel and dandelion, all of which can be found beside country pathways, in salads; and wild lavender and verbena for flavourings in baking, desserts or drinks. Meanwhile, a trip to the coast can furnish you with the perfect accompaniments to fresh fish in the form of seaweeds and samphire. Remember, what grows together goes together.

FORAGING IN SUMMER

IN THE WOODS

Bilberries	Like blueberries but red in flesh	Use instead of blueberries in desserts and baking
Wild cherries	Juicy, dark red	Rabbit and Wild Cherry Casserole (page 100)
Elderflowers	Sweet, fragrant, perfumed	Elderflower Champagne (page 64)
Cobnuts	Soft, hazelnut-y, milky	Warm Salad of Roasted Pumpkin and Cobnuts with Pearled Spelt and Leeks (page 134)
Borage, lemon balm, lemon verbena	Fragrant, colourful	Good for garnishing drinks

ON LEAFY BANKS

Wild fennel	Aniseed, sweet, liquorice	Use in pasta, soups or add to Gentleman Farmer's Relish (see page 128)
Wild rocket	Mustard, peppery, hot	Serve with grilled meat such as lamb or add to frittatas or risottos
Wild oregano	Fragrant, sweet	Use in summer salads
Sorrel	Zingy	Summer Chicken Broth with Hazelnut Pesto and Lardo Dippers (pages 98-99)
Rose geranium	Perfumed	Heritage Tomato Salad with Rose Geranium Dressing (page 80)

IN THE MEADOWS

Field mushrooms	Meaty, rich, filling	The Mushroom Forager's Ragù with Celeriac Purée (page 136)
Puffballs	Spongy, clean	Pan-fried Puffballs (page 86)
Meadowsweet	Herby, acidic	Use to flavour summer salads

BY THE SEA

Rock samphire	Salty, crunchy	Hake, Samphire and Red Pepper Salsa (page 140)
Sea purslane	Salty, delicate, leafy	Add to fritters or partner with fish
Sea cabbages	Tough, bitter, wild	Toss in summer salads
Seaweeds	Slimy, salty	Use to season soups and stocks
Sea Aster	Soft, textured	Serve with fish such as sea bass

SUMMER MOUTHFULS

QUEEN SCALLOPS WITH CITRUS BUTTER

The Isle of Man, in the middle of the Irish Sea, is famous for its delicate little Queenie scallops, which, thanks to careful controls and conservation, remain a sustainable product. They even have a Manx scallop festival in the middle of June each year to celebrate their provender.

There are a number of shellfish around the British Isles that make perfect individual mouthfuls served in their own shell. These include cockles, clams, mussels, oysters and these little Queen scallops. Queenies are very succulent and tender, they cook in a few seconds and are beautifully complemented by this pungent citrus butter. Makes 12 mouthfuls

12 Queen scallops, cleaned but still in their shells
30g marsh samphire, rinsed in cold water

FOR THE CITRUS BUTTER
3 tablespoons crème fraîche
zest of ½ orange
zest and juice of 1 lime
salt
a few drops of Tabasco sauce
½ teaspoon caster sugar, to taste
60g unsalted butter, cut into small knobs

Preheat the grill to high.

Arrange the scallops, still sitting on their shells, on a baking tray that will fit under the grill. Add a few sprigs of samphire to each scallop shell.

Put the crème fraîche, orange zest, and lime zest and juice in a small saucepan and warm over a low heat until hot but not boiling. Season the mixture with salt, Tabasco and a little sugar, to taste.

Put the butter in a mixing bowl. Pour the hot crème fraîche mixture over the butter and beat vigorously with a wooden spoon to form a smooth, glossy sauce.

Spoon 2–3 teaspoons of the butter sauce over each scallop. Then cook under the hot grill for 2–3 minutes until just cooked. Serve immediately.

MACKEREL SASHIMI

Mackerel is a wonderful, versatile fish, full of healthy natural oils. The Japanese dish sashimi refers to thinly sliced raw fish (or meat), which is traditionally served at the beginning of a meal as a great delicacy. We serve raw mackerel sashimi as a mouthful at The Shed, accompanied by peppery fresh radishes, English mustard and a little soy sauce. So the sensation is fresh, clean textured fish, complemented with hot English mustard, peppery radish, then a little soy for seasoning. It is incredibly simple to prepare and well worth a try.

Mackerel is a sustainable shoaling fish available in many different parts of the world and bountiful in British waters in the warmer months of the year when they come in close to the shoreline to feed. I would only recommend preparing any raw fish dish if you are confident that the fish is incredibly fresh. Makes 20 mouthfuls

2 x 200g very fresh mackerel fillets

1 bunch of radishes, washed, trimmed and cut lengthways into quarters

2 tablespoons light soy sauce

1 teaspoon English mustard

The skill of sashimi is in the perfect slicing of the fish. Lay the mackerel fillets, skin-side down, on a chopping board. Insert a very sharp knife just above the skin at the tail end. Holding the tip of the tail skin in one hand, and keeping the knife totally horizontal, draw it along the fish – away from your hand – to remove the skin in one piece. Cut the fish widthways on the diagonal into even slices so that each slice is at least twice the depth of the fillet.

A very stylish presentation is to use the blue and silver fish skin as a little serving mat. Arrange the radishes along it and carefully drape a slice of fish on top of each one. Pour the soy sauce and mustard into little bowls to serve alongside.

MINTED PEAS ON CHEESE CRISPS

We make these cheese crisps with a local hard cheese called Twineham Grange, which is somewhere between Cheddar and Parmesan in style. The cheese bakes to a slightly chewy, brûléed base which is then topped with a really fresh, minty pea purée. They are a perfect combination washed down with a summer cocktail such as Richard's Summer Rose Royale (see page 114).
Makes 20 mouthfuls

200g Parmesan cheese (or Parmesan-style hard cheese such as Twineham Grange)
250g garden peas
2 sprigs of fresh mint, one kept whole and the remaining leaves finely shredded
salt and coarsely ground black pepper
2 tablespoons double cream

Preheat the oven to 180°C/gas mark 4 and line a baking tray with baking parchment.

Grate the Parmesan by hand on a box grater to fine shavings rather than powder. Using a small round 4cm cutter as a guide, make even little piles of Parmesan approx. 1cm deep in rows across the lined baking tray. Don't press the cheese down – just gently lift the cutter off and move on to the next one.

Bake the cheese piles for 8 minutes until crisp and lightly singed around the edges. Set aside to cool.

Meanwhile, cook the peas along with a large sprig of mint in a small saucepan of lightly salted water for 1 minute; drain and refresh under cold water. Return the peas to the pan, add the cream and season with plenty of black pepper. Using a hand-held immersion blender, purée the peas and cream together, but leave some texture.

Remove the cheese crisps from the baking parchment using a palette knife and arrange them in a single layer on a serving dish. To serve, spoon a dollop of the pea purée onto each cheese crisp and top with some shredded mint. Serve with a glass of sparkling wine.

GREEN HERB MACAROONS WITH SOFT CHEESE

Why the whole world is obsessed with brightly coloured macaroons full of E-number colouring, I just don't know. A traditional soft almond meringue is a delicious thing and I'm not sure the commercial addition of bright blue or purple colouring and white chocolate improves it. However, macaroons do give scope for lovely sweet/savoury combinations and this recipe balances the sweetness of a herby almond meringue with a rich cheesy filling, made with our own 'Nutty' cheese made by our mother in Nutbourne. Makes 20 mouthfuls

50g icing sugar
100g ground almonds
2 sprigs of dried chervil
3 leaves of dried tarragon
2 large egg whites
80g caster sugar
pinch of salt

FOR THE FILLING
100g Nutty Camembert or equivalent, skin removed
a dash of milk
freshly ground black pepper

Line two baking trays with baking parchment.

Put the icing sugar, ground almonds and herbs in a liquidiser or food processor and blitz until the herbs are perfectly blended. Now rub this mixture through a sieve.

Whisk the egg whites in a food mixer until they form soft peaks. Add the caster sugar, a teaspoon at a time, while continuing to whisk. Once all the caster sugar has been incorporated, add a pinch of salt and continue to whisk for a further 5 minutes until the meringue is really thick and glossy.

Remove the bowl from the mixer and, using a spatula, gently fold in the sieved almond mixture. Transfer the almond meringue to a piping bag and pipe 3cm mounds onto the lined baking trays, spacing them apart. Tap the tray on the work surface several times to settle the macaroons, and then set aside to stand at room temperature for 15 minutes.

Preheat the oven to 150°C/gas mark 2.

Bake the macaroons for 10 minutes until crisp on the outside but still soft in the centre. Transfer to a wire rack to cool.

To make the filling, blend the cheese with a dash of milk and plenty of black pepper until it is a smooth, soft consistency. Transfer the mixture to a piping bag and use it to sandwich the macaroons together in pairs.

STUFFED JERSEY ROYALS

My godmother, Penny, lives in Jersey and many a summer holiday was spent running on the beach, throwing stones at the seagulls with my brothers and getting into all sorts of trouble for behaving so badly in front of her good little girls.

Jersey's number one export is their famous 'Royal' new potato. (That's probably not true in economic terms - the number one export is probably tax avoidance - but farming-wise it is definitely potatoes.) A Jersey Royal is very distinctive both in shape (like a small kidney) and for its sweet, earthy flavour. In this recipe the potatoes are stuffed with anchovies and ricotta so that they become a mouthful sensation, however, they are definitely good enough to serve simply on their own. Makes 12 mouthfuls

12 even-sized Jersey Royal
  potatoes, washed but kept
  whole
salt and freshly ground black
  pepper
3 marinated anchovy fillets,
  cut into small slivers
80g. ricotta
pinch of nutmeg
1 teaspoon chopped dill

Preheat the oven to 150°C/gas mark 2.

Put the potatoes in a medium saucepan of lightly salted water and bring to the boil over a moderate heat. Simmer for 8 minutes, and then drain and refresh under cold running water.

Meanwhile, mix together the anchovies, ricotta, nutmeg and chopped dill in a small bowl and season carefully with a little salt and plenty of pepper – try it for taste.

Using a melon baller, scoop out a hole in the top of each potato. Fill this with a teaspoonful of the ricotta mixture.

Arrange the filled potatoes on a roasting tray and reheat in a low oven (160°C/gas mark 3) for 10 minutes before serving.

HERITAGE TOMATO SALAD
WITH ROSE GERANIUM DRESSING

Our local tomato grower down at Nutbourne cultivates a wonderful variety of orange, brown, golden, green and, of course, red tomatoes. The range of shapes and flavours is magnificent - and if left to ripen properly on the vines, the different levels of acidity and sweetness really capture the essence of summer.

I serve the tomatoes as a simple salad and complement their flavours with a rose geranium dressing. Don't muddle rose geranium with the brightly coloured Mediterranean geraniums you often see in window boxes - they are not the same plant and the latter, though not inedible, taste of detergent! Rose geraniums are said to have healing and calming properties; they are easy to grow, even indoors, and the leaves and petals give a deliciously atmospheric smell - the perfume of summer. This simple marriage on a plate between the tomatoes and the dressing will transport you to a country garden on a perfect summer's day, even if it is cold and rainy! Serves 6 as a side dish

1kg assorted ripe heritage or
   heirloom tomatoes

FOR THE ROSE GERANIUM DRESSING
60ml rapeseed oil
6 rose geranium leaves, finely
   shredded
30ml cider vinegar
1 tablespoon caster sugar
pinch of salt and freshly
   ground black pepper
6 chives, chopped
12 rose geranium petals,
   to garnish

Slice the tomatoes according to their different sizes and shapes. Try to maintain the character of each variety, and arrange them on a serving platter.

Heat the oil in a small pan over a very gentle heat until it is warm but not too hot. Remove the pan from the heat and add the rose geranium leaves, vinegar, sugar, salt and pepper. Set aside for an hour or so to infuse until cool.

To serve, stir the dressing and pour over the tomatoes. Sprinkle with chopped chives and dot with some individual geranium petals to garnish.

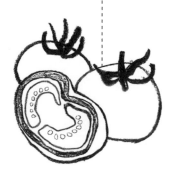

BROAD BEAN HUMMUS
WITH BARBECUE-BAKED FLATBREADS

A barbecue is a great versatile outdoor cooker and you can do so much more on it than just grill meats. Twice each year down at Nutbourne we stage major open days called 'Jazz in the Vines'. The events take place right in the centre of the vineyard where guests come to relax in this fabulous setting, enjoy English wine in its natural surroundings and listen or even dance to some local jazz bands. Of course, when it came to photographing this event for the book it poured down with rain, but in the end that only enhanced the atmosphere and demonstrated great British spirit with everyone thoroughly enjoying themselves in spite of the appalling weather.

The Shed team puts on a range of local fare all cooked in the open air on large-scale barbecues. The menu includes Nutbourne lamb and pork, local asparagus, and these delicious flatbreads, filled with broad bean hummus and salad. Rain or shine.

Serves a generous 6 to share

FOR THE BROAD BEAN HUMMUS
4 sprigs of fresh mint
1kg broad beans, podded
50g unsalted butter
3 garlic cloves, peeled
2 tablespoons tahini paste
zest and juice of 1 lemon
2 tablespoons crème fraîche
salt and freshly ground black
  pepper

FOR THE FLATBREADS
500g plain flour
600ml water
10g fast-action dried yeast
  (or 20g fresh yeast)
20g salt
60g semolina flour, for dusting

TO SERVE
1 red pepper
2 heads of Little Gem lettuce,
  coarsely shredded

Put a medium saucepan of salted water over a moderate heat, add the mint and bring to the boil. Drop in the broad beans and cook for 3 minutes; drain and refresh under cold running water.

Squeeze out the inner kernel from each bean, discarding the outer layer, and put in a food processor. Add the butter, garlic, tahini, lemon zest and juice and crème fraîche and blitz to a coarse purée. Season with salt and pepper. Spoon into a serving dish, cover with clingfilm and set aside in the fridge until ready to serve.

To prepare the flatbreads, mix the flour, water, yeast and salt in a large mixing bowl to form a dough. Turn out onto a floured work surface and knead for 5 minutes until the dough becomes elastic and smooth. Return the dough to the bowl, cover with a dry tea-towel and set aside to prove for 1 hour in a warm place.

Light the barbecue (or preheat a griddle pan) so it is nice and hot.

Break the dough into 6cm pieces and roll into balls in the palms of your hands. Dust a work surface with semolina flour and roll out the balls into ovals, approx. 5mm thick.

Cook the breads over the hot embers of the barbecue (or on the griddle) for 1–2 minutes on each side.

Meanwhile, roast the red pepper on the barbecue until it softens and blackens on all sides, approx. 10 minutes. Cut the pepper in half, discard the seeds and core, then peel off the blackened skin and slice the flesh into thin strips.

To serve, split the breads open and fill the pockets with a generous dollop of broad bean hummus, some shredded lettuce and a few strips of red pepper. Serve while the bread is still warm.

COURGETTE FLOWERS FILLED WITH RICOTTA, LENTILS & PINE NUTS

The joy of growing your own vegetables is not only that you get very fresh ingredients, but also that you can choose exactly when you wish to pick them. Courgettes are easy to grow and take no time at all to develop from seed to fruition (yes, they are a fruit) but the real bonus is the flowers. Courgette flowers are a truly delicious delicacy. They are often served deep-fried, but they can also be baked, blanched, or stuffed and pan-fried, as in this recipe.

Be careful that you don't pick all the flowers from your garden, or you won't get any courgettes in a couple of weeks' time. There are both male and female flowers and the courgette itself grows from the base of the female flower - it is interesting to see how the flowers differ. The male flower grows directly from the stem with no swelling behind it to develop into a courgette, while the female has a very golden blossom and grows further out on the plant with the beginnings of a courgette at its base. Both are edible and equally delicious. Serves 6 as a starter

100g Puy lentils
salt and freshly ground black
  pepper
80g ricotta cheese
1 tablespoon pine nuts, toasted
1 garlic clove, crushed
6 courgette flowers
30ml rapeseed oil
40g hard cheese (such as
  Twineham Grange or Parmesan),
  finely grated
home-grown lettuce leaves (such
  as Little Gem, rocket, lollo
  rosso), to serve

Put the lentils in a small saucepan of lightly salted cold water and cook over a moderate heat for 20 minutes. Drain through a sieve and rinse well under cold running water.

Combine the cooked lentils in a bowl with the ricotta, pine nuts and garlic and season well.

Carefully open the courgette flowers just enough to fill them with some of the lentil mixture, and then gently squeeze them shut again around the stuffing.

Heat the rapeseed oil in a heavy-based frying pan over a moderate heat. Carefully lay the flowers in the hot oil and cook for 2—3 minutes on each side.

Sprinkle the grated cheese onto a flat plate and lift the fried courgettes from the pan onto the cheese. Roll and coat them in the cheese before serving straight away with some green salad leaves.

KOHLRABI, ALEXANDER & ROCK SAMPHIRE SALAD

Our menu at The Shed changes every day according to the best ingredients. We always incorporate one or two very simple salad dishes, which are hugely popular. This is a recipe that really allows each ingredient to speak for itself, capturing the natural flavours and character of the three ingredients. Alexander is an ancient herb somewhere between parsley and celery. It grows abundantly on wild cliff tops near the sea and is a forager's favourite, being quite rare and therefore very rewarding when found. Rock samphire is another delicacy from the seashore and these two treats marry perfectly with the crisp, sweet juicy flesh of kohlrabi.
Serves 6 as a sharing plate

1 kohlrabi, peeled
100g rock samphire
20g sunflower seeds, lightly
   toasted
2 sprigs of Alexander, leaves
   and stems shredded together
Juice and zest of 1 lemon
a drizzle of rapeseed oil

Cut the kohlrabi into really thin slices, using a very sharp knife or mandolin. Assemble the slices as a flat, even layer on a serving plate and sprinkle the samphire over the top. The samphire's natural salt will bring out the juices from the kohlrabi.

Sprinkle over the sunflower seeds and Alexander, and dress with the lemon juice and zest and a drizzle of rapeseed oil.

PAN-FRIED PUFFBALLS

If you come across a puffball mushroom you are very lucky. Puffballs are found in open meadows and often in cow fields, even on woodland edges. There are several different types of puffball and not all are edible. Rule 1: if it's got a stem don't pick it or eat it. Rule 2: if it looks discoloured (not pearly white) it is maturing ready to spore, so don't pick it. And, finally, to see if the puffball is a true puff, cut it in half to make sure it does not have gills. It is important to only pick mushrooms if you can confirm their type from a description and photo.

Serves 4 as a main course or more as a sharing plate

400g young spinach, washed and picked
1 large puffball mushroom (weighing approx. 400g)
100g unsalted butter
2 garlic cloves, finely chopped
salt and freshly ground black pepper
60g pine nuts
juice of 1 lemon

Put the spinach leaves in a dry saucepan and wilt over a moderate heat for 2–3 minutes. If the leaves are a bit tough, you may need to add a little water to the pan. Drain well, and then return the cooked spinach to the pan and keep warm on the side of your cooker with the lid on.

Cut the puffball into even 1cm slices ready to cook at the last possible moment.

Heat the butter in a large frying pan over a moderate heat. Add the garlic and season with plenty of salt and pepper. Once the garlic starts to colour, toss in the pine nuts and cook for 1 minute. Add the mushroom slices and cook evenly for 2–3 minutes on each side, allowing them to brown but not shrivel up. Add the lemon juice at the last moment and immediately remove the pan from the heat.

To serve, arrange the spinach on a serving plate, heap the mushrooms on top and pour over the juices and pine nuts from the pan – lucky you!

SALMON & POUTING CEVICHE

Tender raw fish with a piquant, citrus marinade full of vibrant colours and textures is a perfect summer treat. This simple ceviche is easy to prepare and can be adapted to use with many different fishes and vegetables. For example, trout, sea bass, mackerel, mangetout, kohlrabi and courgette are all delicious variations. Serves 6 as a starter or light lunch

300g skinless salmon fillet
300g skinless pouting
  (or pollock or coley) fillet
juice and zest of 1 large orange
juice and zest of 2 lemons
juice and zest of 2 limes
60ml dry white wine
30ml rapeseed oil
1 red chilli, diced
1/2 teaspoon paprika
1 teaspoon caster sugar
1/2 teaspoon salt
6 radishes, sliced into thin
  discs
1 tablespoon chopped fresh
  chives
1 tablespoon chopped fresh
  coriander

Slice the fish lengthways/crossways into thin strips, approx. 5mm thick, and lay them out on an attractive serving platter. Cover with clingfilm and set aside in the fridge until 10 minutes before serving.

To make the marinade, combine the citrus juices and zests, white wine, rapeseed oil, chilli, paprika, sugar and salt together in a deep bowl. Set aside for 30 minutes to allow the flavours to develop, then check the seasoning and adjust if necessary.

Ten minutes before serving, scatter the radishes, chives and coriander over the fish. Pour over the marinade and toss everything gently together. The acidity will immediately tenderise the fish.

Note: If you leave the fish in the marinade for too long it will go flabby and bland, however, served after 10 minutes, it will be sensational. Accompany with a quinoa salad, some boiled new potatoes or a few crisp leaves.

MACKEREL, PEACH & DANDELION SALAD

This lovely fresh and colourful summer salad came about by accident. It was one of those rare, glorious summer days when we had all been getting on with various jobs in the garden and just wanted a very light Sunday lunch before going swimming in the lake. There were mackerel in the fridge and a bowl of peaches on the table and we just decided to put them together.

The delicate fruity sweetness of the peach was a perfect balance to the oily, textured fish and then the slightly peppery dandelion leaves weeded straight from a rose bed made a salad worthy of featuring on The Shed menu. Some crusty bread, a glass or two of Pinot Noir Rosé and family together in the garden – what could be better? Serves 6-8 as a large sharing salad

2 mackerel, filleted into 4 pieces
a little rapeseed oil, for brushing
60ml dry white wine
juice of 1/2 lemon
2 sprigs of fresh tarragon, stems removed and leaves finely chopped
salt and freshly ground black pepper
3 peaches, halved, stoned and cut into wedges
1 bunch of young dandelion leaves, washed and dried
1 curly endive lettuce, broken into pieces
250g punnet of cherry tomatoes, halved
linseed oil, for drizzling

Preheat the oven to 180°C/gas mark 4.

Brush the mackerel fillets lightly with oil and put them, skin-side up, on a baking tray. Bake for 6 minutes or until the flesh is just cooked, but still pearly. Set aside to cool.

Meanwhile, heat the white wine, lemon juice and tarragon in a small saucepan over a low heat. Season well with salt and black pepper. Just as the mixture comes to the boil, remove the pan from the heat and add the peaches. Set aside to marinate and cool.

Carefully remove the skin from the mackerel and gently break the flesh into flakes.

To assemble the salad, toss the dandelion leaves and endive together and arrange on a serving platter. Top with the flaked mackerel, peach wedges and cherry tomatoes. Pour over the peach cooking liquor and finish with a drizzle of linseed oil and some extra freshly ground black pepper.

1.

GRILLED SEA BASS WITH SAUCE VIERGE

A bike ride down to the beach with just a worm and a hook on a line, early enough to catch the first light of a summer dawn, can provide the thrill of catching your own wild sea bass. When I lived down in Dorset the best treat on a day off was not to have a lie-in, but to go early morning fishing on Chesil Beach.

Sea bass is an exquisitely textured, sweet-fleshed fish that needs careful treatment in the kitchen. It should be plain baked to just 'pearly' in colour and served with very simple accompaniments. For me, a sauce vierge – 'virgin sauce' – made from virgin unprocessed oil and delicate baby vegetables, is perfect.

Serves 4-6 as a main course

a little rapeseed oil,
  for brushing
1-1.5kg whole sea bass
watercress and boiled new
  potatoes, to serve

FOR THE SAUCE VIERGE
300g broad beans in their
  pods
300g peas in their pods
150g pomodoro cherry
  tomatoes, quartered
2 large sprigs of basil,
  leaves removed and
  finely shredded
4 large sprigs of chervil,
  picked into tiny leaves
125ml linseed oil
juice of 1 lemon
salt and freshly ground
  black pepper

First make the sauce vierge. Fill a medium saucepan with boiling water, put in the whole broad bean pods and pea pods and cook for 4 minutes. Drain and refresh under cold running water.

Pod the broad beans and also remove the husks by squeezing out the small, delicious kernels from inside each one. Pod the peas and put these in a bowl with the bean kernels. Discard the pods and husks.

Add the tomatoes, basil, chervil, linseed oil and lemon juice to the bowl, stir everything gently together and season with salt and pepper. Cover the bowl with clingfilm and transfer it to the fridge for at least an hour to allow the flavours to develop.

Preheat the oven to 190°C/gas mark 5.

Heat a heavy-based frying pan over a moderate to high heat. Brush a little oil onto both sides of the sea bass, and then fry it quickly for 1–2 minutes on each side to allow the skin to crisp. Put the whole pan in the oven – if you don't have an ovenproof pan you can transfer the fish to a roasting tin – and bake for 6–8 minutes.

Serve the sea bass and the sauce vierge as a central sharing dish, garnished with watercress and accompanied by some boiled new potatoes.

3.

4.

SCALLOP & CRAB FLORENTINE

While lots of really inexpensive or even foraged ingredients are undervalued, there are some very special ingredients that command very high prices but are still worth every penny. A fresh, diver-caught King scallop is just such an indulgence. In this recipe, the richness of the crabmeat combined with the sensual texture and delicacy of the King scallop makes for a sublime dish. It can be cooked within the individual scallop shells or in little ovenproof dishes. If you are serving it as a central sharing dish, you may wish to slice the scallops into pieces.

Serves 6 as a starter

400g spinach, washed and picked
250g cooked white and brown
   crabmeat
a few drops of Tabasco sauce
6 King scallops, coral bit
   cleaned and side muscle
   removed
400ml whole milk
1/2 medium onion,
   peeled but kept whole
a few cloves
2 bay leaves
a scattering of black
   peppercorns
30g unsalted butter
30g plain flour
50ml double cream
50g Cheddar cheese, grated
2 medium egg yolks
salt and freshly ground black
   pepper
a few wild chervil leaves,
   to garnish

(You will need 6 gratin-style dishes or 6 cleaned out scallop shells)

Put the spinach in a large, heavy-based pan over a moderate heat and toss until it wilts; drain well and set aside to cool.

Meanwhile, put the crabmeat in a bowl, season it with the Tabasco and set aside. Arrange the spinach in little nests inside 6 individual dishes or scallop shells. Fill each spinach nest with a spoonful of the crabmeat, and then put a scallop in the centre. Arrange the filled dishes or shells on a grill tray and set aside while you prepare the sauce.

Heat the milk in a small saucepan over a low heat with the onion, cloves, bay leaves and peppercorns. Simmer for 5–10 minutes to allow the flavours to infuse, and then strain the milk and discard the flavourings.

Preheat the grill to moderate.

Melt the butter in a small, heavy-based pan over a moderate heat. Stir in the flour, cook for 1 minute and then stir in the infused milk. Whisk to remove any lumps. Finally, stir in the cream and cheese and cook for a further 5 minutes. Remove the pan from the heat, whisk in the egg yolks and season carefully with salt and freshly ground black pepper.

Spoon the sauce over the scallops and cook under the hot grill for 5 minutes until bubbling and golden. Garnish with chervil and serve immediately.

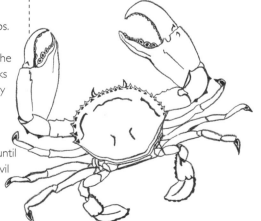

PLAICE STRAWS

This is another Shed classic and if I try to move it off the menu our regulars immediately complain. Everyone secretly likes fried fish in batter, but these are a more elegant version. Served upright in a china mug, they create a real 'wow' when presented to a restaurant table. Then dipped in our fresh dill mayonnaise, the rest is history - they have all disappeared. Serves 6

6 skinless plaice fillets
200ml rapeseed oil, for
   deep-frying
Dill Mayonnaise, to serve
   (page 66)

FOR THE BATTER
200g self-raising flour
200g rice flour
zest of 2 lemons
350ml lager
1 teaspoon rock salt
freshly ground black pepper

Cut the plaice fillets lengthways into approx. 12 long, wide strips. Set aside on kitchen paper to absorb any excess moisture.

To make the batter, put the self-raising flour and rice flour in a large mixing bowl. (The addition of rice flour helps the batter stay crisp after cooking.) Add the lemon zest and, using a balloon whisk, mix the dry ingredients together. Slowly add the lager, whisking constantly until the batter is smooth and the consistency of thick cream. Season with salt and pepper.

Pour approx. 1cm of oil into a large, heavy-based frying pan and heat over a moderate heat. Either use a thermometer to measure the oil up to 175°C or drop a small piece of bread in. If the oil is ready, the bread will brown after 1 minute.

Dip the strips of plaice into the batter a few at a time, making sure that they are evenly coated. Lay them out straight in the hot oil and fry for approx. 2 minutes on each side until golden brown. Drain on kitchen paper while you fry the rest.

Serve your plaice straws with Dill Mayonnaise or a similar dipping sauce such as sweet chilli dipping sauce, chimichurri or caper tartare.

SUMMER CHICKEN BROTH
WITH HAZELNUT PESTO & LARDO DIPPERS

FOR THE BROTH

1 free-range chicken carcass

1.5 litres water

200ml white wine

3 shallots, peeled and sliced

3 garlic cloves, sliced

2 sprigs of thyme

1 teaspoon black peppercorns

1/2 teaspoon salt

150g garden peas

6 radishes, topped, tailed
    and sliced

In Britain we eat more chicken than any other meat but so much is sold off the bone or in joints that buying a whole chicken is becoming a rarity. The real plus of buying a whole bird is that whatever you do with it the first time around you still get a second meal when you turn the carcass into a good broth.

This little feast came together when we were all doing some tree clearing down at the farm. We lit the barbecue and chilled some beers. Then came a Summer Chicken Broth with a spicy hazelnut pesto and chargrilled sourdough lardo dippers, long homemade breadsticks wrapped in thin cured pork fat then cooked on the fire. Serves 6 as an informal meal

FOR THE PESTO
100g sorrel leaves, finely
    shredded
50g blanched hazelnuts, crushed
30g Cheddar cheese, finely
    grated
1 tablespoon cider vinegar
1 tablespoon caster sugar
pinch of salt and some freshly
    ground black pepper
50ml rapeseed oil

FOR THE SOURDOUGH LARDO DIPPERS
1 crusty loaf of sourdough bread
12 strips of lardo (or air-dried
    ham or streaky bacon)

First make the broth. Put the chicken carcass, water, wine, shallots, garlic, thyme, black peppercorns and salt in a large saucepan over a low heat. Cover with a lid and simmer for 3 hours. Pour the liquid through a fine sieve and discard all but the stock. Keep the stock in the saucepan ready to reheat.

Prepare the pesto by blending all the ingredients together to form a coarse paste in a large pestle and mortar or food processor. Spoon this into a bowl, cover with clingfilm and transfer to the fridge until you are ready to serve.

Assemble the dippers by cutting the sourdough bread into long fingers and winding the slices of lardo around them in a spiral.

Reheat the chicken broth on one end of the barbecue if you're outdoors (or on the hob). Meanwhile, grill the lardo dippers for 1 minute on each side until crisp and

golden. Add the peas to the hot broth and cook for 5 minutes. Throw in the radish slices at the last moment, just before you ladle the broth into bowls. Finish with a good dollop of pesto in each bowl and serve the lardo dippers on the side.

RABBIT & WILD CHERRY CASSEROLE

I wrote a dramatic piece about stealthily hunting down and shooting a rabbit the moment it poked its head out of the burrow. Then I went on to explain how to gut it, skin it and chop it up in graphic detail. But Richard and the publisher vetoed all this from the book! Let's talk about the cherries instead. We have some massive old wild cherry trees down at Nutbourne, which yield a bountiful crop of very small, sour, bright red fruits. The longer we leave them on the trees the sweeter they become, but the race to harvest is pitted against the local blue jays who are also waiting for their moment to feast. The answer is to get in first and we have a hilarious session with ladders, baskets and girlfriends to gather up the fruit while we climb and shake the trees. The result is delicious free food to steep, bottle or cook with.

This unusual recipe uses the acidity and natural sweetness of the cherries to complement the delicate flavour of the wild meat. Serves 4-6 as a main course or more as a central sharing dish

30ml rapeseed oil

2 medium red onions, finely chopped

2 garlic cloves, finely chopped

1 large rabbit (weighing approx. 800g) skinned, gutted and jointed by your butcher

20g plain flour, for coating

120ml white wine

120ml cranberry juice

200g wild cherries, stoned and halved

salt and freshly ground black pepper

fresh pasta and summer greens, to serve

Preheat the oven to 180°C/gas mark 4.

Heat a heavy-based ovenproof casserole over a moderate heat, add the oil and fry the onions and garlic for 3 minutes until soft and lightly browned. Coat the rabbit pieces in flour and add them to the pan. Cook the meat for 3–4 minutes until browned on all sides.

Stir in the wine and cranberry juice. Toss in the cherries and season well. Bring up to simmering point, put on the lid (or cover the pan with foil) and transfer the casserole to the oven to braise for 30 minutes.

Once the casserole is cooked it can be eaten right away or reheated later. Serve with some fresh pasta and summer garden greens.

LAMB CHIPS

We came up with this dish at The Shed because of our determination to use up every possible part of the animal in our cooking. A hogget lamb (one year old) has a lot of flavoursome meat in the shoulders, belly, neck and shanks and by braising this meat slowly for many hours we create the most wonderful tender pulled lamb to then transform into 'chips'.

These chips are The Shed's number one bestselling dish - I suspect it is the naughty 'chip' word that first attracts our customers to order it, but then they come back and order it again and again. There are several stages to the preparation and we have therefore made quite a large quantity but it will be worth it as you can freeze some Lamb Chips for future occasions. Makes 24 (Serve 2 per person as a sharing dish)

2 x 1kg lamb shoulders (on the bone)
rock salt and freshly ground black pepper
1 medium onion, halved
1 whole head of garlic, halved
3 large sprigs of rosemary
3 sprigs of thyme
2 tablespoons tomato purée
125ml red wine
30ml sherry vinegar
1 litre water
200g plain flour
3 large eggs, beaten with a pinch of salt
300g fresh sourdough breadcrumbs
rapeseed oil, for deep-frying
Shed Harissa (see page 115), to serve

Preheat the oven to 220°C/gas mark 7.

Put the lamb shoulders in a deep roasting tin with high sides and season well with salt and pepper.

Roast the lamb for 15 minutes until it begins to brown. Remove from the oven and add the onion, garlic and herbs. Mix together the tomato purée, red wine, sherry vinegar and water in a measuring jug and pour the whole lot over the lamb.

Put on a good-fitting lid (or cover the tray with a layer of greaseproof paper and some foil) and reduce the oven temperature to 120°C/gas mark ½. Return the lamb to the oven to braise very slowly for 4 hours, by which time the meat should be falling from the shoulders. Remove the lamb from the oven and set aside until the meat is cool enough to handle.

Meanwhile, pour the braising liquid into a saucepan, set over a high heat and boil rapidly until it reduces by approx. one-third. While the sauce is boiling, line a 15 x 20cm roasting tin with clingfilm, making sure it comes up and over the sides.

The lamb is best dealt with while still warm. Pull the meat off the bones in strands, discarding any pieces of tough cartilage or sinew, and lay it in the roasting tin to form an even layer approx. 3cm deep. Add the reduced braising liquid over the top and find a smaller baking tray that will fit neatly inside the tin in order to compress the meat. Weigh this down with a couple of tins or jars and transfer to the fridge overnight, during which time the gelatinous stock in the lamb will solidify.

The following day, turn the tray of set lamb out onto a large chopping board and remove the clingfilm. Cut into 24 even finger-sized pieces.

Put the flour, beaten egg and breadcrumbs in separate bowls ready for coating. Roll the lamb pieces first in the flour, then in the beaten egg and finally in the breadcrumbs. Arrange the 'chips' on a baking tray, cover with clingfilm and transfer to the fridge or freeze in batches until needed.

Fill a large frying pan with oil, approx. 5cm deep, and heat over a moderate to high heat. To test the temperature, put in a small cube of bread, which should turn golden in 30 seconds. Fry the chips a few at a time in the hot oil until golden brown all over, approx. 5 minutes, and then drain on kitchen paper while you cook the rest. Serve with Shed Harissa.

DUCK LIVER, SMOKED BACON
& SULTANA SALAD WITH A
HONEY MUSTARD DRESSING

DUCK LIVER, SMOKED BACON & SULTANA SALAD WITH A HONEY MUSTARD DRESSING

I bend my own rules about always using whole animals when it comes to duck livers. They are a good by-product to purchase and you would need to serve a lot of whole ducks to accumulate enough livers for a decent salad! A lot of poultry farmers sell duck breasts and leg joints, but the livers are usually dealt with separately - making them relatively inexpensive. This salad could be served as a whole meal in itself. The livers work well with the bacon and croûtons, which contrast with the bitter salad leaves and the sweet sultanas and dressing. It is very moreish, so be prepared for a demand for second helpings. Serves 6 as a starter

3 tablespoons rapeseed oil

200g smoked bacon lardons

100g white or brown bread, cut into 1cm cubes

1 curly endive lettuce, torn into bite-sized pieces

2 heads of radicchio, finely sliced

400g duck livers, cleaned of any sinews and cut in half

80g yellow sultanas

FOR THE HONEY MUSTARD DRESSING

100ml water

pinch of salt

50g black mustard seeds

50g yellow mustard seeds

1 tablespoon English mustard

2 tablespoons runny honey

1 tablespoon sherry vinegar

1 teaspoon chopped rosemary

200ml rapeseed oil

Start by making the dressing. Put the water and salt in a small saucepan over a low heat, add the black and yellow mustard seeds and simmer for approx. 5 minutes until tender. Pour the contents of the pan into a bowl and add the English mustard, honey, sherry vinegar and chopped rosemary. Whisking constantly, slowly add the rapeseed oil in a steady trickle so it combines with the other ingredients and emulsifies into a dressing. Set the dressing aside while you cook the duck livers.

Heat a heavy-based frying pan over a moderate heat. Add 2 tablespoons of the rapeseed oil and fry off the lardons until golden and crisp. Add the bread cubes and fry them in the hot bacon fat until crisp. Remove the lardons and croûtons with a slotted spoon and set aside on kitchen paper to drain.

Arrange the salad leaves in a serving bowl.

Return the frying pan to a moderate heat, add the remaining oil and fry the duck livers for approx. 1 minute on each side until browned all over. Toss in the sultanas, add the dressing to the pan and simmer for a moment.

To serve, spoon the duck mixture over the salad leaves and top with the fried lardons and croûtons. Serve immediately.

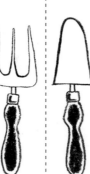

6 x 120g pork chops
salt and freshly ground black
    pepper
2 heads of kohlrabi, peeled,
    thinly sliced and cut into
    5mm matchsticks
400g marsh samphire, washed and
    picked
2 tablespoons Honey Mustard
    Dressing (see page 106)
    or Mustard Seed Emulsion
    (see page 51)

FOR THE PICKLED GIROLLES
150g caster sugar
100ml white wine vinegar
100ml water
6 sprigs of thyme
3 bay leaves
peel of 1 lemon
6 cloves
1 teaspoon black peppercorns
1 teaspoon salt
200g girolle mushrooms, gently
    cleaned of any soil with a
    damp cloth

BARBECUED PORK CHOPS
WITH PICKLED GIROLLES

A warm daybreak in late summer, but it has started damp and misty. There has been some light rain in the night. I get out early into the silent wood of beech and silver birch. There is a wild bilberry crop to forage, growing in small bushes scattered among the trees, then out of the corner of my eye on a mossy bank I spot a tiny 'village' of bright, apricot-coloured, delicate mushrooms. They are chanterelles or European girolles - the ultimate prize for summer foragers.

I have given warnings elsewhere about being 100 per cent sure of the identity of a foraged mushroom before you eat it, but the thrill of finding your own little treasure trove is second to none. For me, it is back home for a breakfast of pan-fried girolles on hot, buttered toast - there is nothing more delicious. The remainder of your bountiful hoard can then be lightly pickled, and once preserved in this way will last for several weeks in the fridge to use as a wonderful and unusual accompaniment to this barbecued pork dish.

Serves 6 as a main course

First prepare the pickled girolles. Put the sugar, vinegar, water, herbs, lemon peel, cloves and seasoning in a small saucepan over a moderate heat and bring to the boil. Stir to make sure that the sugar has dissolved. Remove the pan from the heat and set aside to cool for 5 minutes.

Put the girolles in a sterilised glass, ceramic or plastic bowl and pour over the warm pickling liquid. Cover with a clean tea-towel and set aside to cool and steep for a minimum of 6 hours in a cool, dark place. Remove the mushrooms from the pickle before serving. (Any leftover mushrooms can be stored in their liquid in a sealed container in the fridge for several weeks.)

Light the barbecue and make sure it is really hot.

Season the pork chops with salt and pepper, and then chargrill them on the hot barbecue for approx. 2 minutes on each side. Render the fat by tilting the chops against one another on their sides over the hottest part of the fire. Move the meat to the side of the barbecue, away from the direct heat (but still warm) and leave to rest for 5–10 minutes before serving.

Meanwhile, mix the strips of kohlrabi with the samphire in a serving dish and toss lightly in the Honey Mustard Dressing.

To serve, arrange a bed of the kohlrabi and samphire salad on each plate, top with a pork chop and spoon over some of the pickled girolles.

CHOCOLATE & RASPBERRY PAVLOVA

This dessert is difficult to beat. It has all the right components for those with a sweet tooth, including rich dark chocolate ganache, chewy meringue, indulgent double cream and the glorious flavour and acidity of tangy raspberries.

If you want to be a little bit restrained, make small bite-sized ones like we do at The Shed. Your guests can just take a small portion but I bet they have more than one. For a celebratory birthday bash, make a great big pavlova with a few candles stuck in the top. There are several stages to this recipe, but don't let that put you off - it is incredibly easy.

Serves 6-12 depending on how greedy the guests are!

FOR THE PAVLOVA
4 medium egg whites
220g caster sugar
1 teaspoon cornflour
1 teaspoon white wine vinegar
1 teaspoon vanilla extract

FOR THE CHOCOLATE GANACHE
150g dark chocolate (approx.
   70 per cent cocoa solids)
100ml double cream

FOR THE TOPPING
300ml double cream
250g raspberries
a small bunch of mint,
   to garnish (optional)

Preheat the oven to 150°C/gas mark 2 and line a baking tray with baking parchment.

Put the egg whites in a large mixing bowl (or the bowl of a food mixer) and, using an electric whisk, beat until they hold soft peaks. Slowly add the caster sugar, a tablespoon at a time, while continuing to whisk. Mix the cornflour, vinegar and vanilla together in a small cup, making sure there are no lumps. Once all the sugar has been incorporated into the egg whites, add the cornflour mixture and whisk this in.

Spoon the meringue into a piping bag and pipe 24 individual meringues, approx. 6cm in diameter, or one large round base (20cm) onto the lined baking tray.

Put the meringue(s) in the oven and reduce the temperature to 130°C/gas mark 1. Bake the individual meringues for 1 hour or the large one for 1½ hours. Once the meringue(s) are cooked, turn off the heat and leave them to rest and cool inside the oven for a further 30 minutes before taking them out.

To make the chocolate ganache, put the chocolate and the 100ml cream in a heatproof bowl. Set the bowl over a pan of gently simmering water and stir until the chocolate has melted and become smooth.

Spoon the chocolate ganache into a piping bag and pipe a generous layer of chocolate over the base of each meringue.

Whip the remaining 300ml cream until it holds firm peaks and spread a generous layer over the chocolate. Arrange the raspberries on top of the cream and finish with a few sprigs of fresh mint, if you wish.

SHED KISSEL

We Gladwins had a Russian great-grandmother and although this had very little impact on our upbringing there are still a few small quirky things that have crept through the generations. For example, the making of Pashka at Easter time and a predilection for summer fruit kissel, a sort of thick fruit soup - although that description does not do it full justice.

Kissel can be made from whatever soft fruits you have an abundance of - strawberries, gooseberries, cherries, plums, bilberries and more. I use a little spice and red wine to deepen the flavour, but it is really all about the ripe fruits speaking for themselves. Serves 6-8

400g strawberries, hulled
  and diced
200g cherries, quartered
  and stoned
200g blueberries
80ml water
40ml red wine
30g caster sugar
1 stick of cinnamon
1 teaspoon arrowroot

Put half the strawberries, half the cherries and half the blueberries in a medium, heavy-based saucepan. Add 40ml of the water, the red wine, sugar and cinnamon stick. Set over a low heat and simmer for 10 minutes, stirring occasionally, until the fruit becomes mushy and soft.

Put the remaining 40ml cold water in a small bowl with the arrowroot and mix to a smooth paste with no lumps. Stir the arrowroot mixture into the hot fruit – it will thicken immediately – and remove the pan from the heat. Add the remaining fruit to the pan and stir gently to combine. Transfer the kissel to a suitable serving bowl and chill in the fridge before serving.

Kissel is great just on its own or it can be served with a scoop of sorbet, ice cream, whipped cream or crème fraîche.

SHED SUMMER PUDDING

Every supermarket, restaurant and recipe book now has its own version of summer pudding and it's tempting to think that we shouldn't even go there. But what better way to use up stale bread and overripe summer fruits to such outstanding effect? We make our summer pudding a little different by including peaches and apricots as well as berries and lacing it with cassis and elderflower cordial. Serves 6

250g ripe peaches or apricots, stoned and cut into small pieces
150g strawberries, hulled and halved, plus extra to garnish
100g raspberries, plus extra to garnish
250g blackcurrants or redcurrants, de-stemmed, plus extra to garnish
180g caster sugar
100ml crème de cassis
30ml elderflower cordial
12 slices of thinly sliced white bread (slightly stale is best)

(You will need a 1-litre pudding basin)

Put all of the fruit in a saucepan. Add the sugar, crème de cassis and elderflower cordial and mix gently together with a wooden spoon. Cover with a clean tea-towel and set aside to macerate at room temperature for 2 hours.

Put the pan of macerated fruit over a moderate heat and bring to the boil. Once boiling, strain the fruit through a sieve set over a large mixing bowl to collect all the juices. Tip the fruit into a separate bowl.

You now need to make a patchwork of slices of bread to line a 1-litre pudding basin. Trim the crusts off each slice of bread, and then dip one side in the bowl of juice. Arrange the bread, dipped-side outwards, in the pudding basin. For a good fit, use one square slice in the base, 4 square slices up the sides and 4 small triangles to fill any gaps.

Spoon half the fruit into the bread-lined basin, and then lay another layer of dipped bread across the surface. Fill the bowl with the remaining fruit and finish with a top layer of bread. Trim off any excess bread that is sticking out.

Put the basin on a large plate to collect any excess juices. Then find a smaller plate or saucer that fits snugly inside the rim of the bowl to press down the pudding. Put an old-fashioned weight or a large tin of beans on top, and set aside in the fridge overnight.

When you are ready to serve your pudding, remove the top plate, release the edges slightly with a palette knife, and then flip the basin over onto a serving platter. A sharp shake and it should turn out as a perfect dome. Decorate with a cascade of extra berries and serve with some lightly whipped cream.

LAVENDER & HONEY CREME BRULEE

Lavender is a wonderful plant - it grows profusely, fills the late summer air with its gorgeous smell and decorates moorland and gardens with lovely shades of mauve, purple, pink and white. Best of all, if you gather a couple of big bunches just before the flowers go over they can be dried and used in the kitchen throughout the winter as a delightful aromatic flavouring.

This simple crème brûlée recipe could be adapted in many ways by incorporating different seasonal fruits or flavours. Rhubarb, plum, raspberry, cinnamon or basil are all favourites at The Shed, but lavender with honey is probably the most unusual. Serves 6

500ml double cream
6 stalks of fresh or dried
  lavender flowers
6 large egg yolks
80g caster sugar
2 tablespoons honey

(You will need 6 x 125ml china
dishes or 1 x 750ml serving
dish)

Heat the cream and lavender flowers in a heavy-based saucepan over a low to moderate heat. Just before the cream comes to the boil, remove the pan from the heat and set aside to infuse for 1 hour.

Using a balloon whisk, whisk the egg yolks and 40g of the sugar together in a heatproof bowl.

Return the cream to the heat, bring it back up to the boil and then strain it through a sieve onto the egg mixture. Discard the lavender. Stir the honey into the egg mixture.

Prepare a bain-marie by placing the bowl containing the egg and cream mixture over a pan of gently simmering water. Stirring occasionally, allow the mixture to thicken slowly for 15–20 minutes, by which time it should be thick enough to coat the back of a wooden spoon.

Pour the lavender cream into six individual dishes or one large dish and transfer to the fridge to set overnight.

Preheat the grill to high.

Sprinkle the tops of the brûlée(s) with the remaining sugar and put under the hot grill to melt, bubble and brown. Chill and serve later or serve immediately while still warm.

APRICOT & ALMOND TARTE TATIN

Tarte Tatin is one of the great timeless classics. Invented by two sisters of that name, it is a caramelised fruit tart cooked upside down, with the pastry sealing the filling, and then turned over to serve — and that is the stroke of genius.

Once mastered you can make a tarte Tatin in every different season of the year using apples, pears or plums in autumn, bananas or pineapple imports in winter, rhubarb in spring and peaches, cherries or apricots in summer. This recipe combines apricots and almonds. We also make savoury tarts to equally good effect using onion, fennel, parsnip, butternut squash and more. Serves 8

50g unsalted butter
75g demerara sugar
25g flaked almonds
12 fresh apricots, halved
  and stoned
450g rough puff pastry
  (see page 50)

(You will need a 20cm solid-
bottomed cake tin)

Preheat the oven to 200°C/gas mark 6.

Heat the butter and sugar in a small, heavy-based saucepan over a low heat. Stirring occasionally, allow the sugar to dissolve and then turn into a rich dark caramel.

Pour the caramel into the base of the cake tin, sprinkle over the almonds and then immediately arrange half the apricots, rounded-side down, to fill the base. Arrange the remaining apricots in a second layer on top to evenly fill the tin.

Roll out the puff pastry to form a circle slightly larger than the tin. Put this over the apricots, tucking the edges down firmly inside the side of the tin.

Bake for 40 minutes. Remove from the oven and set aside on a wire rack to cool for 5 minutes before attempting to turn the tart out. To serve, flip the tart upside down onto a serving dish so the pastry is now on the underside.

The tart can be served right away or a little later. Accompany it with whipped cream or a ball of Ever-So-Easy Tangy Lemon Ice Cream (see page 55).

SUMMER LARDER

RICHARD'S DAILY LOOSENER: SUMMER ROSE ROYALE

Most of our daily loosener cocktails are based around homemade syrups or steeps. The Tractor Bonnet Bar in The Shed is lined with Kilner jars and flip-top bottles containing the different concoctions we have in stock and then comes the inspiration – and, of course, testing and tasting – to choose the loosener of the day.

Summer Rose Royale is based around rose geranium syrup, which we also use as a dressing for salads (see page 80). Royale refers to sparkling wine and, of course, we use our own Nutty Brut. Makes approx. 12 cocktails but syrup for more

1 medium egg white

15g caster sugar

1 bright pink or red rose, broken into individual petals

2 bottles chilled Nutty Brut or other sparkling wine, to serve

FOR THE SYRUP

500g caster sugar

500ml water

20 rose geranium leaves

Begin by preparing the rose petals. Put the egg white and sugar in separate little bowls ready for coating the petals. Carefully dip each petal first into the egg white and then in the caster sugar, coating them thoroughly on both sides. Arrange the petals in a single layer on a small tray and set aside in a warm place (such as an airing cupboard) to dry out for 6–12 hours.

Next, prepare the rose geranium syrup. Heat the sugar and water in a small saucepan over a moderate heat. Stir occasionally until the sugar dissolves, and then bring to the boil and reduce by half. Stir the rose geranium leaves into the hot syrup and remove the pan from the heat.

Cover the pan with clingfilm to stop any flavour escaping and set aside to cool. Once completely cold, pick out the leaves and discard them, leaving the syrup ready for the next stage.

Choose your most elegant Champagne flutes. Measure 25ml rose geranium syrup into each glass. Carefully put one or two of the crystallised rose petals on top. Then slowly pour sparkling wine down the side of the glass to fill to a 175ml measure. Your drink will slowly turn pink from the bottom upwards as the bubbles do their work on the petals.

LEMON BALM & RASPBERRY CRUSH

It is well worth growing a variety of mints and balms in your vegetable plot so that you can use them for drinks and garnishes as well as cooking. Once established, peppermint, garden mint and lemon balm usually come back year after year. This vibrant summer soft drink combines lemon and mint with just a hint of raspberry - ideal for non-drinkers, but even better with the addition of a slug of vodka. Makes 2 litres

3 sprigs of lemon balm, tops reserved to garnish
3 sprigs of mint, tops reserved to garnish
2 litres water
200g caster sugar
3 large lemons, roughly chopped
100g raspberries
ice, to serve

Put the lemon balm, mint, water and sugar in a large saucepan. Stir over a moderate heat until the sugar dissolves, and then bring briefly to the boil. Remove the pan from the heat, cover with a tea-towel and set aside to cool and infuse for 1–2 hours.

Put the chopped lemons and raspberries in a food processor, add 100ml of the lemon balm infusion and blitz until the lemons and raspberries are pulped. Pass the mixture through a sieve into a large jug or mixing bowl, pressing down well with a wooden spoon to extract all of the juice. Discard the pulp.

Mix the juice with the remaining lemon balm infusion and chill well in the fridge. Serve in tall glasses with lots of ice and the reserved leaves for decoration.

SHED HARISSA

Our version of this hot North African cooking paste makes a great dipping sauce and it is also a great accompaniment to The Shed's most popular dish - Lamb Chips (see page 102). Makes approx. 300ml

50ml rapeseed oil
6 garlic cloves, peeled
3 red chillies, halved, deseeded and diced
1 teaspoon fennel seeds
1 teaspoon coriander seeds
6 whole cardamom pods
100g caster sugar
100ml red wine vinegar
250g tinned tomatoes
250g tinned sweet peppers
1 tablespoon tomato purée
juice and zest of 2 lemons
salt and freshly ground black pepper

Heat the oil in a medium heavy-based saucepan over a moderate heat and fry the garlic and chillies until lightly brown. Stir in the spices and cook together for a couple of minutes.

Meanwhile, put the sugar and vinegar in a separate small pan and stir over a low heat to dissolve the sugar. Increase the heat, bring to the boil and reduce by half.

Pour the reduced sugar/vinegar over the fried garlic mixture and stir in the tomatoes, sweet peppers, tomato purée and lemon juice and zest. Season well with salt and pepper. Cook over a low heat for approx. 15 minutes, stirring occasionally, during which time the sauce will reduce by about half and thicken.

Transfer the harissa to a food processor and blitz to a smooth paste. Store in a sealed container in the fridge for up to 3 months. Once opened, consume within 2 weeks.

BÉARNAISE SAUCE

A good Béarnaise is a very useful, adaptable sauce to become expert at making. It complements both fish and meat dishes such as grilled salmon or barbecued steak, adding richness and flavour. Our Shed Béarnaise uses Dijon mustard and shallots as well as fresh herbs for added depth. Makes 450ml

6 tablespoons white wine vinegar
1 shallot, finely diced
225g unsalted butter
8 large egg yolks
1 tablespoon Dijon mustard
salt and freshly ground black
  pepper
1 tablespoon chopped tarragon
1 tablespoon chopped chives

Put the vinegar and shallot in a small saucepan over a moderate heat and boil until the liquid has reduced by two-thirds. Add the butter, reduce the heat and allow it to melt slowly, stirring occasionally.

Prepare a bain-marie by placing a dry, heatproof bowl over a saucepan of gently simmering water. Add the egg yolks and mustard to the bowl and whisk together. Continue to whisk while slowly adding the hot melted butter mixture, a little at a time – the whole process should take approx. 5 minutes.

Once the sauce has thickened, carefully remove the bowl from the heat and season with salt and pepper. Finally, stir in the chopped herbs. Serve warm.

Note: If you have any sauce left over, you can store it in a sealed container in the fridge for up to 2 weeks.

GREENGAGE CHUTNEY

Chutney is very satisfying to produce in your own kitchen and is a great standby to enhance meals or give away as a present for other people to enjoy. How many jars of chutney do you think travel from household to household as dinner party gifts without ever being opened?

The joy of making chutney is that it is so versatile. Once you have grasped the basic principles of spicing, evaporating the liquid, pickling and sweetening you can apply them to almost any combination of vegetables, fruit and spices.

Greengages are wonderful green plums that ripen in late summer to a subtle yellow. The shame is that the whole tree tends to ripen at once so, at the same time as scoffing as many as you can manage, it is the ideal time for bottling them and making them into chutney. Makes 6 x 250ml jars

2kg greengages, halved and
  stoned
2 medium onions, chopped
2 red chillies, finely diced
1 tablespoon yellow or black
  mustard seeds
2 teaspoons ground cinnamon
2 teaspoons ground star anise
1 tablespoon salt
500g caster sugar
500ml cider vinegar

(You will need 6 x 250ml sterilised jam jars with lids)

Put all the ingredients in a large, heavy-based pan over a moderate heat. Stir gently to dissolve the sugar, and then bring to the boil. Reduce the heat to low and simmer for 2 hours, stirring every now and then to make sure the chutney does not catch.

Allow the chutney to cool before spooning it into sterilised jam jars. Cover with a small waxed paper disc and seal with a lid. The chutney should last at an ambient temperature for up to a year. Once opened, store in the fridge and consume within 3 weeks.

Cranberry & Elderflower

Apple & Cobnut

Strawberry, Rose & Geranium

Quince & Marjoram

Turnip & Plum

Fodder Beet & Mustard Seed

Parsnip & Honey

Carrot & Blood Orange

Walnut & Cranberry

Rhubarb & Vanilla

Green Tomato

Pumpkin & Date

MORE YEAR-ROUND CHUTNEY IDEAS

SPRING Rhubarb & Orange, Red Onion & Sultana, Carrot & Caraway

SUMMER Courgette & Redcurrant, Tomato & Gooseberry, Apricot & Aniseed

AUTUMN Pear & Raisin, Apple & Blackberry, Plum & Chilli

WINTER Butternut Squash & Thyme, Black Fig & Whisky, Date & Cinnamon, Beetroot & Ginger

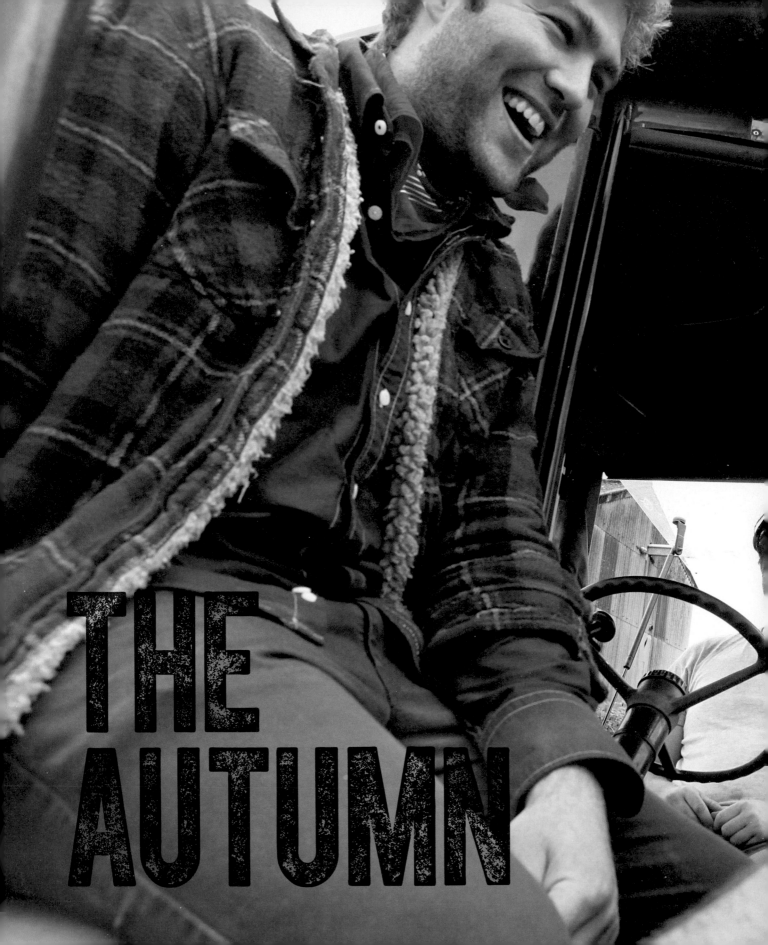

THE
AUTUMN

GREGORY
THE SEASON'S CHALLENGE

For me autumn is like a race or a sporting challenge. You suddenly notice the days are getting shorter, there is a huge amount to get done in order to be ready for the winter, and you have to be constantly alert to the possibility of the weather breaking. How late can I leave the cutting of the maize? Then we need to plough, harrow and drill in grass seed for next spring before it gets too cold. The cows are beginning to churn up the lower meadows and the sheds still need scraping out and re-bedding before we can bring the animals in. Then there are the pigs: Oliver wants more taken to slaughter so he can get his ham cures underway. The sheep are all right, thank goodness, as they are hardy creatures, but they still need checking every day. Then suddenly Dad announces that we are about to start harvesting the grapes!

The Nutbourne grape harvest has always been a family affair. We took on the vineyard when I was less than a year old so I've never known anything different. The process takes two or three weeks and starts at the end of September or in early October. We have a team of approx. 30 pickers all using little scissors to cut each bunch by hand. The problem these days is that with Oliver and Rich so busy with the restaurant, most of the lifting, carrying, and above all clearing up of several tons of grapes falls to me.

At the end of each day's picking the white wine grapes are placed in a mighty stainless steel press, where the whole bunches are gently crushed by a series of enormous cushions to ease the juice out. Then the yeast is added and the ferment begins. The procedure for the red grapes is quite different. The individual fruits are removed from the bunches and their skins are split (thankfully this is all done mechanically). Then the must as it is now called is transferred to a red wine fermenter, where yeast is added and the fermentation begins. To maximise the flavour and colour of the wine, we have to 'punch down' the must several times a day. The days of foot stomping are long gone.

In the unlikely event of a day off, I like to go up to The Shed to drink in the atmosphere. Everyone always seems to be smiling and having such a good time. I think a major part of this is Oliver's theatrical way of cooking. His 'pass' (the place where the food is finished and passed to the waiting staff) is situated bang in the middle of the dining area. This allows guests to see their dishes being carved and garnished just a few feet from where they are sitting. Oliver often brings food to the tables himself, along with a little speech about its origins and how it has been prepared. To be fair, he is very good about giving credit to me and all his other suppliers. There is a gallery on the wall called 'food heroes' featuring photos of our main suppliers of game, fish, dairy products and so on.

FORAGING IN AUTUMN

IN THE WOODS

Ceps, chanterelles/girolles	Strong, meaty, orangey	Barbecued Pork Chops with Picked Girolles (page 107)
Wild apples and crab apples	Acidic, cider, tangy	Crab Apple Autumn Spritz (page 166)
Elderberries	Sweet, perfumed, fragrant	Add to crumbles and pies or preserve as jam, chutney or champagne

ON LEAFY BANKS

Wild chervil/cow parsley	Fresh, slight aniseed finish	Fennel-cured Pollock with Pickled Cucumber (page 38)
Wild rocket	Mustard, peppery, hot	Serve with grilled meat such as lamb or add to frittatas or risottos

IN THE HEDGEROWS

Damsons/bullaces, wild and mirabelle plums	Strong, dark fruit	Giant Plum Meringue (page 163)
Sloes	Strong, dark fruit flavour	Ideal for preserving in jam, jelly and sloe gin
Lavender	Soupy, perfumed	Lavender and Honey Crème Brûlée (pages 112-113)
Blackberries	Strong flavour	Perfect in puddings such as crumbles, cheesecakes or jellies
Quince	Tart, individual flavour	Quince and Rosemary Jelly (page 167)

BY THE SEA

Sea purslane	Soft, leafy, herby	Use in fritters or as natural partner for fish

RICHARD
RECOMMENDING WINES

Oliver's 'flair cooking' often means I never know what is going to be on the menu until the last moment. Even then I have to sneak mouthfuls so I can brief the team on how to describe the dishes to customers, let alone recommend the right wines to drink with them.

With the vineyard harvest about to happen, this is the most exciting time of year for me. A warm sunny autumn is really important but even then it is impossible to know what the wines will be like until the grapes are pressed and the fermenting begins. I've worked in wineries in several parts of the world, including France, New Zealand and California, but the transformation of a basic fruit crop into the most intricate, wondrous beverage known to man never ceases to amaze and enthral me. I make sure I get down to Nutbourne for at least some of the picking just so I can feel part of the new vintage when it is released.

Autumn is also a prime time for foraging. The range of hedgerow fruits, wild herbs and vegetables is irresistible, as are the seashore cabbages, seaweeds and shellfish. At this time of year we take it in turns to undertake foraging expeditions, bringing things you simply can't buy back to The Shed and then featuring them on the menu. The ultimate coup is discovering a little treasure trove of cep mushrooms under a beech tree deep in a moist forest, glistening

in the speckled sunlight. You need to be 100 per cent sure that you have identified them correctly but as long as you are certain, there is nothing more satisfying than cooking with one of the world's great gourmet delicacies picked with your own fair hands.

Many vegetables also come into season in the autumn. With the help of some

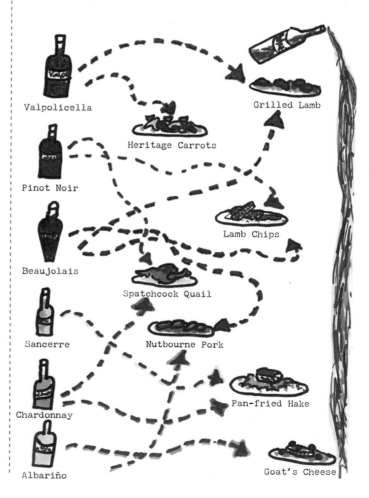

Valpolicella

Heritage Carrots

Grilled Lamb

Pinot Noir

Lamb Chips

Beaujolais

Spatchcock Quail

Sancerre

Nutbourne Pork

Chardonnay

Pan-fried Hake

Albariño

Goat's Cheese

diligent suppliers both in Sussex
and in New Covent Garden Market, we
are able to incorporate a wonderful
variety of squashes, pumpkins, swedes,
turnips, celeriac and cauliflowers into
our menus, along with the last of the
aubergines, tomatoes, and lettuces.
Herbs are still going strong, among
them lovage, dill, oregano and chives
as well as thyme, sage and rosemary,
all of which should last into the
winter months.

Returning to the subject of
recommending wines to go with food,
I am well aware that in the James Bond
novel *From Russia with Love* the bad guy
Nash gives himself away by ordering red
wine with fish. But in reality, certain
reds can be delicious companions for
some fish dishes. It really comes down
to personal preference. Nevertheless,
opposite you'll find what I hope is a
useful illustration on the subject of

food and wine pairing. It was drawn by
Emma, a delightful member of our team
who is responsible for all the pictures
on our blackboards. She came up with
this illustration after one of the
regular 'wine with food' sessions we
hold as part of our in-house training,
which enable staff members to make
their own informed decisions about what
wines to recommend with what dishes.

OLIVER
CIDER PRESSING & PRESERVING

The roots of Richard's enthusiasm for wine stretch back to an autumnal adventure that took place when I was about 12 and Rich a couple of years older. We decided to go into the cider making business. There are a pair of old apple orchards at Nutbourne which produce a bountiful crop that no one does much with, so we thought we could base our new mission on them.

We began by gathering a trailer load of apples, which we shook from the trees and picked up from the ground. Then we got hold of the model traditional oak press that is displayed in the wine tasting room to show visitors how wine used to be made. Richard had done his research and knew that the apples should be chopped or crushed before pressing but that seemed too much like hard work. So we emptied the trailer load onto a plastic sheet and just bashed the fruit with garden spades.

The press was then filled and set into action. After a great deal of strenuous effort a smidgen of juice appeared. Eventually we had a large bucketful of liquid ready to be fermented. We raided Mum's larder for sugar, did a lot of stirring and shaking, and decanted the mixture into three large glass flagons. These were then carefully stored in an outhouse and left to brew. Each time we came home from school the cider was examined. After several weeks we decided it was ready. It had fermented into a cloudy, bitter, foul flavoured sort of sludge. I spat it out right away but Richard was too proud for that and forced down a gulp. He then declared that it needed more time to mature. It remained untouched for many months. In the end I think someone discretely threw it away.

I love each new season as it comes along; the changes in produce and ingredients to be foraged, and the subtle yet definite alteration in style of cooking and eating. The autumn shift is definitely the most pronounced and I think it's my favourite. After a summer of salads, salsas and berries it's really exciting to take delivery of the first few brace of pheasants and put them straight on the menu. The autumn vegetable range is warm, wholesome and plentiful, and within a couple of weeks we are fully into the game season.

At this time of the year I get down to the farm as often as I can. Gregory needs a fair amount of cajoling to keep up the supply of lambs and pork at this busy time. There is a cornucopia of good things to be gathered in the hedgerows and woodlands, and then, of course, there are the demands of the grape harvest. Between 30 and 50 tons of fruit need to be hand-picked and processed in a two to three week period. Last time I put together a hearty venison stew in a massive cauldron, leaving it to brew for most of the day. My brothers accused me of not being much help with the picking but they certainly wolfed down the stew without complaining.

Weigh the meat - most cures are calculated per kilo of meat; pack the meat in salt in an appropriate container; use pure dried vacuum packs of salt for an even cure; leave the meat in a dry place.

CURING & PRESERVING

The great thing about having both a restaurant and a farm is that we can co-ordinate their activities. At The Shed it is unlikely that we will get through as many as three pigs in a week because of the variety of dishes on the menu. Nevertheless, it makes sense for Gregory to take them to the abattoir in groups at least this size. Like humans, animals grow at different rates, so in a litter of 12 piglets, three to six will typically be pushy and grow more quickly than their siblings. This is good for the farmer but there is also something to be said for the piglets who live happily with less food, as this can improve their muscle build up (there is also nearly always one runt per family but I'm not going to mention names!). Naturally the first group will reach slaughter size quicker than the second, so it is logical to cull them in separate batches. But this means that an awful lot of pork arrives at once. Curing is an essential way of preserving meat

from the farm to the table. If it wasn't for this magical process, there would be an unacceptable amount of wastage. Curing also often improves the flavour of meat, for instance in treacle-cured pork, Christmas spiced bacon, and orange juniper bresaola.

So what is this mystical procedure? Curing is simply placing food in a salty environment which draws out its moisture by osmosis. This has the welcome effect of concentrating flavour. I use pure dried vacuum packs of salt, because the crystals are random and sharp in shape, which allow the salt to penetrate quickly and evenly. Curing can be done in many different ways, from wet cures or brines, in which the salt is dissolved in water or other liquids, to dry curing, in which it isn't. For the latter you can use 100 per cent salt, as for air-dried leg of pork (above), a mixture of salt and sugar, or a combination of salt and aromatics, as employed in our

Fennel-cured Pollock (see page 38). For wet cures a good rule is to weigh the meat or fish and then weigh out 20 per cent of this figure in salt. Mix the salt well with enough water to cover the produce you are curing and pour it over until it is submerged. I also like to add sugar or some other sweet substance to my cures. A new favourite is bresaola cured in red wine, coriander seeds, garlic and golden syrup.

Preserving vegetables, fruit and eggs can be just as rewarding as curing meat or fish. At The Shed we ferment, cure and pickle lots of vegetables. We keep the pickling liquor because it tends to improve with usage. I currently have nearly 1,000 cooked and peeled quail eggs pickling in a purple violet liquid, which turns them blue (great fun!). We also make pickled walnuts for the winter and green elderberries in sweetened brine in summer.

Fennel-cured Pollock (see page 38); coppa; a selection of cured meats air-drying at Nutbourne.

AUTUMN MOUTHFULS

PORK SCRATCHINGS & SPICED APPLE DIP

This recipe demonstrates our core principles: waste nothing and make something delicious using every part of the animal. Gregory's pigs are a Tamworth and Gloucester Old Spot cross. Both are traditional heritage breeds - the Tamworth is a small wild-boar-type pig with amazing dark red meat and lots of flavour; the Gloucester is a much bigger breed, which grows quicker and puts on an excellent layer of fat. The result is a great animal - both for cooking and curing. Making your own pork scratchings is a very satisfying thing to do. Makes 20 mouthfuls

20 x 10cm pork skin (available from most good butchers)
600ml rapeseed oil, for deep-frying
rock salt

FOR THE SPICED APPLE DIP
1 large Bramley apple, peeled, cored and cut into chunks
30g unsalted butter
1 tablespoon brown sugar
ground cinnamon, to taste
salt and freshly ground black pepper

Preheat the oven to 120°C/gas mark ½.

Put the skin in a roasting tin, cover with water and cook for 2–3 hours in the oven. Drain off the water, pat the skin dry with kitchen paper and put, skin-side up, on a wire rack. Use a tea-towel or cheese cloth to cover and set aside in a cool, dry place to dry out for 1 week.

To make the spiced apple dip, put all the ingredients in a small saucepan and cook over a low heat for approx. 20 minutes until the apple softens, stirring occasionally. Spoon the apple purée into a serving dish and set aside until you are ready to serve.

Heat the oil in a deep, heavy-based pan until smoking hot. Meanwhile, cut the tenderised dry pork skin into finger-sized rectangles, approx. 5 x 2cm, using a sharp pair of scissors. Sprinkle lightly with salt.

Deep-fry the pork scratchings a few at a time in the hot oil until they puff up like prawn crackers and triple in size, approx. 2 minutes. Lift them out with a slotted spoon and drain on kitchen paper while you cook the rest.

Serve with the spiced apple dip – delicious!

BEETROOT CRISPS WITH GOAT'S CHEESE & HONEYCOMB

Wow, what a mouthful! The crunch of a beetroot crisp combined with creamy goat's cheese and waxy sweet honeycomb will send you to heaven. We get hold of a lavender honey where the bee colony pollinates lavender flowers, giving the honey a lightly perfumed flavour.

The Shed kitchen was working on developing a new autumn goat's cheese salad when we realised that these three simple ingredients were just made to go together as a single bite. Makes 12 mouthfuls

1 medium raw beetroot, peeled
6 tablespoon sunflower oil
30g soft goat's cheese
2 tablespoons double cream
freshly ground black pepper
1 piece of natural honeycomb
12 tiny marjoram leaves,
   to garnish

Very carefully slice the beetroot into 2mm rounds or half rounds – you might want to use a mandolin slicer, if you have one, but be careful of your fingers!

Line a baking tray with greaseproof paper and arrange the beetroot slices in a single layer on top. Set aside in a warm place, such as on a radiator, to dry out for 1–2 hours.

Heat the oil in a heavy-based shallow pan over a high heat and quickly fry the dried beetroot slices until crisp. Drain on kitchen paper and set aside to cool.

In a small bowl, beat the goat's cheese to a smooth paste using a wooden spoon. Stir in the cream and season to taste with black pepper.

Daintily assemble the mouthfuls by placing a teaspoon of the goat's cheese mixture onto each beetroot crisp, followed by a tiny nugget of honeycomb and a small marjoram leaf.

PHEASANT RILLETTE CROUTES

At the Tractor Bonnet Bar in The Shed we have an unwritten offer entitled 'Birds for Beers'. A number of our friends and regulars drop in to see us on their way back into London after a day's shooting to take advantage of this little tradition. They generally have more game birds than they know what to do with and a trade for a Shed Lager Beer or two and some of these delicious little pheasant mouthfuls means everyone comes out a winner. Makes 20 mouthfuls

200g duck fat
4 pheasant legs (save the breasts for roasting)
1 whole head of garlic, halved
3 sprigs of thyme
1 teaspoon black peppercorns
2 tablespoons plum jam
1 tablespoon sherry vinegar
salt and freshly ground black pepper

TO SERVE
1 small baguette, cut in half lengthways and then into thin slices
1 fresh plum, halved, stoned and sliced

Preheat the oven to 120°C/gas mark ½.

Melt the duck fat in a small saucepan over a low heat.

Pack the pheasant legs into a tight-fitting, lidded ovenproof dish and nestle the garlic, thyme and peppercorns around them. Pour in the melted duck fat and cover with a well-fitting lid or foil. Cook in the oven for 4–5 hours, by which time the meat should be really tender and falling off the bones.

Remove the pheasant legs from the fat and set aside on a chopping board until cool enough to handle. Meanwhile, strain the cooking fat into a measuring jug and set aside to cool and harden.

Carefully pick off all the pheasant meat and put in a mixing bowl, discarding the bones, skin and tendons.

As the cooking fat cools it will separate into two layers, with the fat on top and the jellied stock underneath. Carefully scrape away the stock from underneath the fat and add it to the bowl with the pheasant meat. Stir in 1 tablespoon of the cooking fat, the plum jam, sherry vinegar and seasoning. (The rest of the duck fat can be stored in the fridge for up to 6 weeks and used for roasting potatoes, making more confit or for Potted Goose, see page 155.)

To serve, bake the thin slices of baguette in the oven until golden and crisp. Spread each slice with a generous layer of the pheasant mixture and garnish with a little slice of fresh plum. Oh, and don't forget the beer.

GENTLEMAN FARMER'S RELISH (ANCHOVY PASTE)

The original recipe for Gentleman's Relish has been kept secret since 1828 and remains so today. So Dad asked me to come up with my own version of the strong, salty paste that is traditionally spread thinly on hot toast and eaten at teatime after a full day's autumnal shooting by Sussex gentlemen. We serve our relish on thin toast as a afternoon snack, or on savoury scones to complement a mustard leaf salad. It is also a brilliant addition to scrambled eggs. Makes 200ml

100ml rapeseed oil
1 garlic clove, crushed
100g jar of salted anchovies
1 teaspoon caster sugar
1 teaspoon white wine vinegar
zest of 1 lemon
1 teaspoon finely chopped chives
freshly ground black pepper

Pour half the rapeseed oil into a small saucepan, add the garlic and heat gently for 2 minutes to allow the flavour of the garlic to infuse the oil.

Put the anchovies, sugar and vinegar in a liquidiser and blitz to a pulp. With the blade still running, slowly pour in the hot infused oil followed by the remaining oil and blitz to a very smooth paste. Add the lemon zest, chives and black pepper and blitz again.

Transfer the paste to a sterilised jar, seal with a lid and store in the fridge until needed. There is very little in the paste that can turn so it will last in the fridge for a good few weeks.

BAKED OYSTERS

My dad has an old friend, who lives near West Mersea in Essex, with a few hundred yards of beach at the bottom of his garden awash with native oysters. Every Christmas he gathers a few bucket-loads for a special lunch in Livery Hall in the City of London - transporting them up to town in a very old wheelie suitcase on the train. He then goes to the kitchens to help to shuck and clean with the reward of a large glass of Chablis for himself, the chef and helpers. After all this he changes his clothes to become an eminent guest at the lunch. This recipe was a collaboration between Dad and his friend, designed for those who prefer their oysters baked or for those who have access to so many they just enjoy the variety.

For me this is a delicious mouthful to kick off a gourmet meal. Cooked very lightly so that the oysters are warm but not chewy, they are complemented with the addition of some tangy spinach and a rich aniseed butter sauce. Makes 12 mouthfuls

200g baby leaf spinach, washed
   and picked
juice of 1 lemon
salt and freshly ground black
   pepper
12 native oysters, shucked,
   scraped and left in half-
   shell
40ml Pastis
4 tablespoons Béarnaise Sauce
   (see page 116)
2 tablespoons crème fraîche

Put the spinach, lemon juice and some seasoning in a medium saucepan and toss gently over a low heat for 2–3 minutes until the leaves soften; drain well.

Divide the spinach between each oyster shell, tucking it around the oysters to form a little nest – be careful to keep the oyster shells upright so as not to lose any of the natural juices. Drizzle some Pastis over each oyster.

Mix the Béarnaise sauce and crème fraîche together in a bowl and dollop a good-sized teaspoon onto each oyster.

Preheat the grill to very hot. Transfer the oysters to a grill tray and set under the grill for 3–5 minutes until lightly brown and bubbling. Serve immediately with another glass of that Chablis.

SMOKED POTATOES

If you're thinking of getting into home-smoking, you really need to make friends with Henry Williams - a few beers down the Riser (our local pub in Nutbourne) should usually do the trick. Henry is a local Sussex carpenter who specialises in English oak. A couple of bags full of sweepings from his workshop floor will set you up for many months of natural hot-smoking.

I recommend that you do your smoking outside on a barbecue, although the technique we have described below works perfectly well done on the hob if you don't mind the strong smell of wood smoke in your kitchen. You can use this method of hot smoking for all sorts of vegetables, meats and even fish, it just requires experimentation. Serves 6 as a side dish

OAK-SMOKED POTATOES, CURED
TROUT & WILD LEAVES

salt
1kg waxy potatoes (such as
  Pink Fir or Maris Peer or
  Charlotte), washed and cut
  into large chunks
300g untreated oak chippings
  (or other hardwood chippings)
1 lemon, halved
1 whole head of garlic, halved

TO SERVE
a few knobs of unsalted butter
a sprinkling of paprika

Put a large pan of salted water over a moderate heat, add the potatoes and bring to the boil. Simmer for 15 minutes or until the potatoes are just cooked but still firm; drain and set aside. (Note: For smoking onions or most other vegetables, pre-cooking is not necessary.)

Assemble your smoker by putting an even layer of wood chippings across the bottom of a deep, heavy-based roasting tin. Put a pebble at each corner, rest a wire rack on top, and put the cooked potatoes, lemon and garlic onto the rack. Make a domed lid of foil, leaving room for air to circulate above the potatoes but ensuring it is tightly fitted around the edges.

Put the smoker over a hot flame and heat for 5–6 minutes until you can smell the wood beginning to singe. Then move the smoker to a cooler part of the fire (or reduce the heat) and cook for a further 30 minutes, during which time the wood chippings should slowly burn to embers.

Lift the potatoes out of the smoker and transfer them to a serving dish. Add a few knobs of butter to glaze the potatoes, sprinkle with some paprika and serve as a side dish or just as a treat on their own.

BULLS BLOOD BEETROOT & BLUE CHEESE TARTLETS

Our dish development at The Shed is, of course, all about the seasons and what are the best ingredients available on a given day. But we also have to focus on how easy a dish is going to be to share. One of the things that generates such an atmosphere in the restaurant is the constant sharing, passing and discussing individual dishes and flavours around the table. There are things that naturally divide and are easy to share and others that simply aren't. These small beetroot tartlets presented on a large salad bed are perfect to place in the middle of a table for everyone to just tuck in to.

Bulls blood beetroots are a fabulous vegetable because the highly coloured baby leaves are as sweet and tender as the beets themselves. In this recipe I use both. The young beets are served in crumbly blue cheese sablé cases on a salad of their own leaves combined with fresh lesser celandine leaves.

Makes 12 tartlets

FOR THE PASTRY CASES
150g plain flour, plus extra for dusting
150g blue cheese, grated
150g unsalted butter, grated
1 medium egg yolk
salt and freshly ground black pepper

FOR THE FILLING
4 Bulls Blood beets
1 tablespoon rapeseed oil
3 sprigs of thyme, finely chopped

TO FINISH
50ml crème fraîche
a small bunch of Bulls Blood leaves
a small bunch of lesser celandine leaves
20ml virgin linseed oil

Preheat the oven to 180°C/gas mark 4.

Sieve the flour into a mixing bowl and work in the cheese and butter with your fingertips. Now knead in the egg yolk and season with salt and plenty of black pepper until the dough comes together.

Turn out onto a floured work surface and roll out to 5mm thickness. Using an 8cm pastry cutter, make rounds and fit these into a tartlet baking tin. Reform the offcuts and re-roll so that you use all the pastry.

Bake for 10 minutes, then set aside ready for the beets.

Cut the beets into wedges, season with salt and pepper and roll in the rapeseed oil and thyme. Put in a small roasting tin and bake for 30–40 minutes until tender.

Fit the wedges of beetroot into the tartlet cases and finish with a teaspoon of crème fraîche in each. Put back in the oven to keep warm before serving.

Arrange the salad leaves on a large serving plate, drizzle with a little linseed oil and put the warm tartlets on top.

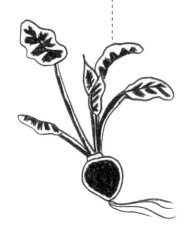

WARM SALAD OF ROASTED PUMPKIN & COBNUTS WITH PEARLED SPELT & LEEKS

These four very simple ingredients are natural autumnal partners. The farmer is harvesting his grain crops; the market gardener's pumpkins are ripe and he is pulling his first new leeks; and the forager is finding cobnuts in the hedgerows. They go together to create a delightful warm seasonal salad.

A lot of people only buy pumpkins to carve scary faces into them at Halloween, but the flesh itself is actually really flavoursome and delicious. Pearled spelt is another underrated ingredient. Gill Meller of River Cottage raves about it for its nutty character and we value it for its strong natural flavour, sweetness and texture. Leeks are at their youngest and most tender in autumn, making them a perfect ingredient in salads. And finally, cobnuts are a type of hazelnut, but with the essence and sweetness of coconut. They grow in abundance in Southeast England; perfect for foraging. Serves 6 as a sharing dish

600g peeled pumpkin flesh
40g pumpkin seeds
60g blanched cobnuts or
    hazelnuts
2 tablespoons rapeseed oil
1 tablespoon honey
1 teaspoon chopped thyme
salt and freshly ground black
    pepper
200g pearled spelt
250g leeks, sliced into 1cm
    discs

Preheat the oven to 180°C/gas mark 4.

Cut the pumpkin flesh into bite-sized cubes and put it in a roasting tin with the seeds, cobnuts, oil, honey and thyme. Season with salt and freshly ground black pepper. Toss everything together so that the pumpkin is evenly coated in the oil and herbs and roast until tender, approx. 20 minutes.

Meanwhile, put the pearled spelt in a medium saucepan, add enough cold water to cover and season with a pinch of salt. Simmer over a moderate heat for approx. 20 minutes until the grain is tender but still has a bit of texture; drain and rinse under cold running water until cool.

Put a separate pan of water over a moderate heat, add the leeks and simmer for 6 minutes until tender; drain well and keep warm.

To assemble the salad, spoon the spelt onto a serving dish, scatter over the warm leeks and pile the hot roasted pumpkin and nuts on top.

THE MUSHROOM FORAGER'S RAGU WITH CELERIAC PUREE

I will repeat my warning that poisonous fungi can be highly dangerous; only pick or even touch a wild mushroom if you are certain of its identity and even then check with a guidebook or expert. That said, the countryside in early autumn is alive with a veritable mushroom feast. They grow everywhere on the farm, each variety with its own special habitat in which it flourishes: flat blacks and puffballs in the cow fields; parasols and chanterelles in the woods; chestnut and hedgehog under the hedgerows.

If you are not confident as a forager, or simply don't have the opportunity or time, a wide range of wild mushrooms is now available in good food stores. The joy of this simple ragù is that you can make it using whatever looks best on the day. It is a bestseller at The Shed, not just for the way Richard talks up his foraging expeditions but as a great flavoursome alternative to meat. Serves 6 as a main course or more as a sharing plate

FOR THE CELERIAC PURÉE
1 large celeriac, peeled and cut into 3cm cubes
200ml single cream
3 sage leaves
rock salt and freshly ground black pepper
juice of ½ lemon

FOR THE FRIED SAGE LEAVES
2 tablespoons rapeseed oil
6 sage leaves

FOR THE MUSHROOM RAGÙ
1kg assorted wild mushrooms
2 tablespoons rapeseed oil
3 garlic cloves, finely chopped
1 tablespoon coriander seeds
2 tablespoons Worcestershire sauce
200ml red wine
80g unsalted butter

Begin by preparing the celeriac purée. Put the cubed celeriac in a medium saucepan with the cream, sage leaves, some salt and plenty of pepper. Cook over a gentle heat for 30 minutes until tender.

Remove the celeriac from the heat and blitz to a smooth purée using a hand-held immersion blender. Stir in the lemon juice, cover the pan with a lid and transfer it to a low oven 110°C/gas mark ¼, to keep warm.

Meanwhile, prepare the sage leaves. Heat the oil in a small pan over a moderate heat and fry the remaining 6 sage leaves until crisp. Remove from the pan and set aside on kitchen paper to drain.

Treat your mushrooms with great care. Brush off any outer particles of soil with a damp cloth, but avoid fully washing if you can – although smaller chanterelles may need a quick dip to remove any grit. Dry them gently with a tea-towel. Cut the larger mushrooms into even slices and sprinkle all of them with rock salt and black pepper.

Heat the oil in a large, heavy-based frying pan over a moderate heat. Add the garlic and coriander seeds and fry gently for 1 minute. Add the large, more robust mushrooms to the pan first, followed by the smaller, more delicate ones at the last moment. Toss them gently in the pan but be careful not to crush or damage them. The whole cooking time should be no more than 5 minutes – we don't want shrivelled, just lightly fried. Transfer the mushrooms to a serving dish using a slotted spoon and set aside while you finish the sauce.

Return the pan to a moderate heat, pour in the Worcestershire sauce and red wine and boil rapidly until reduced by half (approx. 1 minute). Remove the pan from the heat and stir in the butter, a few small knobs at a time, to form a glossy sauce. Check the seasoning.

To serve, pour the thickened sauce over the mushrooms. Accompany with the celeriac purée and garnish with the fried sage leaves on top. A delicious forager's feast!

BROCCOLI & STILTON SOUP

Because The Shed is all about sharing plates, soup is a difficult dish to include on our menus. But for the home cook soup is a perfect starter, lunch dish or whole meal in a bowl. This is a classic recipe for a lovely bright green, smooth soup with plenty of punch. I make it partly to use up leftover Stilton rind (any blue cheese will do) but also because, for me, it does everything a soup should do in terms of body, flavour, consistency and nourishment. Serves 6

50g unsalted butter
2 tablespoons rapeseed oil
2 teaspoons ground coriander
1 large onion, diced
2 garlic cloves, finely chopped
400g 'old' potatoes (such as Maris Piper), peeled and diced
1 litre water
2 teaspoons Dijon mustard
salt and freshly ground black pepper
1kg broccoli, cut into bite-sized pieces
50g Stilton cheese (rind and all)
250ml double cream

Put the butter, oil and coriander in a large, heavy-based saucepan and stir over a medium heat until it starts to brown. Add the onion and garlic and cook for 5 minutes until soft and caramelised.

Add the potatoes, water, mustard, a pinch of salt and some freshly ground black pepper. Simmer for approx. 20 minutes, stirring occasionally, or until the potatoes are tender. Add the broccoli, crumble in the Stilton and cook for a further 6 minutes.

Remove the pan from the heat and liquidise the soup using a hand-held immersion blender. Finally, stir in the cream. (If necessary, you can prepare the soup to this stage in advance and refrigerate or even freeze it until ready to serve. It will keep in the fridge for 3 days or in the freezer for 2 months.)

To serve, reheat the soup in a saucepan over a gentle heat. Accompany with homemade bread or Sourdough Crumpets (see pages 218–219).

COLMAN'S MUSTARD

HAKE, SAMPHIRE & RED PEPPER SALSA

I love hake because of its sweet white flesh and versatility. It is a great 'carrier' of other flavours, but that can sound a bit derogatory and hake should not be underestimated as a great fish in its own right. Ask your fishmonger to fillet the fish, but make sure he gives you the bones and head as well, because you will need all the trimmings to make the poaching liquor.

I have used vibrant green rock samphire here, which is often available as a free food from the seashore (but can also be bought). The red pepper salsa then gives the dish great visual appeal with a 'tricolore' of red, white and green.

Serves 6 as a main course

800g hake fillets, plus all the fish trimmings to make the poaching liquor
50ml sunflower oil
150ml water
a small bunch of tarragon
a good pinch of white pepper
zest and juice of 1 lemon
300g rock samphire, rinsed in cold unsalted water
1 tablespoon capers

FOR THE SALSA
2 tablespoons rapeseed oil
3 sweet Romano peppers, chopped (seeds and cores removed)
1 large onion, chopped
salt and freshly ground black pepper
125ml white wine

Preheat the oven to 180°C/gas mark 4.

First make the poaching liquor for the hake. Put all the hake trimmings in a medium saucepan with the oil, water, tarragon and white pepper. Heat gently for 25 minutes to allow the gelatin from the fish to release into the liquid. Then boil hard for 5 minutes until the oil emulsifies and combines with the water to thicken the mixture.

Strain the poaching liquor through a sieve into a bowl and stir in the lemon zest and juice. Set aside while you prepare the salsa.

To make the salsa, heat the oil in a frying pan over a moderate heat. Add the chopped peppers and onion, season well and cook for approx. 5 minutes until they soften. Pour in the white wine and continue to cook until the liquid has reduced by half. Tip the pepper mixture into a food processor and blitz to a smooth purée. Set aside.

Arrange the hake fillets in a single layer in an ovenproof dish. Pour over the hot poaching liquor and bake for 10 minutes until the fish is just cooked but still pearly in colour.

Meanwhile, blanch the samphire in unsalted boiling water for 2 minutes then drain. Taste the samphire – if it is still very salty, you may want to pour another kettleful of boiling water over it to rinse off as much of the natural sea salt as you can.

Transfer the cooked fish to a serving platter and dress with the samphire. Serve with the red pepper salsa and a sprinkling of capers.

POLLOCK SOUFFLE
WITH COCKLES & SEA ROSEMARY

I did my first cooking apprenticeship at our dad's catering company assisting at royal palaces, state banquets and all sorts of grand occasions. There were some great chefs there, including Emma Spofforth, who took me under her wing and taught me the art of soufflé-making - savoury, sweet, straight from the oven or twice-baked like this one. So to carry on the family tradition we had to include one in our book.

A twice-cooked soufflé is a useful dish to perfect because it can be adapted to include many different vegetables, herbs, cheeses, fish or even meats. Try bacon and spinach or chicken and tarragon, for example. Our inspiration here, however, is from the sea - pollock is a sustainable fish still abundant in our coastal waters, while sea spinach, cockles and sea rosemary can all be gathered from the seashore. The Magna Carta grants every citizen the right to collect up to 8lb of cockles a day - any more and you're going into business! Serves 6 as a starter

60g sea spinach (or leaf spinach)
30g unsalted butter, plus extra for greasing
30g self-raising flour
250ml whole milk
150g skinless pollock (or hake) fillet, cut into 1cm cubes
60g Cheddar cheese, grated
salt and freshly ground black pepper
2 large eggs, separated

FOR THE COCKLES
400g fresh cockles
2 sprigs of sea rosemary (or standard garden rosemary)
100ml white wine
100ml double cream

(You will need 6 x 125ml ramekins)

Preheat the oven to 180°C/gas mark 4 and grease the ramekins with a little butter.

Blanch the sea spinach in boiling water for 2 minutes; drain and refresh under cold running water. Squeeze the cooked spinach dry, transfer to a food processor and blitz to a smooth purée. Set aside.

Melt the butter in a heavy-based pan over a low to moderate heat. Stir in the flour with and allow the mixture to cook for 4–5 minutes and bubble like honeycomb. Pour in the milk, stirring constantly to avoid lumps, and bring to the boil. Add the fish, cooked spinach and cheese and fold in carefully. Season with salt and pepper.

Remove the pan from the heat and mix in the egg yolks. Spoon into a large mixing bowl to halt the cooking.

Whisk the egg whites in a separate bowl until they form soft peaks. Using a metal spoon, gently fold the whites into the fish mixture and combine carefully.

Divide the mixture between the ramekins and arrange them inside a roasting tin. Pour in enough just-boiled water from a kettle to come halfway up the sides of the ramekins. Carefully transfer the tray to the oven and bake the soufflés for 25 minutes until risen and golden on top.

Remove the soufflés from the oven and set aside to cool for 5 minutes before attempting to remove them from their ramekins. Meanwhile, line a baking tray with greaseproof paper.

Once the soufflés have cooled down slightly, run a palette knife around the inside edge of each ramekin and turn them out onto the prepared baking tray. (If necessary, the soufflés can be prepared in advance to this stage and reheated later. Cover them with clingfilm and store in the fridge for up to 2 days.)

Increase the oven temperature to 200°C/gas mark 6.

To make the cockle sauce, put the cockles, rosemary and white wine in a small pan over a moderate heat. Cover with a tight-fitting lid and cook for 5 minutes until all the shells have opened. Remove the cockles from the pan using a slotted spoon and transfer them to a mixing bowl. Reserve the cooking liquor in the pan.

Remove the cockle meat from the shells and add it back to the pan. Discard the shells along with any cockles that failed to open.

Bake the tray of soufflés for 10 minutes in the hot oven, during which time they will rise again. Meanwhile, reheat the cockle mixture and stir in the double cream. Season with a little salt and plenty of black pepper to taste.

Serve the soufflés as soon as they come out of the oven with the cockles and sauce spooned around them.

PAN-FRIED CUTTLEFISH
WITH BLACK BEANS,
PAPRIKA & ALMONDS

PAN-FRIED CUTTLEFISH
WITH BLACK BEANS, PAPRIKA & ALMONDS

Cuttlefish is one of the sea's great underrated treasures. It is plentiful in British waters, has a really meaty character and is a great principal ingredient for a wide variety of different dishes.

The secret of preparing it is to marinate it with something naturally acidic, such as kiwi fruit or pineapple, to tenderise it before cooking. This dish also uses the fish's black ink to stain the cannellini beans for a very stylish presentation and rich flavour.

Serves 6 as a starter or light lunch

2 x 800g cuttlefish, prepared by
    your fishmonger (see right)
4 kiwi fruit, sliced into
    5mm rounds
400g tin of cannellini beans,
    drained and rinsed
1 tablespoon fennel seeds
salt and freshly ground black
    pepper
80ml sunflower oil
150g flaked almonds
2 teaspoons smoked paprika
lemon wedges and watercress,
    to garnish

Ask your fishmonger to gut, clean and prepare the cuttlefish, reserving the ink sack. Also ask him to score the body with even criss-cross cuts.

Arrange the cuttlefish body and tentacles in a ceramic dish (not a metal one because the acidity in the kiwi could taint the flavour) and layer the kiwi fruit over the top. Cover the dish with clingfilm and transfer to the fridge to marinate for 24 hours.

The following day, blitz the cannellini beans in a food processor along with a small amount of the cuttlefish ink to blacken the purée – just add a teaspoonful at a time and then taste, as you don't want the ink to overwhelm the flavour of the beans. Stir in the fennel seeds and season to taste. Transfer the puréed beans to a small saucepan and heat through gently over a low heat while you cook the cuttlefish.

Pour the oil into a large frying pan, season with salt and pepper and heat over a moderate heat until smoking hot. Meanwhile, remove the marinated cuttlefish from the fridge, discarding the kiwi, and pat dry with kitchen paper.

Fry the cuttlefish, a few pieces at a time, in the hot oil until lightly coloured, approx. 1 minute on each side. Remove the fish with a slotted spoon and drain on kitchen paper while you fry the rest.

Arrange the cuttlefish on a serving plate and spoon the warm black beans alongside.

To finish the dish, toss the almonds into the same pan that you used to cook the cuttlefish and fry until golden brown. At the last moment, stir in the smoked paprika and then pour the whole mixture over the fish. Garnish the dish with lemon wedges and watercress.

CLAM CHOWDER

Creative cooking is often about taking a great food idea from somewhere in the world, adapting it to your own ingredients and style, and then tinkering and experimenting until you are happy with it and have suddenly created something new.

This is a take on a classic American chowder that should be made when you are sick of your standard repertoire. There are loads of versions of clam chowder and our one is the result of that process of trial and error. It doesn't matter what you use in terms of fish and vegetables - smoked haddock or cod both form a good fish base, while sweet potato, squash or cabbage could all be added for a bit of variety.

Makes 6 hearty portions

24 large clams, scrubbed clean
300ml water
40g unsalted butter
80g smoked bacon, cut into
  2cm pieces
2 celery sticks, finely diced
1 medium onion, finely diced
250g 'old' potatoes (such as
  Maris Piper or Désirée),
  peeled and cut into 2cm chunks
450ml whole milk
1 bay leaf
salt and freshly ground black
  pepper
pinch of chilli powder
150g skinless cod or coley
  fillet, cut into 2cm pieces
200g tin of sweetcorn
2 plum tomatoes, deseeded and
  cut into strips
6 water biscuits, broken into
  pieces
1-2 tablespoons chopped parsley,
  to garnish

Put the clams and 100ml of the water in a large saucepan over a moderate heat and cook for 6–8 minutes until the shells open. Drain the clams through a colander set over a mixing bowl to collect the cooking liquor. Remove the meat from 18 of the clams, reserving the other 6 to garnish.

Melt the butter in a frying pan over a moderate heat. Fry the bacon until it starts to brown, and then add the celery and onion. Cook for a further 5 minutes until the onion has softened. Set aside.

Meanwhile, put the potatoes, milk, remaining 200ml water, bay leaf and clam cooking liquor in a large saucepan and bring to the boil over a high heat. Season well with salt, freshly ground black pepper and a pinch of chilli powder. Reduce the heat and simmer until the potatoes are just tender, approx. 12 minutes.

Add the bacon mixture and white fish to the pan and simmer gently for 5 minutes until the fish is just cooked. Finally, stir in the clam meat, sweetcorn and tomatoes. Bring briefly to the boil.

Spoon the chowder into bowls and garnish each one with a clam in a shell, some broken water biscuits (this is traditional) and plenty of chopped parsley.

A LITTLE ABOUT COOKING OIL & BUTTER

I think there are many amazing oils in the world, all delicious in their individual ways. Rape and linseed fields make the British countryside incredibly beautiful in late spring with fields of vibrant blue and yellow. We are very lucky that real oils are now available in this country, which have not been processed too much. They hold great health properties like omega-3 and omega-9, which our bodies need. So the perfect breakfast bowl would contain 1 spoonful of linseed oil along with a natural mix of cereals, fruits, 2 spoonfuls of natural yogurt and 1 spoonful of wild honey.

We use both rapeseed and linseed oil in our kitchen at The Shed and have no need for imported olive oil. Both are farmed within Sussex. We use an amazing unrefined cold-pressed virgin linseed oil that is golden like late summer straw and perfect for finishing and dressing grilled meat and fish and salads. For cooking, we use a carefully refined rapeseed oil that has a flash point of 220°C, so we can cook with it at high temperatures without the risk of burning.

We also use unsalted butter in the kitchen, so we have complete control of our seasonings. When you baste food in a pan with butter, unsalted foams and holds its heat better.

2kg beef shin, cut into 8cm
    pieces, with the bone left in
salt and freshly ground black
    pepper
350ml red wine
1 litre hot vegetable or beef
    stock
4 garlic cloves, chopped
4 shallots, finely diced
1 tablespoon ground cumin
1 tablespoon ground coriander
1 tablespoon chopped fresh thyme
    leaves

FOR THE PRESERVED LEMONS
4 lemons, cut in half
    lengthways and sliced
    into 5mm half-moons
750ml water
100g caster sugar
40g table salt
3 sprigs of thyme

FOR THE CAULIFLOWER COUSCOUS
1 large cauliflower
100g unsalted butter
2 tablespoons sunflower seeds
2 tablespoons raisins, soaked in
    1 tablespoon hot water
1 red chilli, finely diced
3 sprigs of fresh tarragon,
    leaves removed and finely
    chopped

STICKY BEEF SHIN
WITH CAULIFLOWER COUSCOUS
& PRESERVED LEMONS

Shed cooking is about the whole animal in the kitchen. When new chefs join us from other restaurants they are astonished to learn that the day begins with traditional butchery. Even if they have worked in really smart, well-reputed places, they are used to seeing boxes full of trim fillets, where racks or loins arrive more or less ready for cooking. Some of them don't even know you only get 2 fillets from one cow and then 300 plus kilos of other meat to deal with. So, the key is how do we achieve the very best culinary result from every single cut of a carcass?

Shin of beef is an inexpensive cut that slow cooks down beautifully with a natural, sticky, intense flavour. This recipe marries the beef with the lightness and freshness of raw cauliflower 'couscous' and some quick homemade preserved lemon slices.

Serves 6-8 as a main course

Preheat the oven to 120°C/gas mark ½.

Season the beef shin and put it in a deep roasting tin with the wine, stock, garlic, shallots, spices and thyme. Cover the tin with a layer of greaseproof paper and a tight-fitting lid or foil. Transfer the beef to the oven and braise slowly for 6 hours until it is moist, succulent and tender, and the flesh is falling off the bones.

Meanwhile, prepare the preserved lemons. Put the lemon slices, water, sugar, salt and thyme in a small ceramic ovenproof dish. Cover with a lid and put in the oven alongside the beef shin for 6 hours.

Just before you are about to serve, prepare the cauliflower by grating the heads on the largest holes of a box grater – it will resemble couscous. Put the butter in a large saucepan and stir over a moderate heat until it starts to brown but not burn. Remove the pan from the heat and toss in the sunflower seeds and grated cauliflower, stirring to coat them in the hot butter. Finally, stir in the soaked raisins, chilli and tarragon. Cover with a lid to keep warm while you finish the beef.

Transfer the pieces of braised meat to a chopping board and use 2 forks to pick the flesh off the bones in long strands. Remove the lemons from the oven and drain.

To serve, arrange a bed of cauliflower couscous on each plate, pile the strands of beef shin on top and finish with a scattering of preserved lemon slices.

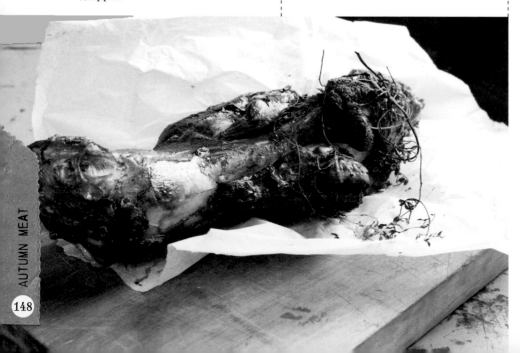

HOG'S WHITE PUDDING

I have a friend in Devon called Robbie Rea, who I know as the 'Master of the Pig'. He breeds, rears, butchers, cures and cooks pork in every conceivable way. We exchange text messages and send one another pictures of our latest creations and it is great to know that someone else is feeling as enthusiastic and inspired by their day in the kitchen as I am by mine. This simple white pudding recipe is perfect as a cold sharing plate accompanied by pickles, or it can be fried like black pudding and served with spinach and poached eggs as part of a full-blown breakfast.

Serves 8-10 as a starter

800g minced pork (60 per cent
  lean meat to 40 per cent fat)
100g fresh white breadcrumbs
100g porridge oats
100ml cider vinegar
1 tablespoon salt
1 teaspoon ground white pepper
pinch of ground mace
2 teaspoons chopped fresh
  thyme leaves

(You will need a 1kg loaf tin
or terrine tin)

Preheat the oven to 160°C/gas mark 2 and line the loaf/terrine tin with three layers of clingfilm, leaving plenty of overlap for the top.

In a large mixing bowl, mix together the pork, breadcrumbs, porridge oats, vinegar, salt, white pepper, mace and thyme. Transfer the pork mixture to the prepared tin and wrap the clingfilm over the surface.

Put the filled terrine tin in a deep roasting tin. Fill the roasting tin with boiling water from the kettle so it comes about halfway up the sides of the terrine tin. Cover the roasting tin with a layer of foil and transfer it to the oven to cook for 1 hour 20 minutes.

Remove the pudding from the oven and set aside on a wire rack to cool. Once it is completely cold, transfer to the fridge to chill and set overnight.

To serve, cut the pudding into thick slices. Accompany with some pickled walnuts, onions and chutney.

AUTUMN MEAT

152

HARVESTERS' VENISON STEW

All wild game needs hanging to allow the flesh to mature and tenderise. The simple rule is that if the animal has two legs, hang it by its head; if it has four, hang it by the hind legs.

The little beauty that inspired this dish strayed into the vineyard last September - an absolute no-no when there was a valuable crop of sweet grapes for him to indulge in. After a little stalking he ended up hanging for two weeks with the fur still on, and then we cooked him in a huge cauldron over an open fire to serve as Harvesters' Stew. Serves 6 as a main course

1kg venison shoulder meat, trimmed and cut into 10cm dice
salt and freshly ground black pepper
10 juniper berries, crushed
a handful of thyme sprigs
60g unsalted butter
60ml rapeseed oil
3 medium onions, peeled and chopped
1 whole head of garlic, peeled and chopped
1kg floury potatoes (such as Maris Piper), peeled and cut into 3cm chunks
500ml red wine
500ml water
1 tablespoon Dijon mustard
1 teaspoon tomato purée
300g carrots, peeled and sliced
300g parsnips, peeled and sliced
2 hard Conference pears, peeled and sliced
600g curly kale, washed and picked
soured cream and chopped parsley, to serve

Put the diced venison in a large mixing bowl and season well with salt, pepper, the juniper berries and thyme. Heat the butter and oil in a deep, heavy pot over a moderate heat and fry the meat, a few pieces at a time, until sealed and caramelised. Each batch will take approx. 5 minutes.

Return all the meat to the pot and add the onions, garlic and half the potatoes. Stir well over a moderate heat for 5 minutes. Pour in the red wine and water and stir in the mustard and tomato purée. Cover the pan with a good tight-fitting lid and simmer over a steady gentle heat until the meat is tender, approx. 2 hours.

After 2 hours, add the remaining potatoes along with the carrots, parsnips and pears. Put the lid back on the pot and leave to cook for a further hour.

Just before you are about to serve, blanch some curly kale in a large pan of salted boiling water for 6–8 minutes; drain well.

To serve, pile the stew onto serving plates, top each portion with a dollop of soured cream and a sprinkling of freshly chopped parsley and serve the kale alongside.

CROWN OF PHEASANT WITH PUY LENTILS, AUTUMN GREENS & ROSE HIPS

We have talked a lot about slow-cooking, marinating and tenderising game. However, pheasant that has been properly hung for 4-7 days in a cool airy place (ideally around 10°C) only require minimum 'fast' cooking and serving thinly sliced and rare. The word 'crown' refers to the two breasts still on the ribcage, which both protects and adds flavour to the meat while it is cooking. In this recipe only the pheasant breasts are used and the other meat can then be used for rillette (see page 128) or ravioli (see page 200). The sliced breast is served on a bed of lentils and greens with a delicious sweet rose hip reduction to finish. Serves 2 as a main course or 6 as a sharing dish

250g rose hips or cranberries
125g caster sugar
250ml water
1 crown of pheasant (2 breasts on the bone)
1 tablespoon rapeseed oil
2 sage leaves, shredded
1 garlic clove, crushed
salt and freshly ground black pepper
200g Puy lentils
300g autumn greens, washed and shredded
25g unsalted butter

Begin by preparing the rose hips. Remove any stalks or loose leaves, and then blitz the rose hips in a food processor until pulped. Put the pulp in a small saucepan with the sugar and water and bring to the boil over a moderate heat. Reduce the heat and simmer for 20 minutes. Transfer the mixture to a fine sieve or muslin bag, placed over a small bowl to collect the juices, and set aside to drain overnight. The following day, discard the pulp and reserve the juice for the sauce.

Preheat the oven to 200°C/gas mark 6.

Put the pheasant crown in a small roasting tin, brush the top lightly with the oil and sprinkle with the shredded sage, garlic, salt and black pepper. Roast for 20 minutes.

Meanwhile, cook the lentils in a medium saucepan of lightly salted water over a moderate heat for 15 minutes. Then add the greens and cook together for a further 5 minutes. Drain, return the lentils and greens to the pan and stir in the butter. Keep warm on the side of the hob while you finish the dish.

Remove the pheasant from the oven onto a carving board and set aside to rest while you make the sauce. Put the roasting tin over a moderate heat, add the reserved rose hip juice and bring to the boil, stirring to capture all the meat juices from the bottom of the pan. Season with salt and freshly ground black pepper.

Cut the pheasant breasts off the bone by sliding a sharp boning knife under each one. Then carve each breast into thin slices.

To serve, arrange a bed of lentils and greens onto plates. Put the pheasant slices on top and spoon over the hot rose hip jus.

POTTED GOOSE

Gregory is determined to get some geese at the farm, I think mainly to warn off unwanted visitors who walk through uninvited and then appear to have all the time in the world to chat about this and that, preventing him from getting on with his work. He also likes them because they represent the archetypal image we all have of a farmyard - proud, bad-tempered birds that don't really take any s**t from anyone. In the kitchen however, geese change character completely and transform into something rich, mellow, succulent and desirable. Throughout the summer months they eat and eat in readiness for winter and therefore become rich in fat, making goose meat ideal for slow-cooking and potting. Potting basically means preserving in fat and this recipe can be equally effective using duck or even pork. Potted meat can be made well in advance and should keep in the fridge for up to a month.

Serves 6 as a starter or more as a sharing dish

200g caster sugar
250g rock salt
zest of 2 oranges
2 teaspoons coriander seeds
a bunch of thyme
2 goose legs
250g goose or duck fat
  (or unsalted butter)
300g shallots, finely chopped
4 garlic cloves, finely chopped
a bunch of parsley, finely
  chopped
salt and freshly ground black
  pepper
pinch of grated nutmeg
1 tablespoon sherry vinegar
sourdough toast and Pear Jam
  (see page 180), to serve

In a large mixing bowl, mix together the sugar, salt, orange zest, coriander seeds and whole thyme sprigs to create a dry cure. Add the goose legs and rub the cure all over them. Cover the bowl with clingfilm and set aside to cure in a cool place for 6 hours. This process penetrates sweetness and flavour into the legs.

After 6 hours, wash the dry cure off the goose legs and pat them dry with kitchen paper.

Preheat the oven to 120°C/gas mark ½.

Put the goose legs in a deep baking dish together with the fat (or butter) and cover with a lid or foil. Cook in the oven for 3–4 hours until the meat is tender and falling off the bones.

Transfer the goose legs to a chopping board, reserving the goose fat, and set aside until cool enough to handle. Once cooled, pick the tender meat off the bones and chop into small pieces.

Set aside in a bowl, discarding the skin, fibrous sinews and bones.

Heat a frying pan over a medium heat with 2 tablespoons of the reserved goose fat and fry the shallots and garlic for 3–5 minutes until lightly browned. Stir in the chopped goose meat along with the parsley and 150ml of the reserved fat. Season to taste with salt and pepper, and then add the nutmeg and sherry vinegar (this will help balance the fat with some acidity). Once you are happy with the flavour, spoon the goose mixture into ramekins and transfer them to the fridge to set for a minimum of 2 hours.

The potted goose is best served at room temperature with very good sourdough toast, accompanied by some Pear Jam.

FRANGIPANE PEAR & CHOCOLATE TORTE

My mother used to make all sorts of marzipan and almond cakes and desserts and I claimed to have a typical childhood dislike of all things almond-based. I don't know why, now I see that our Shed recipes are full of almonds so my attitude has obviously changed.

This glorious rich chocolate torte would not be the same without the zesty frangipane cream. Once you have tried it and loved it with pear, try it with ripe, dark plums. Serves up to 12

FOR THE PASTRY
225g plain flour
110g chilled unsalted butter,
    cut into small knobs, plus
    extra for greasing
80g caster sugar
1 large egg

FOR THE FRANGIPANE
60g unsalted butter,
    at room temperature
120g icing sugar
1 large egg
120g ground almonds
zest of 1 orange

FOR THE CHOCOLATE
& PEAR FILLING
225ml double cream
125ml whole milk
300g dark chocolate (approx.
    70 per cent cocoa solids),
    broken into chunks
3 large eggs
3 ripe pears, peeled, cored
    and quartered

crème fraîche, to serve

(You will need a 25cm
loose-bottomed tart tin)

First make the pastry. Put the flour, butter and sugar in a large mixing bowl and rub together with your fingertips until the mixture resembles breadcrumbs. Make a well in the centre and break the egg into it. Gradually blend the egg into the flour using a palette knife to begin with and then your hands to draw the dough together into a ball.

Turn out the dough onto a floured surface and knead gently into a smooth ball. Wrap the pastry in clingfilm and chill in the fridge for 30 minutes before use.

Preheat the oven to 200°C/gas mark 6. Line the tart tin with greaseproof paper and grease the edges to stop the pastry from sticking.

Roll the pastry out into a 30cm circle, carefully lift it into the prepared tin and pinch it into the edges using two fingers and a thumb. Prick the base. Crumple up a sheet of greaseproof paper, flatten it out again and use it to line the pastry case. Fill with baking beans or uncooked rice; this is called baking 'blind'. Cook the pastry for 10 minutes in the hot oven, and then remove the beans and paper and cook for a further 10 minutes.

Meanwhile, prepare the frangipane filling. Beat the softened butter and icing sugar together in a bowl until light and fluffy. Beat in the egg, and then carefully fold in the ground almonds and orange zest. Set aside.

Once the pastry case is cooked, remove it from the oven and set aside on a wire rack. Reduce the oven temperature to 130°C/gas mark 1.

To make the chocolate filling, heat the cream and milk in a medium-sized saucepan over a moderate heat. Just before the mixture comes to the boil, add the chocolate and stir over a very low heat until it has completely melted. Remove the pan from the heat and beat in the eggs.

To assemble the tart, spoon the frangipane in an even layer over the pastry case. Arrange the pear slices in a Catherine wheel shape on top. Pour the chocolate sauce around the pear slices to completely fill the inside of the pastry case.

Bake the tart for 40 minutes until set.

Serve warm or cold with a dollop of crème fraîche.

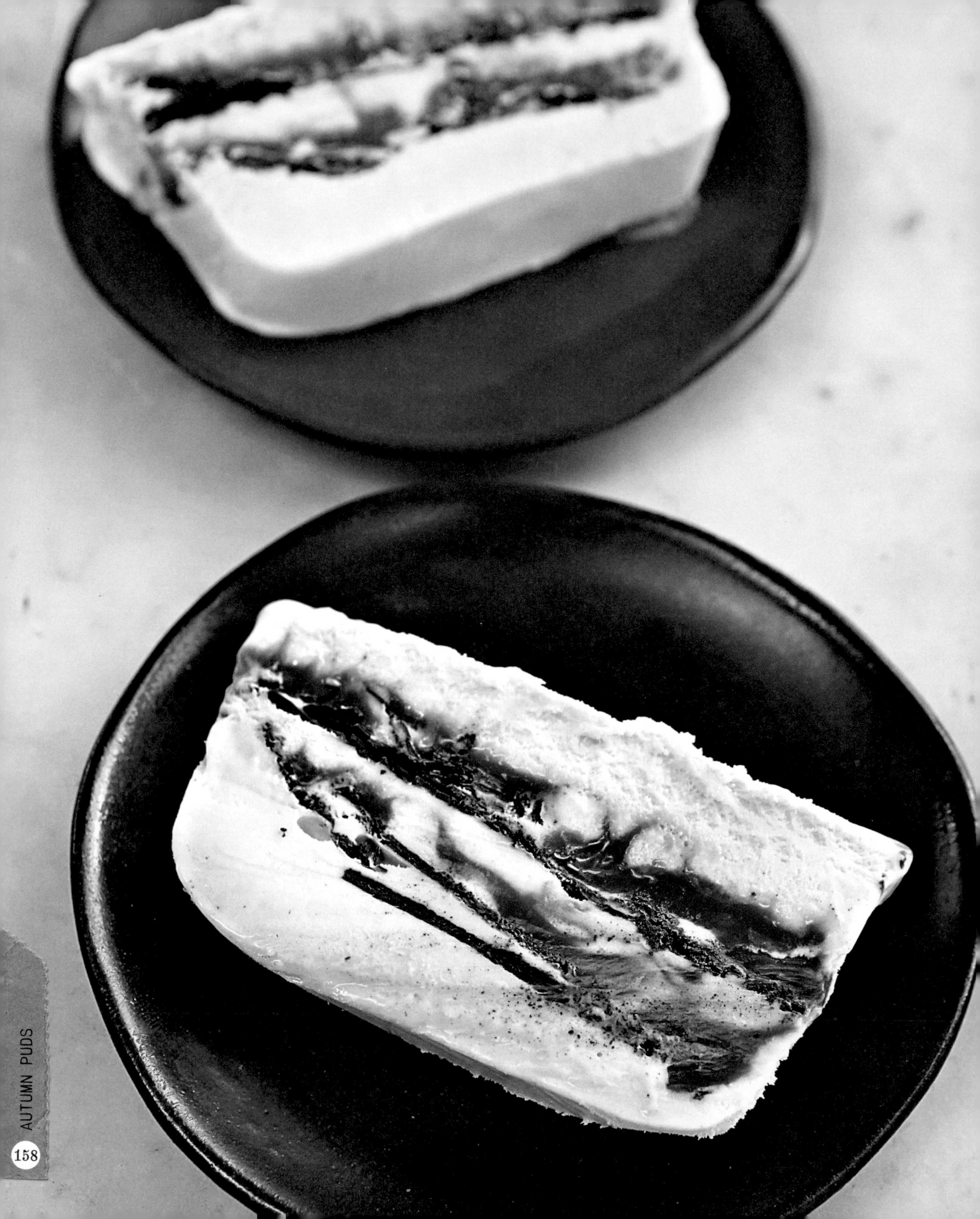

THE SHED VIENNETTA PARFAIT

I first made this hugely indulgent dessert to impress my girlfriend while we were in the building phase of The Shed. Although we three brothers were building, painting, doing woodwork, and everything else, I was frustrated not to be in the kitchen. So for relaxation, I would go home and cook elaborate suppers - just to show I could still do it.

There is a well-known commercial ice cream with a similar name, so for copyright reasons I am going to reassure you this recipe is nothing like it - think homemade double cream ice cream, ripples of salty caramel butterscotch and crunchy rich dark chocolate - you've got it. Serves 12

200g dark chocolate (approx. 70 per cent cocoa solids), broken into small pieces

FOR THE BUTTERSCOTCH
250g caster sugar
70g unsalted butter
375ml double cream
salt

FOR THE ICE-CREAM PARFAIT
150g caster sugar
3 tablespoons water
6 large egg yolks
500ml double cream
1 vanilla pod, seeds scraped out

(You will need a sugar thermometer and a 1-litre terrine tin)

Start by tempering the chocolate. Prepare a bain-marie by setting a heatproof bowl over a pan of gently simmering water. Put the chocolate into the bowl and stir until it has fully melted; it should be glossy and very smooth. Meanwhile, line the terrine tin with clingfilm.

Pour the chocolate onto a cold marble slab, or a large tray lined with clingfilm.

Spread the melted chocolate out to a very thin layer with a palette knife and set aside to cool. Once the chocolate has set, cut it into random shards.

To make the butterscotch, put the sugar in a dry, heavy-based saucepan and dissolve over a low heat – jiggle the pan rather than stirring so that the sugar does not catch or form lumps. Once the sugar has dissolved and become pale golden in colour, remove the pan from the heat and stir in the butter and cream. Season with salt to taste. Set aside to cool, and then chill in the fridge until needed.

To make the ice cream, put the sugar and water in a small saucepan and dissolve over a moderate heat. Do not stir. Using a sugar thermometer, bring the temperature up to 120°C. Meanwhile, put the egg yolks in a food mixer and whisk until thick and fluffy. Once the sugar syrup reaches 120°C, slowly pour it over the beaten egg yolks, whisking all the time until pale and mousse-like.

Whip the double cream and vanilla seeds together in a separate bowl until they form soft peaks. Carefully fold the cream into the frothy egg mixture. Set aside to chill in the fridge.

Make sure the cream and butterscotch are completely cold before you assemble the parfait, otherwise the chocolate shards will melt. Pour one-third of the chilled cream into the prepared tin, cover with one-third of the chocolate pieces and top with one-third of the butterscotch sauce. Repeat the layering process two more times until you have filled the terrine. Cover the filled terrine with clingfilm and transfer it to the freezer to set for a minimum of 8 hours.

To serve, turn the parfait out of the mould and cut it into 8 thick slices using a hot, thin knife. Serve with absolutely nothing at all.

ORANGE & PEANUT NOUGAT BALLS

This exciting confectionery recipe will really impress your family and friends. Rather than making conventional nougat, with nuts running through it, I make individual nougat balls, which I roll in crushed peanuts afterwards. They are a sumptuous whole mouthful sensation. Makes 20-30 nougat balls

400g caster sugar
440g golden syrup
180ml water
3 large egg whites
1/2 teaspoon cream of tartar
zest and juice of 2 medium
  oranges
20g toasted unsalted peanuts,
  finely chopped
2 heaped tablespoons icing sugar

(You will need a food mixer, a sugar thermometer and a non-stick baking tray)

Put the sugar, golden syrup and water in a heavy-based saucepan and dissolve over a moderate heat. Using a sugar thermometer, monitor the temperature as it rises. It will thicken, darken and begin to rise up the pan.

Have the egg whites ready in the bowl of a food mixer. Once the sugar syrup reaches 120°C, start to whisk the egg whites. Carefully watch both the sugar thermometer and the egg whites. When the egg whites form soft peaks, add the cream of tartar. When they become stiff, add the orange zest (but not the juice).

When the sugar syrup reaches 135°C, remove the pan from the heat. It will now be bubbling and golden. Keeping the motor running, very slowly pour the sugar syrup onto the egg whites and continue whisking for a further 5 minutes.

Using a spatula, scoop out the fluffy nougat mixture onto a non-stick tray and set aside for 30 minutes, during which time the nougat will harden slightly. Meanwhile, squeeze the oranges into a little bowl. Put the nuts and icing sugar into separate little bowls ready for coating the nougat balls. Using a 3cm melon baller, scoop out

20–30 little balls of nougat and arrange them on a clean baking tray. Dip each one first in the orange juice, then in the chopped peanuts and finally in the icing sugar. Repeat the coating process again to get a really good crust.

Arrange the coated nougat balls on a serving plate and transfer to the fridge for 40 minutes to firm up before serving.

PINOT NOIR JELLY, VANILLA CUSTARD & SEEDED CRUMBLE

Pinot Noir is an amazing wine grape which successfully grows all over the world but develops a different character, style and flavour according to its root stock and the *terroir* where it is planted. In France, Pinot Noir is the only ingredient of red burgundy and is a key part of most Champagne. It can be delicate, light and fruity, or intense, complex and lasting. We are delighted that Pinot Noir grows incredibly successfully at Nutbourne, where we use it as the base for our award-winning Nutty sparkling (Gold medal-winner last 2 years in a row) and for our Blush rosé and red.

I first made this dish down at the vineyard with the first run off of the Pinot Noir grape pressing, before the juice was fermented. To make it at home you may need to choose a tangy eating grape and press your own juice in a juicer. Carton grape juice is definitely not the same; it tends to lack the acidity and character of a fresh pressing. Serves 6

3 sheets of bronze leaf
  gelatine
600ml freshly squeezed Pinot
  Noir grape juice (see right)

FOR THE CRUMBLE
50g sunflower seeds
50g pumpkin seeds
50g porridge oats
100g plain flour
100g soft brown sugar
pinch of salt
50g unsalted butter, at room
  temperature, cut into knobs

FOR THE CUSTARD
1 vanilla pod
300ml whole milk
150ml double cream
4 large egg yolks
100g caster sugar

(You will need 6 x 125ml dariole
moulds)

Soak the gelatine leaves in a dish of cold water for 10 minutes.

Put half the grape juice in a small saucepan over a gentle heat and bring almost up to the boil (but don't let it actually boil). Remove from the heat.

Remove the gelatine leaves from the water and squeeze out any excess water. Add the leaves to the hot grape juice and stir until fully dissolved. Stir in the remaining grape juice. Divide the mixture between 6 dariole moulds and transfer them to the fridge to set for at least 2 hours.

Preheat the oven to 160°C/gas mark 3 and line a baking tray with greaseproof paper.

To make the crumble, mix together the seeds, oats, flour, sugar and salt in a large mixing bowl. Add the butter and rub it in with your fingertips until the mixture resembles coarse breadcrumbs. Spoon the crumble onto the prepared baking tray and bake for 20 minutes until crisp. Remove from the oven and set aside to cool.

To make the custard, cut the vanilla pod in half lengthways and scrape out the seeds. Put the milk, cream, vanilla seeds and pod in a heavy-based pan over a low heat and slowly bring up to scalding point. Meanwhile, whisk the egg yolks and sugar together in a mixing bowl until pale and frothy. Pour one-third of the hot vanilla cream over the egg mixture and whisk together. Then transfer the mixture back to the pan and stir over a low heat until the custard thickens. Strain through a sieve into a jug, discarding the vanilla pod.

To serve, turn the jellies out of their moulds onto individual plates. Top each jelly with some of the crumble mixture and pour the warm custard around the outside.

GIANT PLUM MERINGUE

You see those amazing colourful, swirling giant meringues in deli shop windows and go 'wow!'. They are actually very simple to make, but there are a couple of meringue secrets we would like to share with you. The first is to heat the sugar before it is added to the whipped egg white. This has the effect of slightly cooking the egg white as it is blended and thus holding air bubbles extremely well. The second is to always cook meringue on a declining temperature so that it dries slowly, forms a nice crust but remains sticky in the centre.

   This recipe uses plum purée for colour and flavour, however, you could use strawberry or raspberry purée — or include nuts, cocoa, chocolate or coffee flavourings instead. Makes 6 giant meringues

6 ripe red plums, quartered
   and stoned
350g caster sugar, plus
   1 tablespoon
50ml water
6 large egg whites

Preheat the oven to 110°C/gas mark ¼ and line a baking tray with greaseproof paper.

Choose the ripest, brightest coloured plums for maximum effect. Put the plums and 1 tablespoon of sugar in a small, heavy-based saucepan. Stirring occasionally, simmer over a low heat until the plums have reduced to a thick purée, approx. 15 minutes. Strain through a sieve into a small bowl, discarding the skin and pulp. Set aside to cool.

Put the 350g caster sugar and the water in a heavy-based saucepan and dissolve over a moderate heat. Using a sugar thermometer, monitor the temperature as it rises.

Meanwhile, put the egg whites in a food mixer and whisk at top speed until they form and hold stiff peaks, approx. 5 minutes.

Keeping the motor of the food mixer running, and once the sugar syrup reaches 120°C, add to the egg whites, one spoonful at a time, and keep beating until the meringue becomes very stiff. Continue to whisk for a further 5 minutes until the meringue is really thick and glossy.

Remove the bowl from the mixer and gently fold in the plum purée using a spatula – don't overmix it, you're aiming for a nice rippled effect with swirls of colour. Spoon 6 large mounds of the rippled meringue onto the lined baking tray, keeping them well apart

Bake the meringues for 2 hours. Then, without opening the oven door, switch off the heat and leave the meringues to cool down inside for a further 3 hours, or even overnight.

The finished meringues should be crisp on the outside and chewy in the middle, with the lovely tang and colour of plum running through them.

BASIC BRIOCHE & CHELSEA BUNS

This recipe gives you basic instructions for making your own brioche dough. This can either be proved and baked in a loaf tin as it is, frozen in small batches to use on other occasions or used in the production of these moreish homemade Chelsea buns.

Makes 1 large brioche loaf or 10 Chelsea buns

FOR THE BRIOCHE DOUGH
500g strong white flour, plus
   extra for dusting
150g caster sugar, plus extra
   for dusting
6g salt
30g fresh yeast (or 15g
   fast-action dried yeast)
4 medium eggs, lightly beaten
300ml whole milk
120g unsalted butter, at room
   temperature, plus extra for
   greasing

FOR BRIOCHE LOAF
1 batch of brioche dough
   (see above)
1 small egg, beaten with a pinch
   of salt, to glaze

FOR CHELSEA BUNS
1 batch of brioche dough
   (see above)
150g fresh blueberries
120g raisins, soaked in
   1-2 tablespoons hot water
150g chopped hazelnuts
1 small egg, beaten with a pinch
   of salt
100g icing sugar
1-2 tablespoons water
1/2 teaspoon vanilla bean paste

(You will need a 600g loaf tin
if you're making a brioche loaf
or a baking tray for Chelsea
buns)

First make the brioche dough. You will need a food mixer fitted with a dough hook set on a slow speed. Put the flour, sugar, salt and yeast in the bowl of the mixer and mix until everything is combined. Add the eggs and milk and continue to mix for 5 minutes. Add the butter, a few small knobs at a time, and continue to mix until the dough becomes elastic and smooth, approx. 5 minutes.

Cover the bowl with clingfilm and transfer the dough to the fridge to relax for a minimum of 1 hour. (If necessary, the brioche dough can be stored in the refrigerator for longer, up to 48 hours, or it can be frozen for up to 2 months.)

BRIOCHE LOAF

Preheat the oven to 180°C/gas mark 4. Grease a 600g loaf tin with a little butter, and then dust it with some flour and caster sugar.

Turn out the dough onto a floured surface and repeatedly pull it from the edges to the centre to form a tight ball. Put the dough, smooth side up, inside the prepared tin, cover with a clean tea-towel and set aside to prove in a warm place for 45 minutes. To test your prove, press your finger gently into the dough: if the indent bounces out you should prove for a little longer, if the indent holds you are ready to bake.

Brush the brioche loaf with the eggwash and bake for 40 minutes until risen and golden. Remove from the oven, turn out onto a wire rack and set aside to cool.

CHELSEA BUNS

Preheat the oven to 180°C/gas mark 4 and line a baking tray with greaseproof paper.

Turn out the dough onto a floured surface and use a rolling pin to roll it into a 30 × 40cm rectangle. Sprinkle the blueberries, raisins and hazelnuts evenly over the surface, leaving a 6cm clear margin along one long edge to seal the roll. Starting at the opposite edge, roll the dough up to form a roulade shape and seal the edge with a brush of water.

Cut the roulade into short lengths, approx. 4cm each, and arrange them well apart on the prepared baking tray, spiral-side up. Brush the tops with the eggwash. Cover the Chelsea buns with a sheet of oiled clingfilm and set aside to prove in a warm place for 1 hour until doubled in size. Remove the clingfilm.

Bake the Chelsea buns for 20 minutes until puffed up and golden. Transfer the buns to a wire rack to cool slightly before glazing them.

To make the glaze, beat the icing sugar, water and vanilla together in a small bowl, and brush over the buns. Serve warm.

AUTUMN LARDER

RICHARD'S DAILY LOOSENER: CRAB APPLE AUTUMN SPRITZ

There are, of course, plenty of hedgerow fruits you can forage for in autumn and many are perfect for preserving, bottling or making into amazing drinks. Sloe gin is a classic, but that is usually drunk as an after-dinner liqueur. As a loosener, we wanted something a bit longer and more refreshing to serve to our customers at The Shed. This recipe uses crab apple cordial, shaken with gin and aromatic white wine (we use our own Nutbourne Sussex Reserve). Makes 1 litre crab apple cordial

FOR THE CRAB APPLE CORDIAL
1kg crab apples, washed
500ml water
300g caster sugar
50g pectin

TO SERVE
lots of ice
gin
dessert white wine (such as
   Nutbourne Sussex Reserve)
sparkling water
oranges or lemons

First make the cordial. Put the crab apples, water, sugar and pectin in a large saucepan over a moderate heat and bring to the boil. Reduce the heat and simmer for 2 hours, by which time the crab apples should be very soft. Pour the mixture into a food processor and blitz to a pulp. Strain through a fine sieve, set over a bowl to collect the juice, rubbing it through with a wooden spoon. Pour the juice into a sterilised Kilner jar, discarding the pulp and skins. (The crab apple cordial can either be used immediately or stored in the fridge for up to 3 months.)

Use a cocktail shaker to build your drink. Fill it with plenty of ice, add 25ml crab apple cordial, 25ml gin and 75ml dessert wine. Pour into a tall stylish glass, filled with more ice, and top up with approx. 50ml sparkling water. Add a squeeze of orange juice and garnish with a wedge of orange or lemon.

CHESTNUT FUDGE

As kids, we used to hunt for conkers (horse chestnuts) and would avoid the prickly sweet chestnuts which were absolutely no use for conker fighting. The biggest nut you could find had to be drilled, then threaded onto string to be swung at another in a challenge of strength and durability. Now of course, it is the sweet chestnuts we gather, roast and peel. Makes 50 squares

200ml tinned evaporated milk
200ml water
100g unsalted butter
450g granulated sugar
100g peeled and cooked
  chestnuts, chopped

(You will need a sugar thermometer)

Line a 20 x 30cm baking tin with greaseproof paper.

Put the evaporated milk, water, butter and sugar in a medium, heavy-based saucepan over a low heat. Stir over a low heat to dissolve the sugar and then bring to the boil without stirring. Use a sugar thermometer to monitor the temperature as it rises. The fudge will darken to a rich golden colour. When the fudge reaches 115°C, remove the pan from the heat.

Using a hand-held electric whisk, beat the hot fudge for 5 minutes until the mixture thickens and goes shiny. Stir in the chopped chestnuts. Pour the fudge into the prepared tin and leave to cool and set for a minimum of 2 hours.

To serve, turn out the fudge onto a chopping board and cut it into even squares or diamonds. This will keep for up to 2 months stored in an airtight container.

QUINCE & ROSEMARY JELLY

One of the great traditions in autumn is bottling and preserving fruit in order to stock up on treats to take us through the lean winter months ahead. Of course, we can buy almost any ingredient at any time of the year nowadays, but that's not quite the same. We have apple, plum, pear, quince and even a medlar tree at home in Nutbourne, all of which make fabulous jellies and preserves.

This jelly recipe is flavoured with the herby tang of rosemary, which makes it a perfect accompaniment for roast meats and terrines. Makes 4 x 250ml jars

1.75kg quinces
zest and juice of 3 lemons
3.5 litres water
approx. 1.25kg preserving sugar
8 sprigs of fresh rosemary

(You will need 4 x 250ml jam jars with lids)

Wash the quinces and roughly chop them, leaving the pips and cores in. Put into a large saucepan with the lemon zest and juice. Cover with 2.5 litres of the water and simmer over a low heat for 1 hour until tender.

Meanwhile, sterilise the jam jars by placing them on a baking tray in a cool oven (130°C/gas mark 1) for 30 minutes. Take care that the oven isn't any hotter than 130°C or the jars will explode!

Strain the cooked quinces through a jelly bag set over a large bowl to collect all of the juices. Return the pulp to the pan, add the remaining 1 litre of water and bring to the boil. Simmer for 30 minutes.

Strain the quince pulp through the jelly bag a second time into the same bowl, and then discard the pulp. Measure the total volume of liquid in the bowl and calculate how much sugar you need. For every 500ml liquid, you will need 450g sugar.

Put the quince juice and sugar in a large preserving pan over a moderate heat and stir to dissolve the sugar. Bring the sugar syrup to the boil and cook vigorously for 15–20 minutes until reduced by half, removing any scum as it rises to the surface. Meanwhile, put a small saucer in the fridge ready for testing the jelly later.

Once the juice has reduced by half you can start testing the jelly for a set. Trickle a few drops of the hot quince jelly onto the chilled saucer – it should set immediately. Drag your finger across the surface of the cold jelly to see if it wrinkles. If it does, the jelly is ready for bottling. (If your jelly is still very runny, return the pan to the heat for a further 10 minutes and then repeat the setting test.)

Carefully remove the sterilised jars from the oven and put two sprigs of rosemary inside each one. Pour the hot jelly into the jars and cover the tops with a little disc of waxed paper. Set aside to cool before sealing the jars with tight-fitting lids. Store in a cool, dark place.

The jelly should last in dry storage for years. Once opened, store in the fridge and consume within 3 weeks.

GREGORY'S SMOKED BARBECUE SAUCE

Gregory does not consider himself to be much of a cook, but when it comes to lighting a good cooking fire he is definitely a supremo and this presents the perfect opportunity to brew up a batch of smoked barbecue sauce.

Hot-smoking can be done on the hob in your kitchen (see Smoked Potatoes page 130), but the smell can linger for several days, so if you have the opportunity to do it outside I would always recommend that you do so. After cooking a wood fired barbecue, it is very little trouble to lay out a range of vegetables and let them smoke away on their own to use as the base for this sauce. Makes 600ml

2 large onions, halved
3 large red chillies, kept whole
2 whole heads of garlic, halved
250ml rapeseed oil
50g ground coriander
100ml Worcestershire sauce
4 tablespoons English mustard
4 tablespoons Dijon mustard
2 tablespoons red wine vinegar
150g tomato purée
100g caster sugar
1 tablespoon salt
2 tablespoons finely chopped
   fresh thyme leaves

Wait until the main heat has gone out of the big fire and then smoke the onions, whole chillies and garlic over the cooling embers for 1 hour until soft. Use an upside down roasting tin as a lid or a couple of layers of foil to hold the heat and smoke in.

Put the smoked vegetables on a chopping board and carefully remove and discard the blackened outer skins. Roughly chop the vegetable flesh.

Heat 50ml of the oil in a heavy-based saucepan over a moderate heat and stir-fry the chopped smoked vegetables for 5 minutes. Add the ground coriander, Worcestershire sauce, mustards, vinegar, tomato purée, sugar and salt. Simmer together for 20 minutes, stirring occasionally while the mixture thickens and comes together as one.

Transfer the mixture to a food processor, add the thyme and blitz to a purée. With the motor still running, slowly add the remaining 200ml of oil in a steady trickle and blitz until smooth. Check the seasoning. You can always add a little more salt or chilli at this stage if you wish.

Transfer the sauce to an airtight jar and store in the fridge for up to a month. Gregory's Smoked Barbecue Sauce will lift the simplest of grilled meats or vegetables and instantly bring back the taste and aroma of that outdoor cooking fire.

ROMESCO SAUCE

This versatile sauce can be served with all kinds of vegetable, fish or meat dishes, such as stuffed aubergines, grilled sea bass or bream, and chicken, pork or veal. We use a combination of hazelnuts and pine nuts for the base, although traditional Spanish recipes are made with almonds. I prefer the sauce a little 'loose' rather than puréed into a paste because it feels less processed and more natural. Makes 300ml

1 head of garlic, broken and peeled into individual cloves
1 red pepper, halved with core and seeds removed
2 ripe beef tomatoes, cut into 1cm slices
100ml rapeseed oil
salt and freshly ground black pepper
60g whole blanched hazelnuts
60g pine nuts
2 heaped tablespoons chopped flatleaf parsley

Preheat the oven to 180°C/gas mark 4.

Arrange the garlic, red pepper and tomatoes in a roasting tin, drizzle with half the rapeseed oil and season well. Roast for 30 minutes until tender.

Meanwhile, heat the remaining oil in a small saucepan over a moderate heat and toast the hazelnuts and pine nuts for 4–5 minutes until golden. Once the nuts are evenly toasted, immediately tip the contents of the pan into a cold bowl to stop the cooking process. Roughly chop the nuts and set aside.

Scrape the roasted garlic, red pepper and tomato, as well as all the cooking juices, into a food processor and blitz until chopped but not pulped. Scrape into the bowl with the nuts and stir in the chopped parsley. Check the seasoning.

Spoon the Romesco sauce into an airtight container and store in the fridge for up to a week. Serve as a gutsy side relish whenever you like.

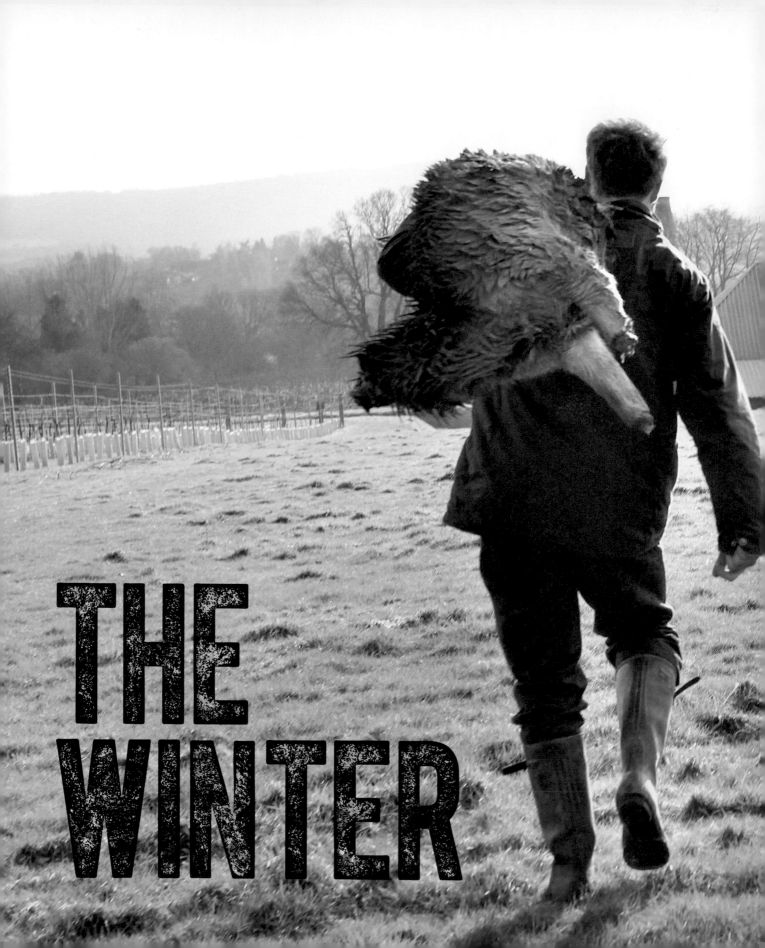

THE
WINTER

GREGORY
WINTER ON THE FARM & TRACTOR BONNET SLEDGING

We three brothers were a bit rebellious as children. We weren't too interested in reading, writing or school. We were much keener on extracting the maximum fun from our environment. It's extraordinary really that we are now all running businesses and have had to become proficient at maths, reading documents and writing things down.

I sometimes accuse Richard of being a boring accountant worrying about his overheads all day long. Meanwhile, Oliver keeps a very close eye on his food costs. And I have to deal with government farming agencies and monitoring running costs on the farm. A bad winter and unbudgeted expenses can make all the difference between profit and loss. People imagine that farming closes down in the winter but there is actually still a great deal to be done. All the cows are in the barns and they require several tons of feed

GREGORY – WINTER

distributed to them each day. They also need new bedding straw and mucking out. The pigs continue to eat for England and they need careful checking if the weather turns nasty. Meanwhile, the sheep are on higher ground across the hill sides but they still need careful daily inspection and supplementary food. I also have to make sure the troughs are all running well with fresh water.

Sometimes I can fall into thinking that all these serious responsibilities have taken over and wayward adventures with my brothers are just a thing of the past. This isn't really the case though.

As part of the fit-out of The Shed, Dad and I installed a John Deere tractor bonnet as the shelf above the bar. It is surprising what you can buy on the internet and bits of old tractor are plentiful. In the event I got overexcited and ended up bidding for and buying two bonnets. So we now have an enormous spare, rounded at the front and cut off at the back. Upside down it looks something like a three man bobsleigh.

It doesn't snow often in West Sussex and when it does you have to take advantage. Last time there was a decent covering my brothers came down from town and we decided this was the moment for a spot of tractor bonnet sledging. We identified an ideal steep slope in a clearing in the woods. The three of us

could all fit on board together, with the front man in charge of the steering (what steering?) and the back man doing the running and push off. It wasn't the fastest mode of transport to be honest but it did actually work. Every time the bonnet rolled over and threw us out we were in hysterics.

RICHARD
CHRISTMAS LLAMAS

Mum's first llama was called Launa. She was secretly delivered by a breeder on Christmas Eve and we managed to hide her down in the old stables without giving the game away. It was just like 'Away in a Manger', except that there probably weren't many South American ruminants in first century Bethlehem. We three small boys sneaked down in the middle of the night with Dad to find Launa lying in the hay. On Christmas morning Dad got a rope around her neck and we successively tried to coax her, then bribe, push, pull and drag her towards the house to be presented as the gift. After an hour of hilarity we got to within 150 yards and had to give up. Gregory was dispatched to bring Mohammed to the mountain.

Since then more llamas and a few alpacas have joined the family, becoming an integral part of life at Nutbourne. Most of them are named after famous Champagne houses: there's Bollinger, Heidi Heidseck, Ruinart and, of course, our very own Nutty. We don't spin their wool and we certainly don't eat them. But each Christmas Day the better behaved ones are put on halters and taken on a Gladwin family walk right through the village. We stick a couple of bottles of our sparkling wine in their saddle bags and deliver cards and good cheer to the neighbours. Launa still stays at home though, having become no easier to manoeuvre over the years.

We wanted our restaurant to always have an atmosphere of celebration about it. Just like Christmas, this involves all the senses. The noise, the smell and the feel are as important in some ways as the taste of the food and its visual appeal. The pass/central cooking station gives off great aromas and the customers are invariably happy if the lighting is right and the room well dressed. Famous politicians or film stars feel comfortable if you smile at them nicely without acting awkwardly or making a fuss. And we like any excuse to celebrate, whether it be the last day of the game season or the first day of marmalade making. We also hike our hard-working pot-washer out of the kitchen for a Shed rendition of 'Happy Birthday' as often as our customers demand it. Sometimes I just stand in the middle of the dining room and close my eyes for a few seconds. If it sounds like a good party is in swing I know we have got things right.

FORAGING IN WINTER

IN THE WOODS		
Pennywort	Green, fresh	Wild Herb Risotto (page 188)
Hairy bittercress	Watercress-y, mustardy	Chargrilled Heritage Carrot, Red Cabbage and Blood Orange Salad (page 182)
Oak moss	Perfumed, fragrant, woody	Serve with game such as venison
Bay leaf	Earthy, strong baseline flavour	Use to flavour sauces and broths
Chickweed	Green, fresh, subtle	Great in winter salads or pancakes
Marigolds	Colourful, sweet, subtle	Perfect to garnish wild winter salads
IN THE HEDGEROW		
Rose hips	Fruity, berry, syrupy	Crown of Pheasant with Puy Lentils, Autumn Greens and Rose Hips (page 154)
BY THE SEA		
Mussels and oysters	Fresh, salty	Baked Oysters (page 129)
Sea spinach	Hardy, strong, bitter	Pollock Soufflé with Cockles and Sea Rosemary (page 142)
Wild horseradish	Powerful, peppery	Beef and Horseradish Cigars (page 204)

OLIVER
MENU PLANNING

Richard tells me that his imaginary vegetable patch has shut down for the winter but it certainly shouldn't have done. Any real gardener knows the importance of continuing home growing action through the cold months of the year. There should be bountiful crops of sprouts, broccoli, leeks, cabbages and perennial spinach. You can also leave some potatoes and carrots in the ground to stay fresh, digging them out as you require them. There is also plenty of prep work to be done. All the

beds need digging over and hoeing to get the soil ready for the spring, plus next year's onions and garlic must be planted. The traditional rule is that you should plant your garlic on the shortest day of the year and harvest it on the longest. I can't verify this, but that's what my mum says!

We are frequently asked how to work out quantities when preparing meals based on sharing dishes. For large parties at The Shed we tend to serve

approx. 15 different dishes but we can't really expect you to do that at home. One of the joys of our sharing plates is that most of them can be incredibly simple. You just need a couple of more sophisticated ones to create a wonderful, memorable meal. So for example a winter sharing meal might consist of a Brussels Sprout and Apple Salad (see page 184), some smoked fish, cured ham and some paprika roasted new potatoes with a Wild Herb Risotto (see page 188) and some Veal Truffle Patties (see page 209) as the main events.

For a celebratory meal for 6-8 people we would recommend you prepare three vegetable-based dishes, two fish and two meat, using half the quantities we give in the recipes for six people. Serve with some homemade sourdough bread and as many desserts as you like to follow. The alternative is to prepare a set of four sharing plates as a starter - two vegetable, one fish and one meat, then a full-sized main course such as our Venison Wellington (see page 206) accompanied by a side salad and Béarnaise sauce. Once again, some good bread with the starters and an array of indulgent desserts afterwards will do the trick.

Winter food is all about warmth and comfort. You really need to have taken part in some healthy outdoor activity to fully appreciate coming in from the cold for a robust stew, a baked crumble or some homemade crumpets. Dad gets his by working in the vineyard.

Each vine has to be pruned by hand and carefully trained to produce the optimum next crop. It also needs to be left with provision to grow the correct new canes for the following summer. Dad is out there in the wind and rain whenever he has a day off. He says it is very therapeutic and a perfect contrast to a life spent in the stress-filled atmosphere of busy kitchens. We brothers have our own form of midwinter therapy when we are all down at Nutbourne together. We challenge one another to dive into the ice-cold lake fully clothed before making a mad dash back to the house to recover. We reckon this sets us up for whatever life is going to throw at us.

WINTER MOUTHFULS

SCOTCH QUAIL EGGS

There are all sorts of theories about the origin of Scotch eggs, including a claim by the famous gastronomic food store, Fortnum & Mason in Piccadilly, that they invented them as a traveller's picnic snack in the 18th century. In our 21st century they have become very fashionable again and there are now many varieties to choose from – from wild boar and black pudding to salmon and duck egg. I like to use a little anchovy in the mix, which another historic theory claims is what makes these eggs 'Scotch' – apparently, back in the old days, Scotland was famous for its little fishes rather than its whisky! Makes 12

1.

2.

3.

4.

1 teaspoon red wine vinegar
12 quail eggs, at room
   temperature
300g minced pork
2 salted anchovy fillets, finely
   chopped (optional)
1 spring onion, finely chopped
4 sage leaves, finely shredded
2 teaspoons fennel seeds
salt and freshly ground black
   pepper
40g plain flour
2 medium eggs, lightly beaten
200g fresh white breadcrumbs
1 litre rapeseed oil, for
   deep-frying

Bring a medium saucepan of water to the boil with the vinegar. Carefully add the quail eggs and cook for 3 minutes (soft-boil). Drain and cool immediately under cold running water. Then carefully peel the eggs and set aside.

Put the minced pork, anchovies (if using), spring onion, sage leaves and fennel seeds in a mixing bowl and season with a little salt and plenty of black pepper. Mix well. Divide the pork mixture into 12 even-sized balls and arrange them on a sheet of baking parchment, spacing them apart. Flatten the balls into oval patties using the palm of your hand so that they spread to approx. 8cm at the widest point.

Put a peeled egg in the centre of each patty and mould the pork around it so that the egg is completely encased. Repeat with the remaining eggs.

Put the flour, beaten eggs and breadcrumbs into three separate bowls ready for coating. First coat the Scotch eggs in the flour, then in the lightly beaten egg and finally in the breadcrumbs. Put the Scotch eggs on a plate and transfer them to the fridge to chill for at least 1 hour before cooking.

Preheat the oil in a heavy, deep pan over a moderate heat. Test the temperature by cooking a small piece of bread, which should sizzle immediately when you drop it in the hot oil if the temperature is right. Fry the eggs, a few at a time, for 6 minutes until evenly golden on all sides. Lift them out of the oil with a slotted spoon and drain on kitchen paper to absorb any excess oil. Serve the eggs while still warm, sliced in half.

6.

RED DEER TARTARE
ON ORANGE & JUNIPER SABLES

A mouthful is an instant eating sensation, combining visual appeal and texture with, of course, delicious flavour. These very tasty cheese sablés, flavoured with orange and juniper, could be paired with all sorts of toppings, such as blue cheese, smoked fish or aubergine pâté, but they are equally good on their own. I use them as a base for my raw venison tartare and they make a perfect match - the sablé is rich with butter and cheese to coat your mouth while the seasoned and slightly acidic venison cuts through and balances the richness. Makes 24 mouthfuls

FOR THE SABLÉS
250g plain flour
250g Cheddar cheese
250g unsalted butter, chilled
zest of 2 oranges
2 teaspoons crushed juniper
   berries
2 level teaspoons rock salt
2 level teaspoons paprika

FOR THE TARTARE
300g red deer loin
1 shallot, finely chopped
30g gherkins, finely chopped
2 teaspoons Worcestershire sauce
1 teaspoon Tabasco sauce
salt and freshly ground black
   pepper
1 large egg yolk
1 tablespoon rapeseed oil
fresh chives, to garnish

First make the orange and juniper sablés. Put the flour in a mixing bowl. Using the large holes on a box grater, grate the cheese and chilled butter into the bowl; this method gives you very even dough without having to overwork it. Add the orange zest, crushed juniper berries, salt and paprika and draw the mixture together with your hands to form a ball.

Turn the dough out onto a floured board and knead lightly until smooth. Roll into a long cylinder, approx. 5cm in diameter, and wrap tightly in clingfilm. Transfer the dough to the fridge to chill and set for 1 hour. Preheat the oven to 160°C/gas mark 3 and line a baking tray with greaseproof paper.

Remove the sablé dough from the clingfilm and slice it carefully into 5mm discs. Arrange them on the prepared baking tray and bake for 8 minutes.

Remove the sablés from the oven and set aside on a wire rack to cool. (If you are making them in advance, the cooked biscuits can be stored for several days in an airtight container.)

The deer tartare should be prepared at the last minute, preferably within an hour of serving, otherwise the meat could start to oxidise and discolour due to the salt. Put the venison on a chopping board and cut into as tiny dice as you can manage using a really sharp knife; the secret of a good tartare is the fine dicing (not mincing).

Put the finely diced venison in a mixing bowl and stir in the shallot and gherkins using a wooden spoon. Add the Worcestershire and Tabasco sauces and season with salt and pepper. Finally, mix in the egg yolk and oil.

To serve, put a teaspoonful of the tartare mixture onto each sablé biscuit and top with some small chives to garnish.

MINI KEDGEREE CAKES

Kedgeree is traditionally served as a breakfast dish and originates from the British Raj occupation of India. Usually made with leftover fish, cooked rice and hard-boiled eggs, spiced up with curry powder, kedgeree became fashionable at the end of the 19th century. These little mouthfuls recapture the essence of kedgeree, but in a single spicy bite - great with a beer or two before dinner. Makes 24 mouthfuls

250g skinless smoked haddock
  fillets
3 parsley sprigs
2 bay leaves
½ teaspoon black peppercorns
250ml whole or semi-skimmed milk
100g cooked basmati rice
1 large egg, hard-boiled for
  8 minutes, and then finely
  chopped
2 teaspoons garam masala curry
  powder
½ teaspoon cayenne pepper
1 tablespoon chopped parsley
1 tablespoon chopped chives
80g semolina
4 tablespoons rapeseed oil
plain yogurt, to serve

Preheat the oven to 180°C/ gas mark 4.

Put the haddock in an ovenproof dish, add the parsley, bay leaves and peppercorns and pour over the milk. Cover the dish with a lid or foil and bake for 15 minutes until the fish is lightly poached.

Remove the cooked fish with a slotted spoon and put it in a mixing bowl. Strain the milk through a sieve into a measuring jug to remove the flavourings and set aside.

Break the fish into flakes with a fork, discarding any bones or scales. Add the cooked rice, chopped egg, curry powder, cayenne pepper, parsley and chives. Mix everything together carefully with a wooden spoon, adding 20–40ml of the reserved cooking liquor, a little at a time, until the mixture is moist and malleable.

To form the kedgeree cakes, scoop dessertspoon-sized amounts of the mixture and roll them into balls in the palms of your hands, flattening them slightly. Scatter the semolina onto a plate and roll the cakes in the semolina to coat them evenly on all sides.

Heat the oil in a heavy-based frying pan over a moderate heat and fry the kedgeree cakes, a few at a time, until golden and crisp, approx. 3–4 minutes on each side. Remove them from the pan with a spatula and set aside on kitchen paper to drain while you cook the rest.

Serve straightaway, accompanied by a little plain yogurt for dipping.

CHICORY & BLUE CHEESE MOUTHFULS WITH PEAR JAM

A lot of The Shed mouthfuls are made up of very simple but contrasting tastes and textures, which marry together. Here we have the crunchy, bitter leaf of chicory, the strength and richness of blue cheese and the sweet spice of pear jam. Makes 12 mouthfuls

FOR THE PEAR JAM
2 Conference pears, peeled,
  cored and coarsely grated
100g caster sugar
½ teaspoon ground cinnamon
juice of ½ lemon
2 tablespoons water

FOR THE CHICORY MOUTHFULS
1 head of yellow or red chicory
80g blue cheese
1 tablespoon double cream
freshly ground black pepper
a little hairy bittercress
  (or chervil), to garnish

First make the jam. Put the grated pear, sugar, cinnamon, lemon juice and water in a small saucepan and stir over a low heat until the sugar dissolves. Bring to the boil and simmer until all the liquid has evaporated, approx. 6–8 minutes, stirring occasionally. Remove from the heat and set aside to cool.

Pick off the individual chicory leaves and cut them into even 6cm 'boats'. Using a fork, blend the blue cheese with a little cream in a small bowl and season with black pepper.

To serve, fill each chicory boat with a dollop of the blue cheese mixture and top with a blob of pear jam. Garnish with hairy bittercress (or chervil).

MUSHROOM MARMITE ON OATMEAL FARLS

400g fresh black field mushrooms
6 large egg yolks
2 teaspoons caster sugar
1 teaspoon sherry vinegar
1/2 teaspoon salt
200ml sunflower oil
20ml truffle oil
approx. 1 tablespoon water
a few slivers of cornichon,
    to garnish

FOR THE OATMEAL FARLS
250g oatmeal, plus extra
    for dusting
1/2 teaspoon bicarbonate of soda
1/2 teaspoon salt
50g lard or dripping, melted
2 tablespoons hot water

(You will need an 8cm cookie
cutter)

The classic line about Marmite is that you either love it or hate it, but not my mushroom-flavoured version. This is really a sort of rich mushroom, truffly mayonnaise but with the dark black colour and consistency of Marmite. It works beautifully as an intense flavoured spread on these Scottish oatmeal cakes. Makes 24 mouthfuls, with mushroom marmite to spare

First you need to dry the mushrooms. I do this by threading them onto a string and hanging them high above my cooker for at least a week. Alternatively, you can arrange them on a baking tray and leave them to dry over a radiator or in an airing cupboard. Either way, dry your mushrooms in a warm place for at least a week or until they are fragile and crispy. I've been asked if you can't just pop them in a low oven, but I promise you they won't be the same.

Transfer the dried mushrooms to a food processor and blitz to a fine powder. Keeping the motor running, add the egg yolks, sugar, vinegar and salt through the feeder tube. Then slowly add the sunflower and truffle oil, a little at a time, allowing the mixture to thicken. Check the consistency and if necessary let it down with a little water to the consistency of a thick, sticky spread. Spoon the mushroom marmite into an airtight container and store in the fridge until needed.

Preheat the oven to 180°C/gas mark 4 and line a baking tray with greaseproof paper.

To make the farls, mix together the oatmeal, bicarbonate of soda and salt in a mixing bowl. Pour in the melted lard or dripping and rub together with your fingertips until the mixture resembles breadcrumbs. Finally, stir in the water and mix to a stiff dough.

Dust your work surface with oatmeal, turn out the dough and knead gently until it comes together in a ball. Using a rolling pin, roll out the dough to a thickness of 5mm and stamp out 6 discs using an 8cm cookie cutter. Arrange on the prepared baking tray and bake for 25 minutes.

As soon as the oatcakes come out of the oven, cut them into quarters (it is this shape that makes them farls) and transfer them to a wire rack to cool.

To serve, spread a generous layer of the mushroom marmite onto each farl and top with a little sliver of cornichon.

(Any leftover marmite can be stored in a sealed container in the fridge for up to 2 weeks.)

CHARGRILLED HERITAGE CARROT, RED CABBAGE & BLOOD ORANGE SALAD

Did you know that carrots were not always long, pointed and orange? Heritage carrots are the re-cultivation of ancient breeds that were around hundreds of years ago. They come in many different colours – from white and yellow to pink, purple or even black – and are now available commercially. Heritage carrots are sweeter and stronger flavoured than normal carrots and make a wonderful rainbow ingredient in this robust winter salad full of different textures.

We finish this dish with a sprinkling of hairy bittercress, something we really enjoy foraging for in the winter woodland. However, there are lots of other interesting cresses you could substitute instead if you don't have the time or inclination for a hairy hunt. Serves 6 as a starter

$^{1}/_{2}$ red cabbage, cored and shredded

1 tablespoon red wine vinegar

2 teaspoons ground allspice

salt and freshly ground black pepper

4 yellow or white heritage carrots, peeled

4 purple heritage carrots, peeled

50ml rapeseed oil

1 teaspoon caraway seeds

2 blood oranges, peel and pith removed, cut into segments

1 tablespoon honey

100g blanched almonds

juice of 1 lemon

small bunch of hairy bittercress (or lemon thyme)

Put approx. 2cm water in a medium saucepan over a moderate heat. Add the red cabbage, vinegar, allspice, salt and pepper and cook for 45 minutes, stirring occasionally, until the cabbage is tender and soft. Drain and set aside to cool.

Meanwhile, use a wide-backed peeler to cut the carrots into long, thin strips. Put the carrot strips in a bowl, add 2 tablespoons of rapeseed oil, the caraway seeds and some salt and pepper and toss well together.

Heat a griddle pan over a moderate to high heat and chargrill the carrot strips for 1½–2 minutes on each side until they are nicely grill-marked and tender. Set aside to cool.

Arrange the griddled carrots and red cabbage on individual serving plates and dot with the orange segments.

To make the almond dressing, put the remaining oil in a small saucepan with the honey and almonds, and cook gently over a low heat until the nuts begin to colour, approx. 5 minutes. Squeeze in the lemon juice – it will spit slightly, so stand back – and season with salt and pepper.

To serve, pour the warm almond dressing over the salad and finish with a sprinkling of cress. Serve at room temperature or slightly warm.

BRUSSELS SPROUT & APPLE SALAD
WITH MATURE CHEDDAR & WALNUTS

This is such a great little salad - so simple and yet full of unexpected textures and tastes. Brussels sprouts are a star among British winter vegetables. Why sprouts are normally boiled for so long is quite beyond me. The less cooking the better and for this recipe we don't cook them at all. Serves 6 as a starter or more as a sharing dish

150g walnuts
50ml rapeseed oil
1 tablespoon honey
sea salt and freshly ground
    black pepper
400g tender young Brussels
    sprouts, trimmed with outer
    layers removed
2 eating apples (such as Russet
    or Cox)
juice of 2 lemons
150g mature Cheddar cheese,
    grated

Preheat the oven to 150°C/gas mark 2.

Begin by mixing the walnuts, oil and honey together, season well with salt and plenty of black pepper. Put the mixture in a small roasting tin and cook for 10 minutes until the nuts are nicely toasted.

Meanwhile, shred the sprouts very finely using a sharp knife. Core the apples, keeping the skins on, and cut them into fine matchsticks. Combine the sprouts and apples in a mixing bowl, add the lemon juice and toss together.

To serve, spoon the sprout and apple mixture onto individual serving plates. Sprinkle with grated cheese, scatter over the toasted walnuts and drizzle with the honey-flavoured oil from the roasting tin.

PARSLEY & GINGER BROTH

Parsley is such a versatile herb - no wonder it is the most commonly grown. Just plant some out in a sheltered spot - you can do this in a window box, flower pot or garden bed - and before you know it you will have a ready supply throughout the winter for use as a garnish or to enhance vegetable, meat or fish dishes and sauces. If you find you have a bumper crop to harvest, try this delicious and unusual soup.

We developed this recipe using rice as the thickening agent and ground ginger to complement it. The result is a wholesome broth with the freshness of the parsley but an interesting texture and spice behind it. Serves 6

250g parsley (leaves and
  stalks), washed and dried
25g unsalted butter
1 dessertspoon coriander seeds
1 teaspoon ground ginger
salt and freshly ground black
  pepper
1 medium onion, finely diced
2 garlic cloves, crushed
100g long-grain rice
1 litre hot vegetable stock
1-2 tablespoons lemon juice,
  to taste
crème fraîche, to serve

Pick the parsley leaves off the stalks and set aside separately.

Melt the butter in a deep saucepan over a moderate heat. Add the coriander seeds, ginger and 1 teaspoon of salt and allow the butter to develop to a nutty brown. Add the parsley stalks, onion and garlic, reduce the heat and fry gently for approx. 5 minutes until the onion softens and begins to brown. Add the rice and stock and bring to the boil. Then reduce the heat and simmer for approx. 20 minutes until the rice is soft.

Remove the pan from the heat and add the parsley leaves. Using a hand-held immersion blender, blitz the soup until smooth and then season to taste with a little more salt, some black pepper and a good squeeze of lemon juice. (If you are preparing the soup in advance, it can be chilled down at this stage and stored in the fridge until needed.)

To serve, reheat the soup over a low heat, ladle into bowls and finish with a dollop of crème fraîche on top.

PAN-FRIED GOAT'S CHEESE
WITH HAZELNUTS, HONEY & THYME

This dish has quickly become a Shed classic - so simple to prepare and yet perfect as a sharing plate, starter or supper dish. I have a thing for goat's cheese and honey, but it is the slight burning and caramelisation of the cheese, together with the 'toasting' of the nuts, that make this really special. Serves 6 as a starter

120g unsalted butter
200g blanched hazelnuts
2 tablespoons cider vinegar
3 tablespoons honey
rock salt and freshly ground
    black pepper
300g goat's cheese log, cut
    into 6 even slices
a little rapeseed oil
3 sprigs of fresh thyme,
    leaves removed

Start by preparing the dressing. Melt the butter in a saucepan over a low heat, add the hazelnuts and cook gently until golden brown, approx. 5 minutes. Remove the pan from the heat and stir in the vinegar and honey. Season with salt and coarsely ground black pepper. Set aside.

Heat a separate non-stick frying pan over a high heat until it is very hot. Brush the cheese slices (not the pan) with a little oil, and then fry them quickly on each side for no more than a minute until they are singed, sealed and caramelised.

Transfer the cheese slices to serving plates, spoon over the warm hazelnut dressing and finish with a sprinkling of thyme leaves. Serve with a large glass of a robust red wine.

WILD HERB RISOTTO

My favourite pastime on a dull, rainy midwinter Sunday is to go foraging in the woodland. At first all you will see is a barren landscape of trees, stripped of their leaves, muddy paths and broken branches on the ground. Then, when you look more carefully, the life of the winter landscape is revealed. Suddenly a little clump of pennywort discovered growing under an oak tree, and more… On the trunk there is oak moss gripping to the bark, and further along wild chervil and hairy bittercress. It never ceases to excite and inspire me when I find a secret world of culinary delicacies. This simple risotto can be adapted to include almost any herbs or vegetables, but for me it is the perfect vehicle for my winter woodland treasure trove. Serves 4-6 as a main course

3 tablespoons rapeseed oil
½ large red onion, finely diced
750ml hot vegetable stock
250ml white wine
strips of zest and juice of 1 lemon
350g Arborio risotto rice
1 heaped teaspoon salt
250ml double cream
large bunch (approx. 200g) of foraged herbs (such as pennywort, oak moss, chervil and hairy bittercress), lightly washed and coarsely shredded

Heat the oil in a heavy-based saucepan over a moderate heat and fry the onion until soft, approx. 5 minutes.

Meanwhile, measure out the vegetable stock and white wine and combine them in a large jug with the lemon juice.

Add the rice and salt to the pan and stir well for a couple of minutes to coat the grains in the hot oil. Start adding the liquid to the pan, a cupful at a time, stirring well between each addition. As the rice cooks and absorbs the liquid, you can continue adding more liquid, stirring regularly.

Stop the cooking when the rice has swelled but still has a little bite to it, after approx. 15 minutes. To finish the risotto, stir in the cream and wild herbs, reserving some to garnish.

To serve, spoon the risotto into wide serving bowls, scatter over the strips of lemon zest and garnish with the reserved wild herbs.

SMOKED WHITING WITH WARM POTATO SALAD IN LEMON VINAIGRETTE

You can choose almost any fish to hot-smoke including, of course, salmon and trout. However, a cheaper, more sustainable fish such as whiting can be transformed into something much more exciting by a little home-smoking. The key to smoking your own fish is to marinate it first to draw out the moisture so that the smoke can penetrate the flesh more deeply.

In this recipe the smoked whiting is served on a bed of potatoes dressed with lemon vinaigrette and chives. Chives are one of the few domestic herbs that you can keep growing indoors throughout the winter.

Serves 2 as a main course

1 whole whiting (weighing
    approx. 700g), filleted to
    give 2 x 200g fillets
300g untreated oak chippings (or
    other hardwood)
300g late-season salad potatoes
    (such as Pink Fir), scrubbed
juice and zest of 1 lemon
1 teaspoon caster sugar
1 tablespoon white wine vinegar
salt and freshly ground black
    pepper
60ml rapeseed oil
1 teaspoon chopped chives
pennywort or cress, to garnish

FOR THE MARINADE
200ml cold water
20g rock salt
20ml white wine vinegar

Mix the ingredients for the marinade together in a bowl. Arrange the whiting fillets in a single layer in a china dish and pour over the marinade. Cover with clingfilm and set aside to cure in the fridge for 30 minutes.

Meanwhile, assemble your smoker by putting an even layer of wood chippings across the bottom of a deep, heavy-based roasting tin. Put a pebble at each corner and rest a wire rack on top. Put the tin over a moderate to high heat, either on the hob or outside on a barbecue.

Remove the fish from the marinade and pat dry on kitchen paper. Once the wood chips begin to smoke, singe and smoulder, put the fish fillets on the rack and cover with a tight-fitting lid. (Alternatively, you can make a domed lid of foil, leaving room for air to circulate above the fish but ensuring it is tightly fitted around the edges.) Reduce the heat and smoke the fish for 10 minutes.

Remove the tin from the heat, keeping the lid on, and set aside to cool for 20 minutes; as the fish cools down it will carry on smoking inside its domed tent.

Meanwhile, make the potato salad. Boil the potatoes in salted water until just cooked, approx. 15 minutes. Drain and set aside until cool enough to handle. To make the vinaigrette, put the lemon juice, zest, sugar, vinegar, salt, pepper and oil in a jam jar; put on the lid and shake vigorously. Cut the warm potatoes into 1cm slices and arrange on a serving platter. (You can also mash the potatoes together with the vinaigrette to serve, see photo, left.) Sprinkle with the chopped chives and drizzle the vinaigrette over the top.

To serve, remove the warm whiting from the smoker and arrange the fillets on top of the warm potato salad. Garnish with some pennywort or cress.

FISH & WINTER VEGETABLE PIE

We have a family tradition that we always eat fish pie on Christmas Eve before going to church at midnight. I don't quite know the significance of this - maybe it's meant to be a lighter meal in preparation for the turkey feast and other excesses of the next day, but Mum always makes loads so it certainly isn't fasting. This fish pie includes plenty of different vegetables and a sliced potato topping rather than the more predictable mash. But fish pie is something you can adapt and develop to your individual style. Every good cook should have their own special version. Serves 6 as a main course

500g skinless cod, haddock or
  pollock fillet
150g Brussels sprouts, trimmed
  and halved
150g parsnips, peeled and cut
  into 6cm fingers
150g fennel, cored and thickly
  sliced
60g unsalted butter
30g plain flour
600ml whole milk
150g Cheddar cheese, grated
2 sprigs of fresh tarragon,
  leaves removed and finely
  chopped
salt and freshly ground black
  pepper
700g 'old' potatoes (such as
  Maris Piper or St Gouges),
  peeled and cut into 5mm slices

(You will need an ovenproof pie
dish, approx. 30cm in diameter)

Preheat the oven to 180°C/gas mark 4.

Cut the fish into 3cm chunks and mix it with the raw sprouts, parsnips and fennel in an ovenproof pie dish.

Melt 40g of the butter in a medium, heavy-based pan over a moderate heat. Stir in the flour and allow it to cook for 1 minute. Gradually pour in the milk and continue to stir as the sauce thickens and comes to the boil. Finally, stir in 100g of the cheese, the tarragon and some seasoning.

Pour the hot sauce over the fish and vegetables. Arrange the sliced potatoes on top, overlapping one another. Dot with the remaining butter and sprinkle with the remaining cheese.

Put the pie on a baking tray to catch any drips and bake for 40–50 minutes until the potatoes have browned and are cooked through. Serve the pie as a whole meal in one with perhaps a crisp green side salad.

CLASSIC FISH SOUP

100ml rapeseed oil
1 medium onion, finely chopped
1 large leek, finely chopped
1 fennel bulb, cored and
    finely chopped
3 garlic cloves, crushed
2 litres water
zest and juice of 1 large orange
225g tin of chopped tomatoes
2 bay leaves
2 sprigs of thyme
1.5kg mixed sustainable fish
    (e.g. hake, coley, grey
    mullet, gurnard, etc.),
    gutted and cut into large
    sections, bones and all
pinch of saffron
salt
pinch of cayenne pepper

FOR THE ROUILLE
1 red pepper, halved
    (seeds and core removed)
1 red chilli, finely chopped
1 thick slice of stale white
    bread, crusts removed
3 garlic cloves, chopped
1 egg yolk
salt
100ml rapeseed oil

TO SERVE
1 stale baguette,
    cut into thin slices
2 tablespoons chopped parsley
150g firm full-fat cheese,
    grated

There are some traditional dishes that have lasted the test of time and remain as exciting and delicious today as they were 100 years ago. A really good classic fish soup is hard to beat and ticks all the boxes if you make it with sustainable fish. Feel free to use whatever the catch brings in for this classic soup, including dogfish, gurnard, hake, coley or grey mullet.

Make a big pot and serve the soup with the classic accompaniments of croûtes, rouille and grated cheese.
Serves 6-8

Preheat the oven to 180°C/gas mark 4.

Put the oil, onion, leek, fennel and garlic in a large, heavy-based pan. Stir over a moderate heat for 4–6 minutes until the vegetables soften, but don't let them brown. Add the water, orange zest and juice, tomatoes, bay and thyme and bring to the boil.

Add the fish (bones and all) and season with saffron, salt and cayenne pepper. Reduce the heat, cover with a lid and simmer for 40 minutes.

Meanwhile, put the red pepper on a roasting tray and roast in the hot oven for 15 minutes until the skin starts to blacken. Remove from the oven, scrape off and discard the skin and put the roasted flesh to one side.

Purée the fish mixture – fish skin, bones and all – in an old-fashioned, hand-turned mouli grinder set over a clean saucepan. The advantage of the traditional mouli is that it takes out the most inedible pulp but extracts every inch of goodness. A sieve will never give you so much and liquidising in a machine will include the bits that you don't want. (If necessary, the soup can be chilled down at this stage ready for reheating later on.)

Reduce the oven temperature to 160°C/gas mark 3.

Prepare the rouille in a pestle and mortar – we are being classic, you could do it in a food processor if you prefer. Pound the roasted red pepper with the chilli, bread, garlic and egg yolk to form a smooth paste. Season with salt. Add the oil, a few drops at a time, while continuing to pound; it will take approx. 5 minutes of pounding before all the oil is incorporated and the rouille is complete.

Arrange the thin slices of baguette on a baking tray and bake for 5 minutes until lightly browned.

Meanwhile, reheat the soup in a medium pan over a low heat. If necessary, skim off any foam or impurities that come to the surface using a slotted spoon.

To serve, ladle the fish soup into large bowls and garnish with chopped parsley. Present the rouille, grated cheese and croûtes in little individual dishes alongside so everyone can help themselves.

SALMON & BUTTERNUT GOUGERE

Gougère is a classic rural French dish made with savoury cheesy choux pastry. Traditionally baked in a ring, it usually comes with a mushroom, vegetable or meat filling in the centre. Our interpretation of this dish is to make mini gougère rings suitable as individual starters or to serve as a small sharing plate.

This recipe uses a mixture of smoked and poached salmon with butternut squash, however almost any combination of fish, meat or vegetables such as haddock and spinach, lamb with turnip, or mixed lentils and root vegetables could be used instead.

Serves 6 as a starter or more as a sharing dish

FOR THE SALMON FILLING
25g unsalted butter
25g plain flour
100ml whole milk
50ml white wine
salt and freshly ground black
   pepper
½ butternut squash, peeled and
   cut into 1cm dice
300g fresh skinless salmon
   fillet, cut into 1 x 3cm
   strips
100g sliced smoked salmon,
   cut into 6cm strips
1 teaspoon chopped tarragon

FOR THE CHOUX PASTRY
150ml water
50g unsalted butter
65g plain flour
2 medium eggs, beaten
50g mature Cheddar cheese,
   grated
1 teaspoon Dijon mustard
pinch of cayenne pepper

chopped parsley, to garnish

First make the salmon filling. Melt the butter in a medium saucepan over a moderate heat. Stir in the flour and cook for 2 minutes until it bubbles like honeycomb. Pour in the milk and wine, stirring constantly to avoid lumps, and bring to the boil. Season with salt and pepper. Add the diced butternut squash and cook for 3–4 minutes. Remove the pan from the heat and carefully stir in the salmon, smoked salmon and tarragon. Set aside while you prepare the choux pastry.

Preheat the oven to 200°C/gas mark 6 and line a baking tray with greaseproof paper.

Put the water and butter in a medium, heavy-based pan and bring to a rapid boil over a high heat. Once the mixture bubbles up, remove the pan from the heat and quickly tip in all the flour, beating furiously with a wooden spoon for a few moments until smooth.

Return the pan to a moderate heat and cook for 2 minutes, stirring. Beat in the eggs with a wooden spoon and cook for a further 2 minutes. Finally, stir in the grated cheese and mustard and season well with salt and cayenne pepper.

Using 2 teaspoons (one to spoon and one to scrape), arrange the sticky choux pastry in small blobs to form six rings, approx. 12cm in diameter, on the prepared baking tray. The pastry will puff up in the oven so keep the rings well apart. Carefully spoon the salmon filling into the centre of each of the rings.

Bake the gougères for 25 minutes until the pastry has puffed up and turned golden. Serve straight from the oven, garnished with chopped parsley.

SALT COD & HAZELNUT CROQUETTES

Salt cod is an ancient ingredient that we often forget about now that fish is so widely available refrigerated or frozen. I have experimented with salting and then air-drying my own fish, but there is a lot to go wrong when you're dealing with our variable British climate – too damp, too wet or too hot, and too fly-prone, so I recommend you buy the dried salted cod from a professional. Salt cod has a much more intense flavour than fresh fish, making it a perfect ingredient for these moreish delicious croquettes. Serves 6 as a starter (Makes 12 croquettes)

1.

2.

3.

300g salt cod
400ml whole or semi-skimmed milk
425g tin of chickpeas, drained and rinsed
1 shallot, finely diced
1 tablespoon fresh white breadcrumbs
2 tablespoons natural yogurt
2 tablespoons freshly grated horseradish
20g unsalted butter, melted
freshly ground black pepper
1-2 medium eggs, lightly beaten
150g chopped hazelnuts
plain flour, for dusting
rapeseed oil, for deep-frying
seasoned crème fraîche and salad leaves, to serve

Put the fish in a large dish and cover with fresh water from the tap. Cover the dish with clingfilm and set aside in the fridge to soak for 48 hours; drain and replace the water every 12 hours.

Preheat the oven to 180°C/gas mark 4.

Drain the fish and put it in an ovenproof dish. Pour over the milk and poach in the oven for 20 minutes. Remove the cooked fish with a slotted spoon then scrape off and discard the skin. Transfer the flesh to a food processor, discarding the milk.

Add the chickpeas, shallot, breadcrumbs, yogurt, horseradish and melted butter to the food processor and season with freshly ground black pepper. Using the pulse button, blitz the mixture to a smooth, thick paste. Check the consistency – if it is too thick, you can add a little extra yogurt; if it is too loose, simply add more breadcrumbs.

Divide the mixture into 12 equal portions and roll into even lozenges. Put the beaten egg and chopped hazelnuts into separate bowls. Roll the croquettes first in flour, then the beaten egg and then in the chopped hazelnuts, to coat them evenly on all sides.

Preheat at least 6cm oil to 180°C in a heavy-based saucepan over a moderate heat. Deep-fry the croquettes, a few at a time, in the hot oil for 6–8 minutes until golden brown. Transfer them to kitchen paper to remove any excess oil while you cook the rest. Serve with crème fraîche and some crisp salad leaves.

4.

THE SHED BRESAOLA

Aromatics

You can use a variety of aromatics in your cure, such as garlic, herbs or even orange zest. Spices are also used for flavour; the Mallard Bresaola opposite uses coriander seeds.

The cure

This is made up of the aromatics (see above) plus salt and often black peppercorns. In a wet cure, such as the one used for the Mallard Bresaola, there is also water and our recipe uses red wine too.

Prepare to wait

For any type of curing you have to calculate how long to leave your meat, fish or even vegetables in the cure. This is usually done based on the weight of what you are curing but can also be affected by its size and shape.

Hanging the meat

Once removed from the cure, the meat is left to hang in a cool, dry, shaded area. You can wrap the meat in squares of muslin to protect it if you wish, but often large pieces of meat, such as hams, are left to hang from hooks uncovered (see page 125).

Sliced and ready to eat

Cured meats, such as the Mallard Bresaola (see opposite), are best served thinly sliced.

MALLARD BRESAOLA WITH ONION MARMALADE

We sometimes get inundated with wild duck from a big game shoot and I cannot resist the opportunity to cure some of the breasts to preserve them for serving well after the game season is over.

Curing is not for the faint-hearted, it has several stages and takes lots of patience and care. You will need to find a cool, dry, shaded place to hang the meat for air-drying - high off the beams of a draughty barn is ideal. We use muslin cloth for protection against flies and, during the winter months, it is cold enough to hang somewhere sheltered outside. Failing all that bresaola can be left to dry out in the back of a fridge - it's just not as effective. Makes 24 servings

6 mallard breasts, off the bone

FOR THE BRINE
250ml full-bodied red wine
   (it can be quite cheap,
   but opt for a variety that
   is big and gutsy)
150ml water
100g caster sugar
130g salt
3 sprigs of thyme
1 whole head of garlic,
   cut into 4 slices
1 teaspoon coriander seeds
1 teaspoon black peppercorns
zest of 2 oranges

FOR THE ONION MARMALADE
30g unsalted butter
3 red onions, finely chopped
1 tablespoon soft brown sugar
1 teaspoon red wine vinegar
salt and freshly ground black
   pepper

TO SERVE
large bunch of rocket leaves
small bunch of wild chervil
2 oranges, peel and pith
   removed, cut into segments

(You will need 6 x 20cm squares
of muslin and a cool, dry,
shaded barn or shed where you
can hang your duck breasts to
air-dry.)

First make the brine. Put the red wine, water, sugar and salt in a medium saucepan and bring to the boil over a moderate heat. Stir until all the sugar and salt have dissolved. Add the thyme, garlic, coriander, peppercorns and orange zest and remove from the heat. Set aside to cool.

Score the fat on the duck breasts in a criss-cross pattern. Arrange the duck breasts in a single layer in a plastic container. Pour over the cold brine to cover them completely and put on the lid. Transfer the container to the fridge and set aside to cure for 2 weeks; turn the breasts every 2 days.

After 2 weeks, the duck breasts will be ready for air drying. Remove the breasts from the brine and pat dry on kitchen paper. Wrap them individually in squares of muslin and tie with string at each end. Hang the duck parcels in a cool, dry, shaded area for 3 weeks. (They will keep for several months.)

To make the onion marmalade, melt the butter in a heavy-based pan over a low heat and fry the onion until it is really soft, approx. 10–15 minutes, stirring occasionally. Add the sugar, vinegar, salt and pepper and continue cooking until the mixture is very soft and sticky, approx. 15 minutes. Spoon into a serving dish and set aside to cool.

To serve, unwrap the air-dried duck breasts and slice them thinly with a very sharp knife. Arrange a crescent of slices on individual plates, along with some rocket and chervil. Finish with segments of fresh orange and serve the onion marmalade alongside.

PARTRIDGE RAVIOLI

I wanted to include a recipe for making fresh pasta - it is such a satisfying thing to become expert at and will bring great variety to your cooking.

This recipe uses a partridge stuffing, but ravioli (or tortellini, pictured right) can be filled with almost any flavoursome meat, fish, vegetable or cheese (such as mushrooms and Cheddar or fennel, apple and spiced pork, or scallop and tarragon). The reason I am using partridge is that the breasts can be served on their own for another meal and then all the fiddly bits can be used for these delicious little ravioli, which are cooked in their own partridge stock (so there is no waste!). Serves 6 (Makes 18 ravioli)

FOR THE PASTA

400g Italian '00' flour, plus extra for dusting
3 medium eggs, lightly beaten
1 tablespoon rapeseed oil

FOR THE PARTRIDGE FILLING AND STOCK

4 partridge carcasses without the breasts (or 2 partridges if you are using the breasts as well)
1 onion, diced
4 garlic cloves, crushed
2 carrots, finely chopped
2 leeks, finely chopped
sprig of thyme
1 bay leaf
1 teaspoon black peppercorns
1/2 teaspoon salt
600ml cold water
800g black cabbage, to serve
linseed oil, to garnish

(You will need an 8cm round cookie cutter)

Put the flour in a large mixing bowl, make a well in the middle and pour in the eggs. Using your fingertips, mix the eggs with the flour, incorporating a little flour at a time, until everything is combined. Then work in the oil.

Turn the pasta dough out onto a floured surface and knead away energetically for 5 minutes; this process releases the gluten in the flour, making the pasta elastic and stretchy. Wrap the dough in clingfilm and transfer it to the fridge to rest for 1 hour before rolling it out.

Meanwhile, prepare the filling. Put the partridge carcasses in a large saucepan with the onion, garlic, carrots, leeks, thyme, bay leaf, peppercorns and salt. Cover with the cold water and bring to the boil over a moderate heat. Reduce the heat and simmer for 40 minutes. Strain through a sieve set over a bowl, and return the stock to the pan for later.

Put the partridge carcasses on a chopping board. Pick the meat from the bones and cut it into small pieces, discarding the bones. To make the filling, combine the chopped meat with the poached onion, leeks and carrots in a mixing bowl, season and set aside.

Dust a work surface with flour. Divide the dough into two or three pieces and roll them out with a long rolling pin so they are no more than 2mm thick (that's the tricky bit). Using an 8cm round cutter, stamp out 18 rounds.

To assemble the ravioli, put a dessertspoonful of the partridge filling onto each pasta circle and fold in half to create a half-moon. Pinch the edges together to seal. (If you are making the ravioli in advance, arrange them in a single layer on a baking tray and set aside in the fridge until needed.)

Return the pan of partridge stock to a moderate heat, bring to the boil and check the seasoning. Meanwhile, cook the black cabbage in salted, boiling water for approx. 8 minutes; drain well.

To cook the ravioli, drop them into the boiling stock and cook for 3–4 minutes. Serve the ravioli in large bowls with a side serving of black cabbage. Finish with a drizzle of linseed oil.

THE🍴SHED

daily loosner...

DAMS AWAY

...sea damsons
...hase gin
...emon
...da

£9α

mouthfuls

· mushroom marmite, egg confit
· quails egg. celery salt
· goat cheese, endive, pear jam
· pork scratching. apple

"PEAR" BLU...
COMMIS PEAR, C...
FRESH LEMON.

Nutbourne

BEEF & HORSERADISH CIGARS

I am often asked where my more quirky recipes come from and this particular one has a good story. There is a little outdoor yard at The Shed, which is used for dining in the summer but is the domain of smokers in the winter. After a really busy day in the restaurant, I went out for a breath of air only to encounter an extremely rotund man perched on a very small stool smoking a very fat cigar. He rather disgustingly stubbed it out into the remains of his dessert, which he must have brought outside with him, and we had a chat. By the time I returned to the kitchen the idea of the Beef Cigar was born - it would have nothing to do with fat rude men but would be presented sitting upright like a stubbed-out cigar. This slow-cooked recipe takes a long time to prepare and has several stages, but the result is well worth it. Serves 6-8 as a main course (Makes 20 cigars)

1kg braising beef, cut into
    6-8cm chunks
20g coriander seeds
salt and freshly ground black
    pepper
3 tablespoons rapeseed oil
100g dark brown sugar
100ml red wine vinegar
2 teaspoons chopped thyme leaves
1 litre water
1 whole head of garlic, cut
    in half
Juice and zest of 2 lemons
400g packet of filo pastry
120g unsalted butter, melted
100g grated horseradish
Tarragon Mayonnaise (see
    page 66), to serve
a few tarragon leaves,
    to garnish

Preheat the oven to 120°C/gas mark ½.

Put the beef in a large mixing bowl and season with the coriander seeds and plenty of salt and pepper. Heat the rapeseed oil in a large, heavy-based, ovenproof pan over a moderate heat. Add the beef, a few pieces at a time, and brown all over in the hot fat; set aside while you brown the rest.

Return all the beef to the pan and add the sugar, vinegar, thyme, water, garlic and lemon juice and zest. Stir well. Bring it to the boil on the hob, then cover the pan with a layer of greaseproof paper and some foil, or a tight-fitting lid if you have one, and transfer to the oven. Braise for 4–5 hours or until the meat is so tender it falls apart when poked with a fork.

Remove the meat from the pan using a slotted spoon and transfer it to a chopping board until cool enough to handle. Meanwhile, return the pan to a high heat and boil up the cooking liquor until reduced by half.

Using 2 forks, or your hands, gently pull the beef into strands and transfer to a shallow roasting tin, approx. 20 x 15cm. Strain the reduced cooking liquor over

the meat and set aside to cool. Cover with clingfilm and chill in the fridge for at least an hour, where it will absorb the juices and set.

Preheat the oven to 180°C/gas mark 4 and line a baking tray with greaseproof paper.

Lay a 30 x 40cm sheet of filo pastry on your kitchen surface and brush all over with some melted butter. Sprinkle the surface lightly with grated horseradish. Arrange a second layer of pastry on top, brush again with butter and sprinkle lightly with horseradish. Arrange another sheet of pastry on top to form three layers. Cut in half lengthways.

Remove the 'set' beef from the fridge and turn out onto a chopping board.

Arrange a long strip of the set meat along the length of each piece of filo pastry and roll up tightly to form two long roulades, approx. 3cm thick. Seal the edges with a little water. Repeat the process with the rest of the meat and pastry until it is all used up. Cut each roulade into short 10cm lengths.

Arrange the 'cigars' on the prepared baking tray and brush all over with melted butter. Cover loosely with clingfilm and transfer to the fridge until you are ready to cook.

Bake the cigars for 10 minutes until golden. Serve with Tarragon Mayonnaise, garnished with extra tarragon leaves.

VENISON WELLINGTON
WITH BLACK FIGS & SWISS CHARD

Richard and I went to the same cookery school (in different years) - Leiths in Kensington. Dad likes to tease Rich by telling as many people as possible that he spent his time in the Builder's Arms next door learning to drink while I at least learnt to cook. When it came to Gregs they didn't even bother trying. For my part I thoroughly enjoyed Leiths and the inspiration for a classic dish like this Wellington definitely stems from their training. This is a magnificent dish, but quite an ambitious and complex recipe. Take it step-by-step and you will be fine. Allow yourself a couple of hours, when no one is hassling you about anything. There are several stages - preparing the meat, making the fig stuffing, blanching the Swiss chard, cooking the pancakes to line the pastry and then the final assembly of the Wellington. It will be worth it. Serves 6-8 as a main course

1-1.25kg venison fillet, trimmed
salt and coarsely ground black
    pepper
1 tablespoon sunflower oil
6 ripe black figs, cut into
    quarters
100ml red wine
1 teaspoon crushed juniper
    berries
1 teaspoon mixed spice
6 large Swiss chard leaves
500g ready-to-roll puff pastry
1 medium egg yolk, beaten,
    to glaze

FOR THE PANCAKES
50g plain flour
100ml semi-skimmed milk
1 medium egg
a little sunflower oil,
    for frying

Béarnaise Sauce (see page 116),
    to serve

Season the venison fillet all over with salt and pepper and rub it with the oil. Heat a heavy frying pan or roasting tin over a high heat. When the pan is really hot, put in the meat and seal it quickly on all sides – for no more than 1–2 minutes. Set aside to cool.

Put the figs and red wine in a small saucepan over a moderate heat, season with black pepper, juniper and mixed spice, and simmer for 6–8 minutes until all the wine has been absorbed. Set aside to cool.

Fill a medium pan with lightly salted water and bring to the boil. Meanwhile, fill your sink with cold water. Trim out the white stalks of the chard but keep the leaves whole. Plunge the leaves two at a time into the boiling water for 30 seconds, just until they wilt, and then quickly transfer them to the sink of cold water to refresh them. This will help retain their green colour and freshness. Drain really well on kitchen paper and set aside.

To make the pancakes, put the flour, milk, egg and a pinch of salt in a food processor and blitz to form a smooth batter. Heat a non-stick frying pan over a moderate heat and oil the surface very lightly. Pour in a small ladleful of the batter and tilt the pan

from side to side to spread it out in a thin even layer. Cook the pancakes for 1 minute on each side, and then transfer them to a plate while you cook the rest (the mixture should make 4–6 in total). Set aside to cool. (You may not need all the pancakes for the Wellington; any spare ones will be popular reheated for dessert, served with a sprinkling of sugar and some lemon juice.)

Preheat the oven to 220°C/gas mark 7 and line a baking tray with greaseproof paper.

Make sure all the ingredients are cold before you assemble the Wellington. Roll out the pastry to form an even rectangle on a floured surface. Trim to approx. 20 x 30cm, saving any offcuts for decoration. Arrange the cooled pancakes in a single, thin layer over the pastry, leaving a 5cm margin all around the outside. These form a barrier to protect the pastry from moisture, keeping it crisp. Then arrange the blanched chard leaves in a single layer over the pancakes. Spoon an even strip of cooked figs all down the centre and put the sealed venison loin on top. Bring the long sides of the pastry up and over the meat to form a tight parcel, sealing the pastry overlap by brushing with beaten egg yolk. Tuck in the short ends and seal again.

Transfer the rolled venison Wellington to the prepared baking tray, placing the joins on the underside. Decorate the top with pastry offcuts, cutting them into leaf shapes and sticking them down with beaten egg or water. To finish, glaze the whole thing with beaten egg. Cover with clingfilm and transfer to the fridge until ready to cook.

Roast the Wellington in the hot oven for 15 minutes until golden brown, and then set aside to rest in a warm place next to or above the cooker for a further 15 minutes before carving and serving.

I like to serve this with Béarnaise Sauce.

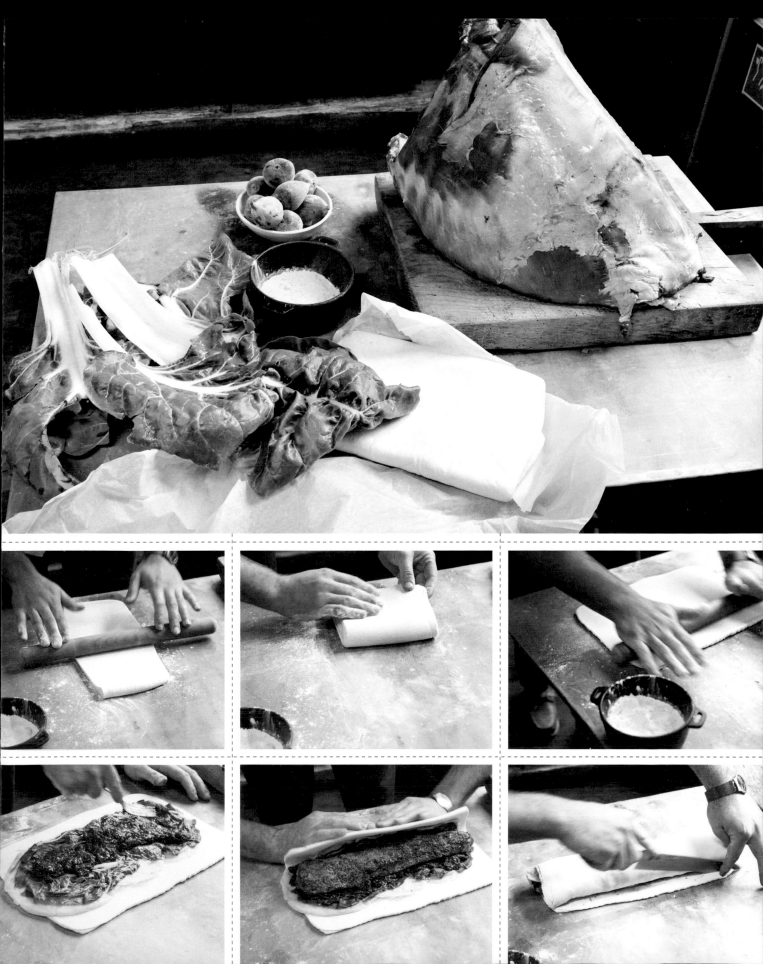

VEAL TRUFFLE PATTIES WITH CARAMELISED CHICORY & WATERCRESS

Gregory rears two to three small herds of veal calves a year on the farm, giving me a steady supply of superbly tender and flavoursome rose veal for each season in the restaurant. The important part of making these veal patties is the ratio of lean meat to fat. We use 75 per cent meat to 25 per cent fat to ensure that the patties remain moist, cook evenly and hold good flavour. I have used truffle oil as a seasoning for the meat, but all sorts of other herbs or flavourings - such as tarragon, balsamic vinegar, lemon, orange or horseradish - could be used in its place. Serves 6 as a main course

1 tablespoon sunflower oil, plus extra for oiling the pan
3 shallots, finely diced
600g minced veal (75 per cent lean meat to 25 per cent fat)
150g fresh white breadcrumbs
50ml water
20ml white truffle oil
salt and freshly ground black pepper
2 tablespoons plain flour
1 teaspoon demerara sugar mixed with a little sunflower oil
2 heads of chicory, separated into individual leaves
large bunch of watercress, washed and picked
50ml veal stock or white wine

Heat the oil in a small frying pan over a moderate heat and fry the shallots for 6 minutes until lightly browned.

In a large mixing bowl, combine the cooked shallots with the minced veal, breadcrumbs, water and truffle oil using a wooden spoon. Season well.

Roll out the veal mixture into a log shape, 6cm in diameter, and then divide it into 12 even pieces. Roll each piece by hand into little patties. Sprinkle the flour onto a plate and coat the patties evenly on all sides.

Lightly oil a ribbed griddle pan and heat over a moderate heat. Meanwhile, use a pastry brush to coat the chicory leaves on both sides with the demerara sugar/oil mixture. Quickly scorch the chicory leaves in the hot griddle pan for 1 minute on each side. Remove the leaves from the pan to a plate and set aside while you cook the veal patties.

Return the griddle pan to a moderate heat and cook the patties, a few at a time, for approx. 3 minutes on each side until evenly cooked. Transfer them to a hot plate and cover with foil to keep warm while you cook the rest.

Meanwhile, arrange the chargrilled chicory leaves and sprigs of watercress on a serving dish.

Remove the last of the patties from the pan and pour in the veal stock or wine. Cook for 1 minute, stirring well to capture all the meat juices from the bottom of the pan.

To serve, arrange the patties on the serving dish and drizzle over the meat juices from the pan.

CINNAMON DOUGHNUTS
WITH RHUBARB COMPOTE

Surely a freshly cooked warm doughnut is just the most delicious thing? If The Shed kitchen is feeling particularly good-natured we will make a batch in the morning for the whole team just to remind them all how lucky they are to work in such a wonderful place!

This recipe uses the same basic brioche dough described in the autumn chapter (see page 164), but for doughnuts I prefer to give the dough a longer prove and time to relax before cooking. These warm cinnamon-coated doughnuts are contrasted with a sour compote of forced winter rhubarb on the side, but they are equally good served just as they are. Serves 6 (Makes 18 doughnuts)

1 batch of Brioche Dough
   (see page 164)
600ml rapeseed oil, for
   deep-frying
100g caster sugar
2 teaspoons ground cinnamon

FOR THE COMPOTE
500g rhubarb, cut into 6cm
   lengths
juice and zest 1 orange
caster sugar, to taste

Line a baking tray with greaseproof paper.

Make up the brioche dough, following the instructions on page 164 and rest in the fridge for 1 hour. Turn out the dough onto a floured work surface and knead for 3–5 minutes until smooth.

Divide the dough into 18 even pieces and roll them in the palms of your hands to form tight balls. Arrange on the prepared baking tray, spacing them apart. Cover loosely with clingfilm and set aside to prove at room temperature until doubled in size, approx. 45 minutes.

Meanwhile, prepare the rhubarb compote. Put the rhubarb, orange juice and zest in a medium saucepan. Simmer over a moderate heat until the rhubarb becomes juicy and begins to break up, approx. 8 minutes. Remove the compote from the heat and sweeten it to taste with a little sugar, adding a teaspoon at a time – remember the doughnuts will be quite

sugary so you want the compote to remain quite tangy in contrast.

Heat the oil to approx. 180°C in a heavy-based pan over a moderate heat. Use a kitchen thermometer or test with a small piece of bread, which should brown in under a minute. Lower the dough balls into the hot oil, a few at a time, and allow them to fry on all sides until golden, approx. 4 minutes. Lift the doughnuts out with a slotted spoon and drain on kitchen paper while you cook the rest.

Sprinkle the sugar and cinnamon onto a plate and roll the freshly cooked doughnuts in it to give a generous coating.

To serve, spoon a base of rhubarb on individual plates, add the warm doughnuts on top and, if you really want to be indulgent, finish with a dollop of clotted cream on the side.

WINTER FRUIT & NUT CRUMBLE

Crumble is one of those puddings that can be enjoyed in every season according to which fruits are available. We are great crumble enthusiasts in our family and could not do a cookbook without including at least one.

This recipe uses a tea-infused fruit compote which makes a really unusual fragrant flavour, together with rolled oats and chestnuts to make the crumble topping extra crunchy. Serves 6

FOR THE FRUIT COMPOTE
100g dried apricots, sliced
50g sticky (dried pitted)
  dates, sliced
50g raisins
1 tablespoon dark brown sugar
1 good-quality Indian teabag
  (such as Assam or Darjeeling)
60ml boiling water
400g Bramley cooking apples,
  peeled, cored and diced
30g unsalted butter

FOR THE CRUMBLE TOPPING
200g plain flour
100g unsalted butter, at room
  temperature
150g demerara sugar
50g peeled and cooked
  chestnuts, chopped
50g rolled oats

(You will need a deep 20cm pie
dish)

Put the dried apricots, dates and raisins in a mixing bowl with the sugar and teabag. Pour over the boiling water and set aside to soak for 1 hour.

Discard the teabag and transfer the mixture to a medium saucepan. Add the chopped apples and butter and cook over a moderate heat until the apples soften and you have a thick compote, approx. 12–15 minutes. Spoon into a deep 20cm pie dish and set aside.

Preheat the oven to 200°C/gas mark 6.

To make the crumble topping, combine the flour, butter and sugar in a large mixing bowl. Rub in the butter with your fingertips until the mixture resembles coarse breadcrumbs. Don't overdo it. Stir in the chestnuts and oats. Sprinkle the crumble topping over the fruit compote in an even layer.

Bake the crumble for 30 minutes until golden on top.

Serve with Vanilla Custard (see page 162) or clotted cream.

BLOOD ORANGE & COINTREAU GRANITA

One of the distinctive things about dining at The Shed is that everyone tends to have a huge variety of things to eat. We encourage everyone to order a range of dishes and then share. When people book the 'Butcher's Table' (which is a big heavy wooden table at the far end of the restaurant used for parties) or on special occasions such as Valentine's Day or the end of the game season, we tend to go a bit over the top and present more than a dozen small sharing courses. Then, of course, you need extra dishes in between the courses to cleanse the palate. We say that our Blood Orange and Cointreau Granita is the perfect intercourse refresher! Serves 6

200g caster sugar
200ml water
juice of 6 blood oranges
50ml Cointreau

Put 6 shot glasses in the freezer.

Heat the sugar and water together in a small saucepan over a moderate heat, stirring until the sugar has completely dissolved. Pour into a shallow plastic container and add the blood orange juice and 30ml of the Cointreau. Cover with a lid and freeze for 2 hours.

After 2 hours, use a fork to scrape the crystallised ice from around the edges of the container, stirring it into the centre. Return the granita to the freezer for a further hour. Repeat the stirring process after 3 hours and return the granita to the freezer for a further hour.

After 4 hours the granita should be set. Give the ice crystals one final stir with a fork and spoon the granita into the frozen shot glasses. Dribble the remaining Cointreau over the top of the granita and serve immediately.

SUSSEX BUN PUDDING

I was trying to come up with a contemporary version of a classic Sussex Pond Pudding but my family told me that without any suet, no whole lemon and not even a 'pond' I couldn't call it that. A Sussex pond pudding is a traditional Sussex dessert made of very heavy, sugary suet, which literally oozes a pond of sweet lemon juice all around it. I just love the name.

My dessert is a delicate almondy sponge presented in crinkly paper with a tangy lemon filling so I call it Sussex bun pudding - not quite the same but I suppose there is no pond! Serves 6 (Makes 12 puddings)

250g unsalted butter, at room
   temperature, plus extra for
   greasing
250g caster sugar
1 teaspoon salt
2 teaspoons baking powder
90g ground almonds
160g plain flour
3 medium eggs, lightly beaten
zest of 2 lemons
100g Lemon and Lime Curd
   (see page 66)
whipped cream or custard,
   to serve

(You will need a 12-bun fairy cake tray)

Preheat the oven to 160°C/gas mark 3 and lightly grease the individual holes of the fairy cake tray.

Put the softened butter and sugar in the bowl of an electric food mixer and beat well until light and fluffy. Sift the salt, baking powder, almonds and flour together in a separate bowl.

Keeping the mixer running on a slow speed, gradually add the beaten eggs and dry ingredients to the butter and sugar mixture. Once everything is incorporated, mix in the lemon zest.

Cut out 12 circles of greaseproof paper, 15cm in diameter. Scrunch them up in your hands to form a ball, smooth them out again and fit them into the holes of the fairy cake tray.

Put a large dessertspoonful of the sponge mixture into each 'cup' and tidy up the mixture into a uniform shape using a slightly wet finger. Bake the buns for 8 minutes until they are lightly golden and doubled in size.

Remove the buns from the oven and set aside to cool in the tin for 5 minutes before transferring them, still in their paper wrappers, to a wire rack.

Insert a small knife into the top of each warm bun to form a little opening and spoon in a generous dollop of homemade lemon and lime curd. Serve warm, still in their wrappers, with whipped cream or custard on the side.

TOFFEE APPLE ICE-CREAM BONBONS

Everyone knows what a toffee apple is, surely? Something sold at fun fairs or carnivals and called candy apples in the US - a hard sour apple on a wooden stick, dipped in a very thick coating of break-your-teeth, highly coloured sugar. Our toffee apples are nothing like that, but they do have some small similarities. These bite-sized toffee and apple ice-cream balls, served on cocktail sticks and coated in milk chocolate, are the ultimate single mouthful dessert. Makes 20 bonbons

FOR THE TOFFEE
100g dark brown sugar
50g unsalted butter
pinch of salt
100ml double cream

FOR THE APPLE ICE CREAM
4 large egg yolks
100g caster sugar
150ml apple purée
150ml double cream

TO SERVE
150g milk chocolate, grated

Start with the toffee, which is a really simple butterscotch. Put the sugar, butter and salt in a medium saucepan and stir over a low heat until the sugar dissolves. Once the sugar has dissolved, stop stirring but continue to heat until the mixture bubbles up in the pan and turns a rich dark toffee colour. Remove the pan from the heat, stir in the cream and set aside to cool.

Meanwhile, make the ice cream. Put the egg yolks and sugar in a food mixer and whisk vigorously until the mixture doubles in volume. Heat the apple purée in a small pan and add it, one spoonful at a time, to the egg mixture, whisking constantly. In a separate bowl, whip the double cream until it forms stiff peaks, then fold the cream into the egg mixture.

Spoon the apple cream into a plastic freezer container, and then carefully spoon the cold toffee sauce in an even layer on top. Swirl the two layers together with a teaspoon so you get a nice rippled effect. Cover with a lid and set aside in the freezer to chill overnight.

Line a baking tray with greaseproof paper. Using a 3cm melon baller, scoop out approx. 20 round balls of ice cream onto the prepared baking tray. Insert a cocktail stick into each ice-cream ball and return them to the freezer to firm up for at least 2 hours.

Make sure that the ice cream has hardened before you attempt to dip the ice-cream balls in melted chocolate. Prepare a bain-marie by placing a heatproof bowl over a pan of gently simmering water. Put the grated chocolate in the bowl and keep stirring until it melts. Remove the bowl from the hot water.

Holding the ice-cream balls by their sticks, dip the bottom half of each one into the melted chocolate to coat it (this will actually be the top half when they are held upright). Arrange the chocolate balls back on the greaseproof paper and return them to the freezer to set.

Serve the toffee apples as delicious after-dinner treats or in place of dessert.

RICHARD'S DAILY LOOSENER: SPICED PEAR & EARL GREY WINTER WARMER

On a cold, dark winter evening a warm loosener is probably just what you need and this gives us the opportunity to experiment with different spices and infusions as well as fruit bases. This recipe combines the smokiness of Earl Grey tea with the sweetness of spiced pear purée. Of course, after your Winter Warmer you might be ready to move onto some cool crisp white wine before a robust red - or maybe not! You might just want another loosener, and another one until you are feeling truly loosened. Makes 600ml pear purée

FOR THE PEAR PURÉE
4 ripe Comice pears, peeled,
   cored and quartered
20g pectin
50g caster sugar
6 cloves
1 cinnamon stick
1/2 teaspoon vanilla bean paste
200ml water

TO SERVE
boiling water
Earl Grey teabag
brandy
long thin slices of pear,
   to garnish

First make the pear purée. Put the pears, pectin, sugar, spices, vanilla and water in a medium saucepan over a moderate heat and cook for 20 minutes. Transfer the mixture to a food processor and blitz together. Pass the mixture through a sieve set over a clean pan to remove the bits of spice. Keep the pear purée warm on the side of the cooker with the lid on.

To make the loosener, pour 100ml boiling water over the teabag in a small pot and set aside to infuse for 30 seconds only; remove the teabag to prevent the flavour from dominating the drink. Pour 50ml brandy into a heatproof glass, add 75ml hot pear purée and top up with the freshly made tea. Stir to combine and garnish with a long slice of pear.

Any leftover pear purée can be stored in the fridge in an airtight container for up to a week and used for a dessert or to make more looseners.

CRANBERRY & WALNUT RELISH

This relish just suddenly appeared at home one winter and we all thought it was fabulous and pestered my mother about where she found it. 'Oh, a friend of a friend told me she makes it and then I changed it a bit.' There appeared to be no recipe as such and no one we can give credit to. So here is my version of this delicious sweet-and-sour relish to serve with cheese, cold meats or even as part of a dessert like rice pudding or panna cotta. Makes a decent-sized bowl (approx. 400ml)

220g fresh cranberries
1 medium orange, cut into
   wedges (skin on)
3 clementines, peel and excess
   pith removed, broken into
   segments
100g dried cranberries
100g chopped walnuts
60ml maple syrup
60ml honey
60ml brandy
1/2 teaspoon ground mixed spice
freshly ground black pepper

Put the fresh cranberries in a food processor and blitz briefly until chopped but not pulped. Scrape into a mixing bowl. Put the orange wedges and clementine segments into the processor and blitz until finely chopped. Add these to the bowl with the cranberries. Stir in all of the remaining ingredients and mix well with a wooden spoon. Cover the bowl with clingfilm and set aside at room temperature to macerate for 4–6 hours. Stir well before serving.

The relish will keep in a sealed container in the fridge for 4–6 weeks. It is a lovely accompaniment to terrines, ham, cold turkey or hard and blue cheeses.

BRIDGET'S ORANGE, GRAPEFRUIT & TANGERINE MARMALADE

My mum has always gone in for the tradition of brewing up several batches of Seville orange marmalade in January to take us through the whole year. When I asked her which recipe she used, she produced a notebook in her mother's handwriting - however, she is keen to point out that it is really her grandmother's recipe we are inheriting. There were also odd notes on the costs - in 1975 the marmalade worked out at 9 pence per lb, but by 1988 this had risen to nearly 20 pence!

There are lots of different methods for making marmalade, but the key is the ratio of fruit to liquid to sugar. The golden rule is 1kg fruit/2kg liquid/2kg sugar. We use the whole fruits method - cook first, cut later. I just think it is more fun.
Makes 6 x 250ml jars

1kg Seville oranges
500g grapefruits
500g tangerines
4 litres water
4 litres preserving sugar

(You will need 6 x 250ml sterilised jam jars with lids)

Put a couple of saucers in the fridge to chill before you begin. These will be used later to check the setting point of the marmalade.

Put the whole fruits in a large preserving pan with the water and sugar. Stir over a low heat to dissolve the sugar, and then bring to the boil. Put on a good-fitting lid and simmer away gently over a low heat for 4–5 hours until the fruit is soft.

Once the fruit has softened, carefully lift it out of the poaching liquid with a slotted spoon. Transfer it to a clean tray to collect all of the juices, and then add these juices back to the pan. Return the poaching liquid to the hob, increase the heat to moderate and boil away vigorously for 30–50 minutes until reduced by about half.

Meanwhile, cut the citrus fruits into quarters and separate the flesh from the skin. Put all the flesh and pith in a nylon sieve and strain it into a clean bowl, pressing down well with a wooden spoon to extract all of the goodness. Using a very sharp knife, cut the peel into long, thin strips. Add the strips of peel and the strained juice back to the pan.

Once the marmalade has reduced by about half you can start checking for a set. Remove one of the saucers from the fridge and drizzle a teaspoon of the hot marmalade onto it. Drag your finger across the surface to see if it wrinkles. If it does, the marmalade is set and ready for bottling. (If it still appears to be too runny, return the marmalade to the heat and continue cooking for a further 15 minutes before testing again.)

Allow the marmalade to cool for 5 minutes in the pan before bottling it into warm, sterilised jam jars (see page 167). Cover with waxed paper discs and fasten the lids.

The marmalade can be stored in a cool, dark place for anything up to 2 years, and even then it will mature and only get better. Once opened, store in the fridge and consume within a month.

SOURDOUGH CRUMPETS

You will find a recipe for making a sourdough 'starter' on page 62 and the great thing about having one on the go is there are all sorts of baking options it can be used for. Crumpets are satisfying to make and using a sourdough starter they have much more character and flavour than standard ones.

To use your crumpets as a wholesome lunchtime dish, serve with a generous topping of wild mushrooms, some grated cheese and a poached egg, accompanied by some peppery green rocket leaves. Makes 12 crumpets

Sift the flour, baking powder, salt and sugar into a large mixing bowl. Using a balloon whisk, slowly stir in the starter followed by the melted butter and thyme (if using). The batter should be a thick pouring consistency. If it is too heavy, you can thin it with a little water – a spoonful at a time – to loosen it if necessary. Cover the bowl with clingfilm and set aside in a warm place to prove for 1½ hours – it will rise slightly.

Heat a heavy-based, oiled frying pan over a gentle heat. Meanwhile, grease the insides of four 10cm metal rings or cookie cutters with a little oil and sit them inside the pan.

To cook the crumpets, spoon a small ladleful of the batter into each ring to fill them by one-third. As the crumpet cooks it will gently rise and start to form air bubbles. Once the crumpets are set, after approx. 6 minutes, you can turn them over to cook on the other side for a further 3–4 minutes.

Remove the cooked crumpets from the pan and set aside on a wire rack while you cook the rest. (If you are preparing the crumpets in advance, you can leave them to cool at this stage ready for toasting later.)

500g strong bread flour
2 teaspoons baking powder
1 teaspoon salt
2 tablespoons caster sugar
200g sourdough starter
  (see page 62)
120g unsalted butter, melted
2 teaspoons chopped thyme
  (optional)
a little water
sunflower oil, for greasing

(You will need four 10cm metal
rings or cookie cutters)

TOP YOUR CRUMPETS WITH GENTLEMAN FARMER'S
    RELISH (SEE PAGE 128) OR LEMON AND LIME
  CURD (SEE PAGE 66)

INDEX

INDEX

ACKNOWLEDGEMENTS

Thinking back to Christmas day 2011 when we announced our plan to open a restaurant in London to where I sit this evening, a week before we open our second restaurant, there are a lot of people to thank!

This book has mentioned many people who have helped us on this path and inevitably some people will have been missed but they are no less important to these last two rollercoaster years.

We would like to start by thanking the book team: Dad, for his wonderful words; Jo Alcott, for making sense of it and us all; Hellie, for spotting us; Kyle, for taking us on; Vicky, for being so patient and working every step of the way with us; the rest of the team at Kyle books who came to our Christmas party and Simon, for not only capturing the story, but also guiding us each step of the way with what to do next. To Cynthia for supplying props and Emma for the illustrations.

Thanks to our mum, Bridget Gladwin, not many people get so many mentions but if it were not for her the story would not have begun. She is a passionate, talented lady and she has taught each of us a remarkable skill.

Roger, Gilly, Nigel and Shane, for giving us guidance and knowledge outside our own field of expertise.

To girlfriends, Jessica and Lucinda, who patiently go out with us while we work for endless hours and get home late and Vicky, who rescues Gregory and even covers his shifts on the farm.

Our inspirations, Gill Meller and Hugh Fearnley-Whittingstall, for giving Oliver the grounding and knowledge to pull off such exciting food. Charlie Gilkes and Duncan Sterling, for believing in Richard and showing him how to run a successful business. Charlie Hughes, for taking Gregory on at 14 in the holidays and making him love farming as much as he does.

Our best customers: Jamie, Henry, Mark, Anistasure, Jo, Gavin and Radha. Plus the many more who come wooing every week.

Our friends: Pierce, Alex, Eddy, Tom, Guy, Guy, Steven, Henry, Charles, Phillip, Kate, Luke and Micky, each one of you have helped us no end in setting up The Shed and writing this book.

Our staff: Carl, Oliver, Theo, Alex, George, Illaria and many more who soldier on day in day out, always beaming and telling this great story. Without them it does not work.

Finally, I would like to thank my brothers and they myself in turn. We may sometimes squabble and sometimes laugh but we are also an excellent team together working daily to achieve our goals.

D0682020

simple japanese

with east | west flavours

Silla Bjerrum

Photography by Lars Ranek

Quadrille

contents

introduction

I returned to London in the early nineties to finish my Bachelor's degree from Copenhagen University as a correspondent student while enjoying the London club scene. To support myself I took a job as a kitchen hand at a friend of a friend's restaurant, Nippon Tuk. This was a small, eccentric place in Chelsea run by Jeremy Rose and Michael Heycock. Michael taught me the basic skills of sushi-making whereas Jeremy taught me about life. I spent four years at Nippon Tuk, picking up techniques and lots of helpful routine, as well as visiting Japan for short periods to work in restaurants serving classical Japanese cuisine and tasting the real deal at source.

During this time I developed a deep fascination not only with Japan's food, but also its culture and people. Initially I wanted to master sushi skills in the traditional way (ie, patiently improving my sushi rice, fine-tuning my knife skills and producing maki and nigiri sushi as close as possible to the authentic original). In 1996 I did a Master of Arts at Goldsmith's College and planned a career in publishing. However the sushi market in London was growing fast and the demand for sushi makers was high. I decided to accept that my fate and my talent was with Japanese food.

I went to work for Birley's in Canary Wharf, hand-producing an outrageous number of lunch boxes Monday to Friday. However repetitive I found making the same three lunch boxes day-in and day-out, it proved an essential experience. It gave me an opportunity to learn more about good routines and the serious side of running a kitchen successfully – things like margin control, staff levels, hygiene, health and safety and so on. The sushi was very popular, pushing me to a five o'clock morning start on a dark industrial estate in Battersea. After two years of this I threw in the towel to work in a more 'human' environment.

Jeremy Rose and I again joined forces as business partners and, together with our financial backers, started Feng Sushi in the summer of 1999. Our first outlet was on Fulham Road; a small local branch with a faithful clientele. During the last seven years we have opened another five branches throughout London, offering a very successful delivery service. From its inception, Feng Sushi has been built on two simple principles: impeccably sourced, quality food made and sold by a young, international, well-trained team.

Starting a small business has been a hands-on experience and provided a steep learning curve. Our strength has been Jeremy's flair for clever locations, good front-of-house management, and my time in the kitchen ensuring that the team understands the product. The rest we picked up as we went along with experiences both hilarious and stressful. Throughout this time Jeremy and I have stuck to two mottos: 'if our fish was any fresher we would have to slap it', and 'you are only as good as your supplier'.

Not being a classically trained chef has been at times difficult: sometimes you feel you lack the lingo and the mannerisms. But never forget that the air of confidence around a good chef often comes from hours spent in the kitchen paying attention to details, not necessarily from catering colleges. In my opinion the growing breed of self-taught 'cooks' brings fresh air to the restaurant scene, and is a healthy alternative to this constant babble from top chefs about who is and who is not a 'real' chef.

My approach to food is based on my eating experiences – past, present and future – plus reading a lot of cookbooks and magazines. The procedure is very simple: 'This tastes or sounds delicious, I wonder if it would work with this…?' And from there it is trial and error. I believe most dishes need to be cooked over and over again before achieving the desired result.

I am also from a large family of foodies. Every seasonal or social event is celebrated with a big feast of new, fashionable cooking. For us this is a serious business: if you invite people around it is to impress and this can be a daunting experience for new members of the family or friends. However, good and constructive criticism is valuable at times. With this background I have always been eager to try new things, in particular when visiting new places or people with a different background to mine.

I like to fuse sushi with Scandinavian and European flavours as it is the food I grew up with and know well. Therefore the sushi and Japanese food in this book is a mixture of classic Japanese dishes and simple tasty new ones with a foreign accent – such as gravadlax

nigiri, which is traditional Scandinavian cured salmon made with Thai herbs instead of dill and served on sushi rice with an Asian-style pesto. Another popular fusion dish is Japanese-style fish and chips with rémoulade, a Japanese interpretation of the traditional British favourite with a Danish detour provided by the rémoulade dipping sauce.

The idea for this book came from my experience training chefs in-house and at the sushi classes I have been running for the general public, businesses and charities since spring 2003. I realised that many of our customers were interested in learning some basic techniques for making their own sushi at home. My strong belief is that anyone willing to learn can be taught how to make Japanese food.

There are two issues about which I am militant: good sourcing of fresh fish (for more on this see pages 10-13) and cooking sushi rice correctly. The former is a given, but the latter is often ignored. Remember: good sushi relies 50 per cent on perfectly cooked sushi rice, so you need to follow the instructions on pages 14-15 with precision, and use proper sushi rice, which is now widely available.

Patience and persistence can make a decent sushi cook of most people and with this knowledge I felt that it would be exiting to put some of my favourite recipes in book form. Japanese cooking requires skill, but once you have mastered a small set of basic techniques the world really is your oyster.

Silla Bjerrum

the starter kit

You need very few tools to make sushi: a bamboo rolling mat for making rolls and a nigiri mould for shaping rice blocks. These are available in most Asian stores. A mandolin cuts julienne of vegetables quickly and easily. It is also worth investing in a couple of Japanese knives. The ones shown here are not expensive, but any good chef's knife and a filleting knife will do. A tamago pan is essential for making rolled Japanese omelettes. Season it by gently simmering 100g salt in a few inches of vegetable oil for ten minutes, cool it and discard the oil and the pan will last you for decades.

The basic ingrdients for sushi are widely available. They are also good store cupboard items (a packet of nori lasts forever unopened) so you can keep them for whenever you feel inspired. Buying sushi vinegar instead of making your own minimises the number of items you need. Finally, make sure you buy proper sushi rice (a short-grained round, polished variety). A mid-priced brand will give excellent results but choose one grown in the hemisphere in which you live because the rice suffers from the high humidity when crossing the equator.

Clockwise from the bottom left: chopping board, bamboo rolling mat, deba knife, sashimi knife, mandolin, nigiri mould, acidulated water, sesame oil, soy sauce, nori, dashi powder, wasabi, pickled ginger, black and white toasted sesame seeds, sushi rice.

fishstory fish for sashimi, sushi and other japanese dishes

I have developed a habit of judging a place and its people by its fish. It may not be a totally fair approach from a sociological perspective, but at least it will get me up early to seek out the local fish market. I have visited markets in small fishing communities with a few boats and a smokehouse, massive frozen warehouses full of imported goods, commercial markets with separate sections for the trade and the public, and all of very different standards.

The one I will always love most is Tsukiji in Tokyo. The first time I went to Tsukiji I was so impressed I went back three times during my trip. Now whenever I go to Tokyo I go there most mornings because it is the most fascinating commercial fish market in the world. Set by Tokyo bay, it has the sea behind it and the city in front. The standard of hygiene is high and I was surprised not to find the sharp smell often associated with fish trading. There I learned the most important lesson: fresh fish does not smell fishy, it smells of the sea, fresh and salty.

Most Tokyo tour guides recommend visiting Tsukiji to see the tuna auction first thing in the morning. This is when the pricy imported bluefin tuna is sold to stallholders in the market and then on to the restaurant trade. However if you miss this, there is

still plenty to satisfy all your senses. The market at first seems chaotic, with people rushing around, traders shouting prices and boxes of fish stacked high everywhere. You have to negotiate a maze of little paths, being careful not to get run over by a trader ruthlessly driving his motorised cart through the market, or standing too close to someone nonchalantly using a chainsaw to cut down a frozen bluefin tuna. There are big stalls offering bright red tuna in glass display cases, as though they were the crown jewels. Then there are stalls specialising in every fish known to Japanese cuisine: one selling sea urchin, another salmon eggs, a third offering mainly squid and octopus, and so on.

On the outskirts of the market there are more opportunities for shopping: greengrocers, cookbook stands, utensil shops, a retailer selling shaved ice, and small sushi bars serving the freshest sushi imaginable. There is an amazing tamago shop that does nothing other than make Japanese omelettes all day: a line of five to six tamago chefs work together, mass-producing beautiful handmade omelettes for the sushi bars in town.

Tsukiji has taught me a lot of what I expect of the fish I buy for my restaurants in London. For sashimi and sushi, most of the fish is eaten raw and therefore the quality and freshness is imperative. To ensure good taste, presentation and food safety, there are some key points to follow:

● Buy your fish from a highly regarded fishmonger or fish market, preferably a shop with which you have some history, or which has been recommended by someone who cares about good quality ingredients.
● Be aware that fish sold on Mondays is often Saturday's stock, as most shops close on Sundays.
● Always make your fishmonger aware that you

intend to serve the fish raw, and ask for 'sashimi-grade' fish, which also indicates that it is going to be eaten raw.
● Very few supermarkets sell sashimi-grade fish. Even though the fish will be perfectly all right to eat cooked, it may not be good enough to consume raw.
● Always buy fish on the same day you want to use it, and put it straight in the fridge when you get home.

In addition, you should follow these basic rules:
● When buying whole fish always ask for it scaled, gutted and cleaned. It saves you the dirty work and you are minimising the risk of cross-contamination in your own kitchen.
● When buying whole fish look for clear eyes and bright red, spongy and odour-free gills.
● When buying filleted fish choose odour-free, firm-textured fillets that still have a natural sheen.
● When buying a loin of fish, ensure that it is cut from the middle of the fish as the tail piece often has a lot of tissue that is of little use.
● A loin should also look fresh and be free of dark patches or dryness.

It is worth taking some interest in how, and from where, the fish we eat arrives. The key issues are fishing methods, handling, distance and transportation. In general, line-caught fish is better than net-caught, providing that the lines are in the water for a minimum of time. The main problem with net-caught fish is the by-catch: sometimes 50 per cent of the fish pulled is dropped back dead into the sea, killed for no purpose. Furthermore, some fish will be damaged by the sheer weight of the nets when they are pulled up from the water.

Fish caught by large commercial trawlers are sometimes fished with so little consideration for fish stocks and the environment that the nets are dragged deeper and deeper, taking everything in their wake, like an evil Godzilla of the sea. I prefer small off-shore day boats, which go to sea for a few days and fish in sustainable waters. With good handling of the fish on

board, the fish is fresher, arrives intact and fetches a better price at the market.

In serving fish every day in our restaurants, I take responsibility for including and promoting locally caught fish wherever possible, to save on air miles. We have got so used to a world of mass-produced, globally transported food that we all expect to be able to eat everything and anything year-round. However the pressure on suppliers and fishermen to get it right can only come from the consumer, whether it is buying fish for home cooking or going out for a meal.

I am a great advocate of sustainable (that is: ecologically friendly) fish farming. Farmed fish can be successful if the producers consider the welfare of the animals and the environment. The salmon farming industry has been under pressure for a number of years to improve its ways. The good initiatives are few and far between, but there are some good products on the market. I choose farmed salmon for various reasons. A good quality farmed salmon is safer to eat raw than a fish caught in the wild as the risk of parasites and fish worm is minimal. Salmon farmed correctly will avoid dioxins in the flesh by using fishmeal made from fish caught in unpolluted waters. Furthermore, giving the salmon plenty of room in their pens (less than one per cent fish to 99 per cent water) will make the fish fit and happy. They not only taste better and have a firmer texture than other farmed fish, they are leaner, and lean fish contain fewer toxins and dioxins because these substances are stored in the fat tissue.

For the last four years I have been fortunate to be using salmon from Loch Duart, a company based at the northwest tip of the Scottish mainland. Loch Duart produces salmon to very high standards and has a fallow system in place for their four farms, so that every year one farm is taken out of production to give the sea bed time to recover from any impact the farming may have had. Furthermore, they do not use chemicals on their pen nets. Instead the salmon are moved to an empty pen every six weeks, and the nets are pulled up to let the algae dry naturally in the sun and wind. The algae are a good source of minerals for the fish. Loch Duart salmon is a little dearer than other farmed salmon, but the difference in taste and texture is outstanding. Hopefully more and more restaurants will demand salmon of this type and quality, and subsequently put pressure on the whole industry to change.

In the case of tuna, it is difficult not to consume air miles. Tuna for the sushi trade in Europe comes mostly from Sri Lanka or the Maldives. As the popularity of sushi has grown worldwide over the past 20 years, tuna fishing has also been intensified. The annual catch is now approximately 1.2 million tons. Japan is catching 350,000 tons of tuna around Japan itself, and importing 250,000 tons annually, therefore taking 50 percent of the global tuna catch.

There are seven known species of tuna, however for sushi the most popular are bluefin, 1000 bluefin, yellowfin and bigeye. The bigeye has a very high fat content and therefore, in one sense, is perfect for sushi. However the flesh loses its colour as soon as it is exposed to air and the fish should be eaten straight after it has been pulled out of the water – making it unsuitable for the European market. Often bigeye is vacuum-packed as soon as it is landed on deck, making it even less suitable to eat raw.

There are two cuts of bluefin very popular on the Japanese market. Most in demand is the belly flap or toro. Toro looks almost like marbled beef and has a pink hue compared to the leaner cut called maguro that comes from the top loin of the fish. Fishing for tuna is a highly technical operation and most tuna for the Japanese market is fished from large boats. The tuna is line-caught and once landed on deck is gutted, bled and then graded. The best fish are nitrogen-frozen as these will fetch the highest price when sold on. This is a very good method of preservation as it helps to kill any bacteria growth in the flesh of the fish. So popular is bluefin tuna in Japan that 80 per cent of the global catch ends up there. Bluefin tuna is only seen on the European market during the summer months when they swim with the Gulf Stream into the Mediterranean Sea.

Unfortunately, due to its high popularity and extreme over-fishing, bluefin tuna is in serious danger of extinction. Some tuna is now being farmed in Croatia, Australia and Italy. Young tuna are taken from the wild and then reared in large fenced areas along the seashore. The problem with this method is that breeding stock is being taken out of the wild stock, which can have consequences for the future population. Around the world various schemes have been devised to help preserve the bluefin tuna. However, as there is still concern about stocks of this species, I prefer using yellowfin tuna.

Mainly from an ecological point of view, but also from a financial and practical standpoint, there are many reasons to favour yellowfin tuna. It is difficult for us to guarantee a stable supply of bluefin as the best quality fish fetch a better price on the Japanese market. Bluefin is often very expensive and the loin, with its highly desirable toro, provides little meat for lean tuna dishes.

Most yellowfin on the European market is from Sri Lanka or the Maldives. The tuna is line-caught and once landed on deck is gutted, bled and kept in an ice slush to cool it down. All tuna prefer warm waters of 17-27°C, however when killed there is a risk of histamine poisoning if they are kept above 5°C, and to some people this can be deadly. All tuna for sushi consumption is checked for safe levels of histamine.

When buying tuna for Japanese dishes always ask for the middle cut as this will provide the greatest yield. You can buy tuna one day in advance of serving providing you wrap it tightly in kitchen paper and then in cling film; kept like this it will firm up overnight in a similar manner to beef.

Yellowtail, or hamachi, is a common name for amberjack fish, which is an oily variety with light grey coloured flesh and a rich, buttery flavour somewhere between mackerel and tuna. Yellowtail belongs to the same family as tuna, bonito and mackerel. Most yellowtail is imported frozen from Japan or Australia, where they are raised in hatcheries and harvested when they weigh 7-10 kilograms. Although yellowtail is sold in frozen fillets it is suitable for eating raw.

Sea bass is another fish being farmed successfully, particularly in Greece, which has become the market leader. As with salmon, farmed sea bass is safer than wild to eat raw, because there is minimal risk of the parasites and fish worm that are often found in the fish but which normally disappear during cooking. In addition, wild sea bass sometimes feed on a green weed containing high levels of bacteria growth, something that can be easily got rid of during cooking, but not when eaten raw. Sea bass are farmed in round cages just offshore in the clean and calm waters of the Greek islands. A good size sea bass for sushi and sashimi is 600-800 grams.

Mackerel is the most underrated fish in Europe and a pertinent example of the bad handling of fish. Often mackerel, because it usually achieves a low price in the market, is just seen as by-catch of other fish. Obviously if the fish is not treated well it will not look presentable at the fish counter and will end up in the stock pot – something I find unbearable as line-caught, well-handled mackerel is the most beautiful fish. An oily fish, high in healthy Omega 3, it is suitable for inclusion in almost any diet. In Japanese cuisine mackerel tends to be pickled or grilled, as this is safer than eating it raw. I am particularly fond of mackerel; it is very common to see a smokehouse by each harbour along the Danish coast, which brings back memories of excellent sailing trips with my father. In Britain, Cornish line-caught mackerel is also excellent and widely available for much of the year. Most comes from the fish market at Newlyn, Penzance, where it is landed by small day boats.

Prawns, especially black tiger prawns, are also popular in Japanese cuisine. In general prawn farms have a very bad reputation, with only a few improving their farming methods in recent years. Ask your fishmonger what he knows about the origin of his tiger prawns. Good quality fresh prawns are often flown in from Nigeria and Madagascar, but this unfortunately consumes many air miles. For acceptable frozen tiger prawns, Malaysia currently has a better reputation than most producing regions and their prawns are transported frozen by sea.

Another delicious ingredient used in this book is the scallop. Hand-diving for scallops is a much gentler method of harvesting these bivalves than trawling. The method was developed in Scotland when the off-shore oil industry was being built. Freelance divers were looking for a way of earning money during the periods when they where not diving for the oil rigs and realised there was a market for hand-dived scallops. Hand-diving has a very low environment impact, because the divers dive the same areas time after time and hand-pick the scallops instead of scraping up everything from the sea bed. Often the divers will keep smaller scallops in underwater cages (a process similar to lobster fishing) until they have grown to a good size. Hand-dived scallops, whether from Dorset or Scotland, are absolutely divine.

fail-safe sushi rice

This method produces 1.1kg of prepared sushi rice; the quantities can easily be doubled or quadrupled.

1 Put 500g sushi rice in a large mixing bowl.

2 The rice needs to be 'rough' washed four or five times. To do this, fill the bowl with cold water and stir the rice with your hand, but not so vigorously that you break the rice kernels. After each wash tip the water out and start again.

3 After four or five washes the water will be cloudy rather than milky white. Now wash the rice another four times, but each time tip the rice into a sieve to get rid of all the water.

4 Leave the rice to rest for 30 minutes in the sieve, then measure the volume of rice in a jug. To cook it, put the rice in a rice cooker or saucepan. Add enough water to give 110 per cent of the volume of rice. Do not add salt. If using an electric rice cooker, turn it on and when it has finished cooking, leave it to rest for 17 minutes. If cooking the rice in a saucepan, bring it to the boil, cover and let it simmer for 17 minutes, then leave to it stand for 17 minutes.

5 When the rice has rested, empty it into a tray and leave to 'steam off' for about 10 minutes, until it reaches 50°C. It is important not to add sushi vinegar to very hot rice or the humidity will cause the grains to collapse.

6 Position a portable fan so that it blows cold air directly on to the rice. Sprinkle 65ml sushi vinegar over the rice and incorporate it by making diagonal strokes across the rice with a spatula. Leave the rice under the fan for about 10 minutes, until it cools to room temperature, or 24-28°C. The rice is now ready to use. If necessary, you can store it up to four hours at room temperature, but do not chill it.

sashimi

Sashimi is the freshest and best quality fish served raw. The cutting technique is vital, because the cut *is* the cooking. Everything must be sliced on the bias, so that you cut through the fibres to make the fish tender. Patience and practice can make any novice a sashimi master. All the recipes in this chapter are for four people, assuming you are serving them in combination with another dish, or as a starter course.

Yellowtail sashimi verde

cutting sides of large fish

In these pictures we are working with a whole side of salmon, however you would use the same technique for sides of other large round fish such as yellowtail.

1. Divide the side of salmon into three by cutting along the line of the spine, then crossways at the tail end. Set aside the tail end (you can freeze it or poach it) for use in other dishes. The thicker, rectangular fillet (on the left hand side of the picture opposite) is for sashimi, the flatter, more triangular fillet (on the right) is for nigiri.

2. Run your hands gently along the sashimi fillet to stretch it. Use a knife to trim off any brown meat as thinly as possible.

3. Trim the sashimi fillet by $^1/_2$-1cm on each side to give a neat rectangular block. Save the trimmings and the brown meat for use in other cooking.

4. When cutting the fish into sashimi pieces you want to slice it across the bias. This means cutting it diagonally along the fillet while at the same time cutting it an angle vertically, always working across the white lines of the flesh. Typically a 45-degree angle is required, but as the lines in the fish vary you may have to reposition the knife periodically so that you keep cutting across the white lines.

5. For nigiri, take the nigiri portion of the side of fish and cut it into blocks of around 6cm. Take the first piece and turn it so that the brown meat is closest to the board. Carefully trim off the brown meat by slicing under the fish as close to the surface of the board as you can.

6. Slice the trimmed block into nigiri pieces across the bias, cutting diagonally with the knife at a 45-degree angle.

classic salmon sashimi

serves • • • •

400g Mooli Salad (see page 45)
400g salmon sashimi block
100g mixed baby salad leaves

to serve
wasabi, pickled ginger and soy sauce

First make the mooli salad using the recipe on page 45 and place in the fridge. Trim the salmon block on each side, saving the off-cuts for another dish. Cut 20 pieces of fish sashimi-style (see page 19), slicing along the bias.

Arrange the salad leaves on serving plates and top with the mooli salad. Place five pieces of fish on each plate and serve with wasabi, pickled ginger and soy sauce on the side.

salmon tartar with spring onions, yuzu tobiko and feng mayo

serves • • • •

200g Mooli Salad (see page 45)
2 tablespoons Feng Mayo (see page 44)
1 cucumber
320g salmon sashimi block
4 spring onions, green tops only, finely chopped
1 tablespoon yuzu juice
1 tablespoon ponzu sauce
freshly ground black pepper
4 tablespoons yuzu tobiko
a few chives to garnish

to serve
wasabi, pickled ginger and soy sauce

Make a half quantity of the mooli salad on page 45, then prepare the Feng Mayo as described on page 44. Peel the cucumber lengthways in long strips, keeping just the skin to use in this recipe – save the flesh for another dish. Cut the salmon into small dice, about $1/2$cm square.

In a mixing bowl, combine the mayo, spring onions, yuzu juice and ponzu sauce, then stir in the salmon and some freshly ground black pepper. Set aside for 4 minutes to let the acid in the citrus 'cook' the salmon. Then transfer the mixture to a sieve to remove the excess liquid and ensure the fish does not overcook. Gently stir in the yuzu tobiko.

Arrange the mooli salad on serving plates. Twirl the cucumber strips to look like a bird's nest and place them on top. Spoon on the salmon tartar (you could shape it using a rice triangle mould, if desired). Garnish with the chives and serve with wasabi, pickled ginger and soy sauce.

yellowtail sashimi verde

serves ● ● ● ●

As most yellowtail is imported frozen, you will need to defrost it in the fridge overnight. Rinse the fish under a running tap and pat dry with kitchen paper before filleting. If yellowtail is not available, you can substitute tuna, salmon or sea bass.

400g Mooli Salad (see page 45)
320-400g yellowtail sashimi block
about 10g chives
about 40g basil sprigs
50g rocket leaves
1 punnet shiso cress

for the dipping sauce
50ml Feng Pesto (see page 44)
2 tablespoons ponzu sauce
1 tablespoon honey
2 teaspoons soy sauce

to serve
wasabi, pickled ginger and soy sauce

First make the mooli salad using the method on page 45 and place in the fridge to crisp.

To make the dipping sauce, prepare the Feng Pesto if you have not already done so (see page 44), then take a 50ml portion of it and mix with the ponzu sauce, honey and soy sauce. Place in a squeeze bottle ready to dress the sashimi.

Drain the mooli salad and arrange it on serving plates. Cut the fish into 20 sashimi-style pieces and arrange five slices of fish on top of each portion of mooli salad.

Cut the chives into pieces about 10cm long and arrange them rustically on top of the sashimi.

Lay the basil leaves on the work surface so that they are just overlapping. Place the rocket in a line down the middle and roll the herbs up tight like a big cigar. Slice the roll very finely on the diagonal and arrange the basil and rocket on top of the chives. Garnish with shiso leaves.

Drizzle a little dipping sauce over each portion of sashimi and serve the rest on the side with the wasabi, pickled ginger and soy sauce

seared salmon sashimi with black pepper and sesame crust

serves ● ● ● ●

This is a variation on a very popular, simple sashimi. I like to incorporate crunch, heat and flavour by adding a sesame and pepper crust, which also gives it a smug healthy status. The recipe also works perfectly with tuna and/or a somen noodle soup with spinach.

100g mixed white and black sesame
   seeds
2 tablespoons black peppercorns
pinch of sea salt
400g salmon sashimi block
400g Mooli Salad (see page 45)
2 teaspoons sesame oil
2 teaspoons olive oil
100g mixed baby salad leaves

for the dipping sauce
20g fresh ginger, finely chopped
1 spring onion, finely chopped
100ml soy sauce
50ml mirin
4 teaspoons runny honey

to serve
wasabi and pickled ginger

Crush the sesame seeds, black pepper and salt together using a mortar and pestle, then spread the mixture in a shallow tray. Trim the sashimi block on each side using the instructions on page 18, then cut the block into two pieces. Press the sesame mixture onto fish so that the four long sides of each block are well coated. Put aside to set.

Make the mooli salad according to the instructions on page 45 and place in the fridge to crisp. To make the dipping sauce, combine all the ingredients in a mixing bowl.

In a frying pan, heat the sesame and olive oils together. When spitting hot, fry each block of salmon for no more than 1 minute on each side, just to sear the edge. Remove the fish from the heat and set aside to rest.

Arrange the baby salad leaves and drained mooli salad on four serving plates. Cut each block of salmon into five pieces, slicing on the bias sashimi-style, then place the fish on top of the mooli salad. Serve with the dipping sauce, plus wasabi and pickled ginger.

upside-down yellowtail sashimi with jalapeño chillies and kimchee dressing

serves • • • •

Japanese food is often paired with Peruvian, Brazilian and Mexican ingredients. It's really no wonder: the passion and fire of South American food is a perfect complement to the controlled nature of Japanese cuisine. I turned this idea 'upside down' to ensure that the yellowtail would not over-marinate. This is the ballerina of sashimi. It takes balance skills to stack this dish, but the result is stunning.

20g dried wakame
small bunch of coriander
50g jalapeño chillies
1 cucumber
1 green-skinned avocado
320-400g yellowtail sashimi block

for the kimchee dressing
40ml yuzu juice
4 teaspoons ponzu sauce
4 teaspoons kimchee base

Place the wakame in a bowl, cover with cold water and set aside to rehydrate. Meanwhile, pick 24 perfect leaves from the coriander and set aside on a piece of kitchen paper.

Finely chop the jalapeños, wearing gloves and using a chopping board exclusively for chillies. Cut the cucumber into 20 slices 1/2cm thick.

Quarter, stone and peel the avocados. Trim and discard the ends from each quarter, then cut each piece diagonally into 5 slices. Drain the rehydrated wakame in a sieve.

To make the kimchee dressing, mix the yuzu juice, ponzu sauce and kimchee base together in a small bowl and place in a squeeze bottle ready for garnishing.

Prepare the yellowtail following the techniques on page 18. Cut each block diagonally to give 20 sashimi-style pieces.

Arrange a row of five cucumber slices on each serving plate. Top with the yellowtail, then arrange a small cluster of wakame on each stack and sprinkle with the jalapeños. Balance a piece of avocado on top, drizzle with dressing and finish each stack with a coriander leaf.

Tip: if the fish is large, you may get a better yield by splitting the 'sashimi' side straight down the middle, rather than trimming off each side to give a sashimi block. This way you could buy just half a fillet, then use the 'nigiri' side and off cuts for other recipes. However remember that if the fish has been frozen, you must not refreeze the off-cuts.

cutting tuna loin

Mature tuna are exceptionally large specimens, so here we are working with a middle cut of tuna loin.

1. You will see a layer of tissue running through the loin. Turn the fish so that the line of tissue is nearest the board and cut along the loin, following the line of the tissue layer, so that it and the flesh underneath it are detached from the rest of the fillet. Set the off-cut aside.

2. Cut a large slice 3cm thick along the leanest side of the loin. This piece is used for sashimi; the remainder of the loin is used for nigiri. Take the sashimi piece and cut it lengthways to give three long fillets measuring about 3cm wide and 3cm deep. Trim as necessary to give neat rectangular blocks, saving any off-cuts for making maki.

3. Slice each block into sashimi pieces, cutting diagonally along the block and downwards at a 45-degree angle.

4. For nigiri, cut the remaining tuna loin into manageable blocks of about 6cm wide. Turn each block on its side and cut into large slices of 1.5cm.

5. Take each slice of tuna and cut into nigiri pieces, working downwards at a 45 degree angle. The finished nigiri pieces should measure about 6x3cm and just 2mm thick.

6. The off-cuts can quickly be made into tuna mince. To do this, use a metal spoon to carefully scrape the meat away from the layer of white tissue.

classic tuna sashimi

serves ● ● ● ●

400g Mooli Salad (see page 45)
400g yellowfin tuna sashimi block
100g mixed baby salad leaves

to serve
wasabi, pickled ginger and soy sauce

Prepare the mooli salad following the instructions on page 45 and place in the fridge to crisp.

Trim the tuna loin into blocks, saving any off-cuts for another dish. Working on the bias, cut the tuna block into 20 sashimi-style pieces (see page 26).

Arrange the salad leaves on serving plates and top with the drained mooli salad. Place five pieces of tuna sashimi on top of each salad and serve with wasabi, pickled ginger and soy sauce on the side.

tuna tartar with ponzu, spring onions and caviar

serves ● ● ● ●

This is the ideal way to use up leftover tuna and makes a perfect starter.

200g Mooli Salad (see page 45)

2 tablespoons Feng Mayo (see page 44)

1 cucumber

350g sashimi-grade yellowfin tuna

4 spring onions, green tops only, finely chopped

4 tablespoons ponzu sauce

2 tablespoons poppy seeds

50g yuzu tobiko

50g Avruga caviar

freshly ground black pepper

to serve
wasabi, pickled ginger and soy sauce

First prepare a half quantity of the mooli salad on page 45 and place in the fridge to crisp. If you have not already done so, make the Feng Mayo as described on page 44.

Peel the cucumber lengthways, keeping the skin and reserving the flesh for use in another recipe.

Mince the tuna, discarding any white tissue. Place in a mixing bowl and add the chopped spring onion tops. Mix in 2 tablespoons of Feng Mayo, plus the ponzu sauce, poppy seeds, yuzu tobiko, Avruga caviar and some freshly ground black pepper and leave to rest for 2 minutes.

Drain the mooli salad and arrange it on four serving plates. Twirl the cucumber strips so that they look like a bird's nest and place on the mooli. Shape the tuna tartar using a mould such as a rice triangle mould, and carefully place each portion on top of the cucumber nest. Serve with wasabi, pickled ginger and soy sauce.

pici-pici sashimi

serves ● ● ● ●

Pici-pici means a friendly slap around the face and this is the ultimate dish for the Feng motto: 'If our fish was any fresher we would have to slap it.' A mixed sashimi such as this is an opportunity to show off your sourcing and carving skills. Use the best and freshest fish available and as many locally fished species as possible. Here I am using salmon, tuna, mackerel and ikura (salmon eggs), but fish such as sea bass, sea bream, snapper and yellowtail would also work perfectly.

400g Mooli Salad (see page 45)
200g salmon sashimi block
200g yellowfin tuna sashimi block
160g marinated mackerel (see page 33)
120g ikura (salmon eggs)

to serve
wasabi, pickled ginger and soy sauce

First prepare the mooli salad following the instructions on page 45 and place it in the refrigerator to crisp.

Cut all of the fish into sashimi pieces following the techniques on pages 19, 26 and 33 respectively. You will need twelve slices of each fish. Keep any off-cuts to make tartar or maki rolls.

Drain the mooli salad and divide it among four serving plates. Arrange three pieces of salmon so that they overlap and lay them together on the plate. Repeat with the tuna and mackerel, then spoon one-quarter of the ikura onto each plate. Serve with the wasabi, pickled ginger and soy sauce.

Tip: I also like to serve this dish with mixed baby salad leaves. To do this, divide 100g salad leaves between the serving plates, top with the mooli salad, scatter the fish across and finish with fresh herbs such as shiso, chives or coriander.

preparing mackerel and other small round fish

Marinating mackerel and other wild, small round fish helps preserve the flesh, makes it safe to eat and easy to cut. Farmed sea bass does not need marinating: fillet it in the same manner, then remove the skin.

1. Start with a fish that has been gutted and had its head removed. Cut along the back and belly of the fish, into the spine. Then hold the fish flat against the board and, keeping the knife flat, cut horizontally along the side of the spine to loosen the top fillet. Repeat on the other side.

2. Working at a 45-degree angle, trim off the thin white tissue layer, keeping as much flesh on the fillet as possible.

3. Use tweezers to remove the pin bones left in the fillet.

4. Place the fillets skin-side down in a baking tray or similar and sprinkle coarse sea salt over them. Set the fish aside for 30 minutes, then rinse off the salt and pat the fillets dry with kitchen paper.

5. Put 300ml sushi vinegar, 20ml soy sauce and a piece of kombu in a large dish. Lay the fillets skin-side up in the mixture and leave to marinate for 20 minutes. Position a cutting board at an angle by sitting an upturned plate under one side. Lay the marinated fillets on the board to drain for a few minutes.

6. Reposition the board so that it is flat. Starting at the bottom corner of each fillet, carefully peel off the papery white outer skin, leaving the silver patterned skin on the fillet. Slice the fish into sashimi and nigiri pieces by working diagonally along the fillet while at the same time cutting downwards at a 45-degree angle.

sea bass sashimi with chilli oil

serves ● ● ● ●

For this dish I favour young sea bass as they have firmer flesh than the older fish. Use a good sustainably-farmed sea bass or, if you are using a wild fish, freeze the sea bass fillets for a few hours to eliminate any contamination from fish worm or parasites. Sea bass is a fish that keeps well even when bought filleted, so you could ask the fishmonger to do the hard work. The chilli oil needs to be made at least one day in advance of serving and will last for up to two months stored in a cool cupboard or fridge.

400g Mooli Salad (see page 45)
small bunch of coriander
100g mixed baby salad leaves
2 small-medium sea bass

for the chilli oil
6 large red chillies
200ml olive oil

to serve
wasabi, pickled ginger and soy sauce

To make the chilli oil: cut the chillies straight down the middle, scrape out and discard the seeds and cut the flesh into chunky pieces. Put the chilli in a shallow ovenproof tray, cover with the olive oil and cook at 70°C/Gas $1/2$ for 1 hour. Leave to rest for a day, then strain the mixture and decant the oil into a squeeze bottle.

Prepare the mooli salad following the recipe on page 45 and place in the fridge to crisp. Meanwhile, pick 20 perfect leaves from the bunch of coriander and set them aside on a piece of kitchen paper.

Divide the baby salad leaves among four serving plates and top with the drained mooli salad.

Fillet the sea bass using the technique on page 32 and skin the fillets. Cut each fillet on the bias to give 5-6 slices per fillet. Place a whole fillet of sea bass on each plate, arranging the slices so that they overlap one another.

Insert a single coriander leaf between each slice of fish, then drizzle with the chilli oil and serve with wasabi, pickled ginger and soy sauce.

Tip: very good quality ready-made chilli oils are widely available. I like the Japanese brand La-Yu, made by S&B.

mr shibushi's mackerel sashimi serves • • • •

This is my tribute to my fish mentor Mr Shibushi, who always takes good care of me when I am in Tokyo. We go together to the fish market in the morning, talk to the best tuna traders and eat the freshest tuna sashimi I have ever had, served with strong black coffee in one of the small sushi stalls surrounding the market. I will pick a fish I find interesting, then we will return to The Quarter House in Akasaka and Mr Shibushi will talk me through every step of preparing this fish. I speak very little Japanese, but food is an international language. 'Watch and learn' has taught me some of my fundamental fish carving skills. Since I met Mr Shibushi in London in 1994 and he taught me to hand-carve mooli, he has opened the world of Japanese cuisine for me, and made me realise that this is a life journey, with ever-new areas and techniques to explore. My gratitude is immense.

4 marinated mackerel (see pages 32-33)
400g Mooli Salad (see page 45)
100g mixed baby salad leaves
12 long chives
1 punnet shiso cress
50g mixed black and white sesame seeds

to serve
wasabi, pickled ginger and soy sauce

Marinate the mackerel using the techniques on pages 32-33. Meanwhile, prepare the mooli salad following the recipe on page 45 and place in the fridge to crisp.

Pull the clear membrane from each fillet of mackerel and cut on the bias to give 7-8 slices per fillet.

Divide the baby salad leaves among four serving plates and place the mooli salad on top. Arrange the mackerel on top of the mooli so that the slices of fish overlap one another.

Decorate each plate of sashimi with three spears of chives, a cluster of shiso cress and finally a sprinkling of black and white sesame seeds. Serve the mackerel with the wasabi, pickled ginger and soy sauce.

scallop sashimi to dive for

serves ● ● ● ●

Scallops are particularly good during the winter months because the colder sea makes them both fresher and safer. It is worth the wait for these tight, succulent pieces of flesh. It pains me to walk along a harbour front seeing the big rusty iron cast nets used for scallop fishing as they literally scrape the sea bed of its life and leave only destruction behind. Fishing for scallops like this is unnecessary and the end product is either frozen or kept in brine, turning them into big fluffy balls. I will only use hand-dived scallops, which makes them a little tricky to get hold of if the weather is very cold and the sea is rough – conditions that are bad for diving. This simple recipe highlights the succulent texture of truly fresh scallops. Buy them ready-shelled from the best fishmonger in your area.

400g Mooli Salad (see page 45)

small handful of coriander

8 scallops

40ml olive oil

4 teaspoons sesame oil

80g mixed black and white sesame seeds

2 spring onions, finely sliced at an angle

to serve

wasabi, pickled ginger and soy sauce

Prepare the mooli salad following the recipe on page 45 and place in the fridge to crisp. Pick the leaves from the coriander and set them aside on a piece of kitchen paper.

Clean the scallops as necessary, removing the intestines and corals. Rinse and pat dry with kitchen paper. Slice each scallop horizontally into three discs.

Drain the mooli salad and divide it among four serving plates. Arrange six pieces of scallop so that they overlap one another and sit them on top of the mooli salad.

In a small saucepan, heat the olive and sesame oils together until smoking point is reached. Drizzle the oil over the sashimi. Sprinkle with the black and white sesame seeds, spring onions and coriander leaves, then serve with wasabi, pickled ginger and soy sauce.

prawn ceviche

As with all shellfish, freshness is the key word here. This recipe is not strictly a ceviche, but the name does emphasise the importance of using only the freshest and best quality prawns. The term 'size 16/20' means that there will be 16 to 20 prawns per kilogram.

200g Mooli Salad (see page 45)
20 raw tiger prawns, size 16/20
1/2 cucumber
2 stalks celery, destrung
1 small red onion, finely sliced
1 pink grapefruit

for the ceviche marinade
2 passionfruit
4 teaspoons ponzu sauce
1 tablespoon red wine vinegar
1 tablespoon honey

If you have not already done so, make a half quantity of the mooli salad on page 45 and place in the fridge to crisp.

Peel the prawns and remove the intestinal threads. Run a skewer through each one to stretch out the body (see picture page 71). Cook the skewered prawns for 4 minutes in a pan of boiling salted water, then plunge immediately into cold water to help preserve the colour and flavour.

For the ceviche marinade: halve the passionfruit and scrape the seeds and juice into a bowl. Add the ponzu sauce, vinegar and honey and stir well.

When the prawns have cooled, remove the skewers and cut each prawn diagonally into four pieces. Add them to the ceviche marinade and set aside for 10 minutes.

Halve and deseed the cucumber. Cut it diagonally into thin slices and place in a mixing bowl. Cut the celery into very thin julienne about 4cm long and add to the mixing bowl with the finely sliced onion. Peel and segment the grapefruit and add the segments to the bowl.

Add half the prawn mixture to the salad and mix gently. Divide among four serving plates, then top with the remaining prawns. Use the excess marinade as a salad dressing and drizzle it over the dish before serving.

salads

Traditional Japanese salads tend to be small and tasty, comprising just a few ingredients such as seaweed, pickles, mooli, spinach and sesame seeds, plus a good dressing. However in Japan it is increasingly fashionable to use vegetables like cherry tomatoes and bell peppers for crunch and flavour. My principle when developing salads for Feng Sushi is that they must include at least three true Japanese ingredients, but the simple, healthy recipes that follow also have a European accent.

Ikura potato salad

dashi dressing
makes 150ml

1 tablespoon dashi powder
1 tablespoon honey
2 teaspoons soy sauce
2 teaspoons sushi vinegar
1 teaspoon wasabi paste
2 tablespoons olive oil
2 tablespoons sunflower oil
4 teaspoons sesame oil

Combine the dashi, honey, soy sauce, sushi vinegar and wasabi in a small food processor bowl or beaker and blend briefly. Mix the olive, sunflower and sesame oils together and gradually add them to the dashi mixture, blending until smooth. This dressing will keep for a week in the fridge.

japanese thousand island dressing
makes 250ml

200ml Feng Mayo
  (see page 44)
4 teaspoons spring water
4 teaspoons yuzu juice
2 teaspoons kimchee base

Make a batch of Feng Mayo as described in the recipe overleaf. Then add the spring water, yuzu juice and kimchee base to the food processor and continue blending for 1 minute or until the mixture is smooth. This dressing will keep for up to five days in the fridge.

japanese vinaigrette
makes 200ml

2 tablespoons yuzu juice
2 tablespoons sushi vinegar
1 tablespoon wasabi paste
2 teaspoons sweet chilli sauce,
  or 1 teaspoon honey
100ml sunflower, grapeseed or
  vegetable oil
50ml extra virgin olive oil

Combine the yuzu juice, vinegar, wasabi and sweet chilli sauce or honey in a small food processor bowl or beaker and blend until the mixture is smooth and light green.

Mix the two oils together in a measuring jug, then add gradually to the wasabi mixture while the machine is running, blending until the dressing has a consistency similar to French vinaigrette. This dressing will keep for up to two weeks in the refrigerator.

miso dressing
makes 200ml

1 shallot, finely chopped
1 large clove garlic, finely chopped
3 tablespoons white miso paste
juice of 1 lemon
1 tablespoon wholegrain mustard
2 teaspoons pumpkinseed oil, or
  sesame oil
1 teaspoon balsamic vinegar
1/2 tablespoon honey
70ml sunflower oil
2 tablespoons extra virgin olive oil

Put the shallot and garlic in a
small food processor with the
miso, lemon juice, mustard,
pumpkinseed (or sesame) oil,
balsamic vinegar and honey
and blend briefly to combine.

Mix the sunflower and olive oils
together in a jug then turn the
machine on and gradually add
the oils to the miso mixture,
blending until the dressing has
the consistency of a thick
vinaigrette – you may not need
all the oil. This dressing will
keep for a week in the fridge.

tahini dressing
makes 200 ml

180ml crème fraîche
juice of 1/2 lemon
1 tablespoon tahini
1 tablespoon runny honey
1 teaspoon cumin
pinch of cayenne pepper
freshly ground salt and pepper

Combine all the ingredients in
a mixing bowl and stir until
well blended. This dressing will
keep for three days in the fridge.

scandia dill dressing
makes 200ml

100g fresh dill sprigs
180ml crème fraîche
juice of 1/2 lemon
1 teaspoon wasabi paste
1/2 teaspoon caster sugar
freshly ground salt and pepper

Discard the stalks of the dill,
then rinse the remainder
thoroughly in cold water and
pat dry with a tea towel. Chop
the dill fronds finely and place
in a mixing bowl. Add the
crème fraiche, lemon juice,
wasabi, caster sugar and salt
and pepper and mix well. This
dressing will keep for three
days in the fridge.

simple teriyaki
makes 250ml

125ml soy sauce
70ml mirin
70ml sake
100g caster sugar
2-3 teaspoons cornflour

Gently heat the soy sauce, mirin, sake and sugar together in a small saucepan, being sure not to let it boil as this will make the soy sauce black and granulated. Meanwhile, in a small dish, blend the cornflour with 20ml cold water.

When the sugar has dissolved in the soy liquid, add a third of the slaked cornflour, whisking constantly as you do so. Repeat this process until the soy mixture is silky smooth and has a consistency similar to double cream. Leave the dressing to cool, then store in fridge, where it will keep for up to two weeks.

Tip: teriyaki sauce will thicken after a couple of days in the fridge, so place it in a saucepan over a low heat, add a splash of soy sauce and a splash of mirin, and give it a good whisk to return the sauce to a silky smooth consistency.

feng mayo
makes 200ml

1 whole free range egg
2 free range egg yolks
2 tablespoons caster sugar
2 teaspoons sushi vinegar
100ml sunflower, grapeseed or vegetable oil
50ml extra virgin olive oil

Combine the whole egg, yolks, caster sugar and sushi vinegar in a small food processor bowl or beaker and blend until white and fluffy. Mix the two oils together in a jug and add to the egg mixture gradually, while the machine is running, to give a rich even mayonnaise. This dressing will keep for up to three days in the fridge.

Tip: I advise using free range eggs from salmonella-free flocks, however it is generally recommended that people who are pregnant or in a vulnerable health group avoid dishes containing raw eggs.

feng pesto
makes 200ml

50g pine nuts
100g coriander sprigs
80g basil sprigs
1 large clove garlic
2 teaspoons sweet chilli sauce, or 1 teaspoon honey
2 tablespoons sunflower, grapeseed or vegetable oil
4 teaspoons extra virgin olive oil

Toast the pine nuts in a dry frying pan over medium heat, stirring often, until golden. Transfer the pine nuts to kitchen paper to cool down. Place the herbs in a food processor with the toasted pine nuts, garlic and sweet chilli sauce (or honey).

Combine the two oils in a small dish. Turn the machine on and gradually add the oils, blending until the pesto is well mixed – you may not need all the oil. This pesto will keep for up to three days in the fridge.

Tip: the herbs can be replaced with fresh parsley, chervil, chives or young rocket leaves. I do not add parmesan to this pesto as the cheese would overpower the raw fish.

mooli salad

serves ● ● ● ●

Mooli, sometimes called daikon or Chinese radish, is a large white radish traditionally used to accompany sashimi. It is an important part of the balance of a Japanese meal as it helps digestion and fat burning, is rich in vitamin C, and can even prevent heartburn. It is also very tasty. I like to add cucumber to the standard mooli salad for extra colour and crispness, and grate both vegetables using a Japanese turner, which makes long curly strands that look good piled high on the plate. This recipe makes about 400g of salad.

1 large mooli
1 cucumber

Peel the mooli and cut into four blocks. Place one block at a time on a Japanese turner, or a mandolin, and grate the mooli into a bowl.

Cut the cucumber into thirds and grate each piece on the turner or mandolin as you did with the mooli, discarding the seeds as you go.

Carefully mix the vegetables together, then cover with tap water and add a handful of ice cubes. Place in the fridge for at least 30 minutes.

Drain the mooli salad – it should be almost translucent and very crisp. It will last for a day covered in water in the fridge, but if you are making it this far in advance, be sure to give it a couple of rinses under cold running water before draining and serving, as the radish will develop a very sharp smell.

Tip: Japanese turners are available from most catering outlets, I prefer to use the medium blade, so that the vegetables are not too chunky but still have a good crunch.

japanese bean salad

serves ● ● ● ●

Edamame are young soy beans and an excellent source of protein. Readily available frozen in Asian stores and supermarkets, they are traditionally served steamed in their shells with a sprinkling of sea salt, or a mirin dip. However as this dish shows, they also make an excellent salad ingredient. For the mixed salad leaves required in this and the following recipes, choose what you prefer from leaves such as baby chard, red mustard, mizuna, baby spinach and young rocket. Cherry tomatoes are generally best from the middle to end of the summer and have the most flavour when bought on the vine.

100g mixed baby salad leaves
500g frozen edamame
200g frozen broad beans
300g cherry tomatoes on the vine
300g feta cheese
freshly ground pepper

to serve
100ml Miso Dressing
  (see page 43)

Prepare the miso dressing using the method on page 43 then decant the dressing into a squeeze bottle. Gently rinse the salad leaves and leave to rest in a colander.

Put a kettle of water on to boil. Place the unshelled edamame in a large heatproof bowl and cover with the hot water from the kettle. Let the edamame steep for 5 minutes, then drain in a colander and pod the beans as soon as they are cool enough to handle.

Meanwhile, bring a saucepan of salted water to the boil and cook the frozen broad beans for 3 minutes. Drain and immediately plunge the broad beans into ice-cold water to help them retain their bright green colour. Rinse the cherry tomatoes and cut each one in half.

In a large bowl, combine the salad leaves, edamame, broad beans and tomatoes. Crumble the feta cheese over the salad. Drizzle with the prepared miso dressing and season with pepper. Arrange the salad on four plates or in a salad bowl and serve as a light lunch.

ikura potato salad

serves ● ● ● ●

Originating in the Americas, potatoes remain a relatively foreign ingredient in the Japanese kitchen, even though they have become a part of the staple diet in Northern Europe. All through my childhood the first small spuds to grow to an eatable size each year were awaited with much anticipation and excitement – they were a real sign that summer had arrived. This salad works best with fresh baby potatoes such as charlotte or juliette.

1kg baby potatoes
100g mixed baby salad leaves
500g frozen edamame
small bunch of chives
zest of $1/2$ lemon
120g ikura (salmon eggs)

to serve
100ml Scandia Dill Dressing (see page 43)

Make the Scandia Dill Dressing according to the recipe on page 43 and set aside. Cook the potatoes in boiling salted water until just tender. Drain, then rinse the potatoes a couple of times in cold water, and leave to dry and cool for at least half an hour.

Meanwhile, prepare the rest of the ingredients. Put a kettle of water on to boil. Rinse the salad leaves gently in cold water and leave to drain in a colander. Place the unshelled edamame in a large heatproof bowl and cover with the hot water from the kettle. Leave for 5 minutes, then drain and pod the edamame. Cut the chives into 5cm pieces.

When the potatoes are ready, cut them in half and place in a large bowl with the salad leaves, edamame, chives, lemon zest. Add the Scandia dill dressing and ikura and toss well. Arrange on four plates or in a salad bowl and serve as a light lunch.

soba noodle salad

serves ● ● ● ●

Soba noodles make an excellent alternative to pasta in salads. They taste delicious and are particularly healthy because they are made from buckwheat, which is a source of slow-releasing carbohydrate. This salad is super simple, but very nutritious.

100g soba noodles
100g chasoba (green tea soba noodles)
100g pine nuts
80g rocket leaves
½ bunch spring onions

to serve
100ml Japanese Vinaigrette
(see page 42)

Prepare the Japanese vinaigrette as directed on page 42 and decant into a squeeze bottle.

Cook the two varieties of soba together in a large saucepan of boiling salted water for 6-7 minutes, until the noodles are al dente – tender but still with some bite. Drain the noodles and plunge them into ice-cold water for a few minutes to help preserve their flavour, then place them in a colander under a running tap for a minute or so, which will add extra shine to the noodles.

Toast the pine nuts in a dry frying pan over a medium heat, stirring often, until they are golden. Transfer them to a piece of kitchen paper to cool.

Remove any thick stalks from the rocket leaves, rinse gently and set aside to drain in a colander. Trim the spring onions and slice them finely on the diagonal.

In a large salad bowl, combine the noodles, vinaigrette, pine nuts, rocket and spring onions and toss well before serving as a light lunch.

x-ray salad   serves ● ● ● ●

In 1999, when we opened the first of our restaurants, we sensed that the Low/No Carb movement was about to take hold. In response, we made this delicious salad with crisp translucent mooli, lots of glorious vegetables and named it after the ultra-thin socialites in Tom Wolfe's **Bonfire of the Vanities**. When preparing the mooli salad, use a Japanese turner or mandolin for the best result.

400g Mooli Salad (see page 45)

500g frozen edamame

2 ripe green-skinned avocados

2 large sweet peppers, ideally one red and one yellow

seeds of 1 pomegranate

40g pickled ginger, finely chopped

finely julienned zest of $1/2$ lemon

100g mixed black and white toasted sesame seeds

to serve

200ml Japanese Vinaigrette (see page 42)

Prepare the Japanese vinaigrette according to the recipe on page 42 and decant into a squeeze bottle ready to serve.

Make the mooli salad as described on page 45 and place in the fridge to chilli. Meanwhile, bring a kettle of water to the boil. Place the edamame in a heatproof bowl and cover with the hot water from the kettle. Leave to stand for 5 minutes, then drain and pod the beans.

Drain the mooli salad and divide it among four serving plates. Halve, stone and peel the avocados, then cut the flesh into cubes and arrange freely on the top of the mooli salad. Cut the peppers into thin julienne at an angle and discard any seeds or white flesh. Again, arrange these freely on top of the mooli salad.

Sprinkle over the pomegranate seeds, edamame, chopped ginger, lemon zest and sesame seeds. Drizzle with the Japanese vinaigrette and serve.

miso and poppy seed salmon with rustic sweet potatoes

serves ● ● ● ●

This is my take on miso-marinated fish. For it I use a good quality farmed salmon or even wild salmon, and it is fine to keep the brown flesh of the salmon in this instance as it is both marinated and cooked. Sweet potatoes are good alternative to normal potatoes as they contain less starch, but also add a natural sweetness to the dish. You will need to start this recipe a couple of days in advance of serving.

200g white miso paste

2 tablespoons caster sugar

2 tablespoons mirin

2 tablespoons sake

400g salmon fillets

2 large sweet potatoes

2 lemons

100ml olive oil

2 tablespoons poppy seeds

salt and pepper

100g baby spinach leaves

extra virgin olive oil, for drizzling

Place the miso paste, caster sugar, mirin and sake in a saucepan over a medium heat and stir constantly until the ingredients have all melted. Set aside to cool.

Cut the salmon into 2cm cubes and place in a non-reactive dish. Pour the cooled miso mixture over the fish and marinate in the fridge for 2-3 days.

On the day of serving, preheat the oven to 250°C/Gas 9. Cut the sweet potatoes into 2cm cubes and place on a baking tray. Squeeze the juice from the lemons and combine with the olive oil, poppy seeds and some salt and pepper. Pour this dressing over the sweet potatoes then, for extra flavour, add the lemon skins to the baking tray. Roast for 25-30 minutes or until cooked through.

Take the salmon from the fridge and rinse off the marinade. Line a baking tray with greaseproof paper and place the fish on it. When the sweet potatoes have been cooking for 20 minutes, place the tray of fish in the oven, turn it down to 220°C/Gas 7 and continue cooking.

Divide the baby spinach among serving bowls. When the potatoes and salmon are cooked, remove from the oven and discard the lemon skins. Gently mix the fish and sweet potatoes together and place on top of the spinach. Drizzle with a little extra virgin olive oil and serve as a main course.

crab claw meat udon noodle salad

serves ● ● ● ●

A dried flat noodle works best in this light lunch or starter dish. Dried udon is a Japanese cousin of Italian taglierini and comes in thin ribbons. Whole crab can be used for this recipe, but I prefer using a good quality pasteurised, ready-picked crab meat such as that sold by Harvey's of Newlyn in Penzance. This makes the salad far less laborious to prepare, but equally tasty.

120g dried udon noodles
1 large, ripe, green-skinned avocado
$1/2$ cucumber
4 spring onions
200g crab claw meat

to serve
100ml Japanese Thousand Island
    Dressing (see page 42)

Prepare the Japanese Thousand Island dressing according to the recipe on page 42 and decant into a squeeze bottle.

Cook the udon for 7-8 minutes in a pot of boiling salted water until they are al dente, or tender but with some bite. Rinse the noodles in cold water and set aside in a colander.

Halve and peel the avocado and cut the flesh into 1cm cubes. Cut the cucumber in half lengthways, scrape out the seeds with a teaspoon and slice the flesh thinly. Trim the spring onions and slice them thinly at an angle.

Pick through the crabmeat carefully, checking for any sinewy pieces or bones. Place in a large bowl with the noodles, half the salad dressing and all the other ingredients. Toss well, then serve the salad in individual bowls, drizzling the remaining dressing on top.

seaweed salad with mooli, edamame and dashi dressing

serves ● ● ● ●

This is pure power food – every ingredient in this salad has beneficial health properties. Seaweed's natural iodine is good for the metabolism and cleansing the blood. Mooli aids digestion and edamame is a low fat protein rich in fibre. Seaweed, dashi and soy sauce are all categorised under the recently discovered 'fifth taste' umami; best described as natural flavour enhancers. Buy your seaweed from Asian or health food stores, where products such as a wakame and kaiso mixture are readily available in dried form.

400g Mooli Salad (see page 45)
50g mixed dried seaweed
400g frozen edamame

to serve
120ml Dashi Dressing (see page 42)

Prepare the dashi dressing following the recipe on page 42 and decant it into a squeeze bottle. Then prepare the mooli salad as per the instructions on page 45 and set aside in the bowl of iced water to crisp.

Place the dried seaweed in a bowl, cover with cold water from the tap and leave to soak for 10 minutes. Meanwhile, put a kettle of water on to boil. Place the edamame in a large heatproof bowl and cover with hot water from the kettle. Leave to stand for 5 minutes.

Rinse the seaweed in a colander and set aside to drain. Drain the edamame and remove the beans from the pods as soon as they are cool enough to handle.

Drain the mooli salad and arrange on four serving plates. Divide the seaweed and edamame among the plates, then drizzle with the dashi dressing and serve immediately.

cornish mackerel ceviche with middle eastern inspired salad and creamy tahini dressing

serves ● ● ● ●

I was looking for a way to combine my two favourite foods, chickpeas and fresh mackerel, and came up with this very tasty salad. You could use dried chickpeas instead of canned. Soak 300g in cold water overnight, then simmer in unsalted water for 40 minutes. Drain and rinse in cold water before proceeding with the recipe below. It's important not to add salt to the cooking water as this will prevent the chickpeas becoming tender.

Prepare the tahini dressing according to the instructions on page 43, then prepare the mackerel as per the instructions on page 33.

Cut the cucumber into three blocks, then lengthways through the middle. Discard the seeds and cut the flesh into julienne, or thin batons. Trim the spring onions, cut each one into three even pieces, then slice into julienne.

Peel the thin membrane from the mackerel fillets. Take four of the fillets and cut into thin strips, slicing across the fillet. Cut the remainder on the bias to give sashimi-style pieces, slicing diagonally at an angle of 45 degrees.

In a salad bowl, mix the baby leaves, drained chickpeas, cucumber, spring onions, and thinly sliced mackerel with two-thirds of the tahini dressing.

Arrange the salad on four serving plates, then put two or three pieces of mackerel sashimi on top. Finish with a dollop of dressing and serve as a light lunch or starter.

5 medium-sized mainated mackerel (see page 33)
1 cucumber
4 spring onions
100g mixed baby leaves
400g can chickpeas, drained

to serve
120ml Tahini Dressing (see page 43)

sushi nigiri

Nigiri (small, oval-shaped portions of rice with a topping) are often regarded as the king of the sushi. The word means 'pressed in the hand', referring to the way in which the nigiri are shaped. In Japan the classic toppings include tuna, mackerel, tiger prawns and tamago omelette, among others, but in the sushi bars of the West salmon nigiri is often the most popular variety. There is also a version called gunkan (meaning 'boat'), that consists of rice balls wrapped with nori and filled with roe such as salmon eggs, or sea urchin. Once you have acquired the basic technique, the possibilities are endless. For extra flavour I like to cure the fish, make tamago with a tasty filling, or add toppings such as chilli oil, pesto, fresh herbs and home-made mayonnaise. For a lunch or light dinner for three to four people, twenty pieces of sushi nigiri will be enough. Start with two or three varieties and, when you have got the knack of it, experiment with different flavours. The recipes in this chapter can easily be cut in half.

Sea bass nigiri with chilli oil and coriander

shaping nigiri

Traditional sushi chefs shape nigiri entirely by hand, but novices can achieve good, consistent results using a mould. The freshly cooked rice should have cooled to about 28°C before you start. Fill a bowl with water and add a splash of vinegar to it – this is used to prevent the rice sticking to your hands or the mould.

1 Dip your hands and the mould in the acidulated water. Take a small handful of rice and gently press it into the nigiri mould, working it lightly into the corners. Do not press hard or the sushi will be too heavy. I think it is best to fill the mould only about four-fifths so the nigiri are not too big.

2 Attach the back of the mould, turn the mould over and use your thumb to scrape any loose rice away from the holes.

3 Take the back off the mould and turn the rice blocks out on to a board, tapping gently through the holes to free the rice.

4 With the topping in one hand, apply a thin layer of wasabi to the underside of the topping. Pick up a rice block using your other hand and gently remould it by cupping your fingers and thumb around it and pressing three or four times. This helps to prevent the rice falling apart.

5 Bring the rice block and topping together and shape the topping down the sides of the rice using your index finger and thumb. The nigiri should be long yet curvaceous.

6 To make gunkan nigiri, cut pieces of nori into strips measuring 7x2.5cm. Wrap one strip around each block of rice (you don't have to reshape the rice in your hand) and secure it by pressing a couple of grains of rice between the seaweed at the top and bottom of the strip. Then fill the boat you have created with the chosen filling.

salmon nigiri with ikura

makes

Salmon nigiri is by far the most popular type of nigiri in the West. To enhance the flavour I have added ikura (salmon eggs) for a hint of salt, and cress for a peppery taste. The real fun is the wonderful sensation the ikura gives when the eggs pop in the mouth, making this nigiri perfect to enjoy with a glass of chilled champagne.

400g Prepared Sushi Rice (see page 15)
300g salmon nigiri block (see page 18)
1/2 teaspoon wasabi paste
2 spring onions, thickly sliced at an angle
100g ikura (salmon eggs)
sprigs of mustard cress

to serve
wasabi, pickled ginger,
grated mooli and soy sauce

Prepare the sushi rice as described on page 15 and allow it to cool. Meanwhile, cut the block of salmon into 20 pieces about 3cm wide, 7cm long and 2mm thick. Store the fish in the fridge until the rice is ready.

When the sushi rice has cooled down to about 28°C, mould it into 20 rice blocks (see pages 60-61). If you do not have a nigiri mould, the hand-shaped rice blocks should measure about 5cm long, 2cm wide and 2cm tall.

Apply a thin layer of wasabi to each slice of fish, then lay one on each block of rice, wasabi-side down, following the shaping technique in the photographs on page 61.

Scatter some spring onion on of each nigiri, then top with a spoonful of ikura. Garnish with cress and serve with pickled ginger, grated mooli, more wasabi and soy sauce.

tuna with shichimi and kimchee
Replace the salmon with tuna sliced nigiri-style (see pages 26-27) then top with a drizzle of kimchee base, strips of red pepper, shiso leaves and sprinkle with shichimi powder.

mackerel with sesame and poppy seeds
Replace the salmon with marinated mackerel (see pages 32-33) then top with shiso and mustard cress and sprinkle with mixed toasted sesame seeds and some poppy seeds.

tuna nigiri with shichimi and kimchee

mackerel nigiri with sesame and poppy seeds

thai-style gravadlax nigiri

This is a Scandinavian salmon sushi with an Asian twist. Gravadlax is cured salmon, an old way of preserving fish for the winter months and a well known deli food throughout the world. Traditionally the curing could last for months, but this recipe takes just seven days and the end result freezes well should you be left with some fish. I use Japanese sake instead of Scandinavian aquavit (water of life), but vodka is also suitable. You can make a faster version using good quality bought gravadlax or smoked salmon instead.

400g Prepared Sushi Rice (see page 15)
50g Chilli Jam (see page 150), or Feng Pesto (see page 44)

for the gravadlax
1 salmon fillet, about 15cm long, scaled
200ml cold sake
2 stalks lemon grass, thinly sliced at an angle
2 garlic cloves, thinly sliced
small piece of ginger, finely chopped
4 kafir lime leaves, torn into small pieces
200g caster sugar
100g fine sea salt
20g basil sprigs
1/2 teaspoon wasabi paste

to serve
wasabi, pickled ginger and soy sauce

To make the gravadlax: use a sharp knife to pierce the salmon flesh in eight places. Pour the sake into a shallow dish and soak the salmon skin-side up for 20 minutes. Combine the lemon grass, garlic, ginger, and kafir lime leaves in a small bowl, and the sugar and salt in another.

Place the salmon skin-side down on a large sheet of greaseproof paper. Rub the herb mixture into the flesh, then cover with a layer of basil leaves. Pour the sugar and salt mixture over the top. Wrap the salmon tightly in the greaseproof paper, then wrap tightly in three or four layers of cling film. Place in a tray skin-side up and leave to cure in the fridge for seven days.

To finish the nigiri: prepare the rice following the method on page 15. Meanwhile, unwrap the fish and discard the herbs and marinade. Cut the fillet into a 7.5cm block and trim away the skin (you can freeze it for use in other sushi). Slice the gravadlax into nigiri pieces (see pages 18-19).

When the sushi rice has cooled down to about 28°C, mould it into 20 rice blocks (see pages 60-61). If you do not have a nigiri mould, the hand-shaped rice blocks should measure about 5cm long, 2cm wide and 2cm tall.

Apply a thin layer of wasabi to each slice of fish and lay the fish wasabi-side down on the rice, shaping it into nigiri. Add a tiny dot of chilli jam (or pesto) to each nigiri. Serve with the pickled ginger, soy sauce and some more wasabi.

seared tuna in pepper and sesame crust nigiri

makes

As with the sashimi version of this recipe, the spiced crust adds extra flavour and depth to the clean taste of the fish.

400g Prepared Sushi Rice (see page 15)
100g mixed black and white sesame seeds
300g tuna nigiri block (see page 27)
2 tablespoons cracked black pepper
1 teaspoon sea salt
olive oil, for frying
1/2 teaspoon wasabi paste

to serve
wasabi, ginger and soy sauce

Cook the sushi rice according to the instructions on page 15. Meanwhile, using a mortar and pestle, crush together the sesame seeds, black pepper and salt, then spread the mixture in a shallow tray.

Cut the tuna block into two equal pieces measuring approximately 12-14cm long, 7cm wide and 3cm deep. Press the sesame mixture onto the long sides of each block, then put aside to set.

When the sushi rice has cooled down to about 28°C, mould it into 20 rice blocks (see pages 60-61). If you do not have a nigiri mould, the hand-shaped rice blocks should measure about 5cm long, 2cm wide and 2cm tall.

Heat a little olive oil in a frying pan and, when smoking hot, fry the two blocks of tuna on each of the four long sides for 1 minute each, so the flesh is seared all around. Leave to rest for a few minutes, then slice the tuna into nigiri pieces.

Apply a thin layer of wasabi to each slice of fish and mould into nigiri as described on pages 60-61, placing the fish wasabi-side down on the rice. Serve with the pickled ginger, soy sauce and some more wasabi

sea bass with chilli oil and coriander

makes

Buy a good quality farmed sea bass for this sushi and ask your fishmonger to scale and fillet the fish for you. If you want to make your own chilli oil you will need to begin it at least one day in advance of serving, but you could use a good bought chilli oil instead.

50ml Chilli Oil (see page 34)
400g Prepared Sushi Rice (see page 15)
4 small sea bass fillets
$1/2$ teaspoon wasabi paste
20 coriander leaves

to serve
wasabi, pickled ginger and soy sauce

If you have not already done so, make the chilli oil according to the recipe on page 34 and decant it into a squeeze bottle.

On the day of serving, cook the sushi rice using the method on page 15. Meanwhile, skin the fish and cut into nigiri slices: you should get five or six slices from each fillet.

When the sushi rice has cooled down to about 28°C, mould it into 20 rice blocks (see pages 60-61). If you do not have a nigiri mould, the hand-shaped rice blocks should measure about 5cm long, 2cm wide and 2cm tall.

Apply a thin layer of wasabi to each slice of fish and place it wasabi-side down on the rice. Mould it into shape as demonstrated on pages 60-61.

Add a coriander leaf to each nigiri and drizzle with chilli oil. Serve with more wasabi, plus pickled ginger and soy sauce.

tiger prawns with feng mayo, shichimi and kimchee

makes

• • • • •
• • • • •
• • • • •

400g Prepared Sushi Rice (see page 15)
40ml Feng Mayo (see page 44)
2 tablespoons kimchee base
1-1.2kg raw tiger prawns, size 16/20
1/2 teaspoon wasabi paste
a little shichimi powder, for sprinkling

to serve
wasabi, pickled ginger and soy sauce

Cook the sushi rice using the method on page 15. Meanwhile, make the mayo following the recipe on page 44 and decant the sauce into a squeeze bottle. Put the kimchee base into a squeeze bottle too.

To prepare the tiger prawns. tear off the heads, then peel off the shells, leaving the last 'jacket' and tail on each prawn. Carefully pull out the intestinal threads. Skewer the prawns along their bellies, stretching them right to the end of their tails to straighten (see picture below).

Cook the skewered prawns in boiling salted water for 4-5 minutes, until bright pink, then plunge them straight into ice-cold water. When cool, remove the skewers and 'butterfly' the prawns by cutting along the belly side, being careful not to cut the whole way through.

When the sushi rice has cooled down to about 28°C, mould it into 20 rice blocks (see pages 60-61). If you do not have a nigiri mould, the hand-shaped rice blocks should measure about 5cm long, 2cm wide and 2cm tall.

Apply a thin layer of wasabi to the underside of each prawn and mould one prawn over each block of rice. Garnish the nigiri with a dot of Feng Mayo, a dot of kimchee base, and a sprinkling of shichimi powder. Serve with additional wasabi, plus pickled ginger and soy sauce.

smoked chicken with white asparagus nigiri

makes

Hot smoked chicken is delicious and surprising in this ambitious, meaty nigiri. Smoking at home is easy as long as the process is followed step by step. In Europe, white asparagus is in season from April to late September. For this dish you could also use green asparagus.

100ml Simple Teriyaki Sauce
  (see page 44)

400g Prepared Sushi Rice (see page 15)

2 organic chicken breasts,
  about 220g each

85g demerara sugar

85g raw long grain rice

4 tablespoons green tea

a little olive oil, for drizzling

salt and pepper

$1/2$ lemon

1 stalk lemon grass

5 spears white asparagus

a few strips of nori

$1/2$ teaspoon wasabi paste

to serve

wasabi and pickled ginger

Make the teriyaki sauce using the recipe on page 44. Meanwhile, cook the sushi rice as described on page 15.

To smoke the chicken: line a wok with a sheet of foil and put a mixture of the sugar, rice and tea in the base. Cover with another sheet of foil and place the wok over a medium heat. When the pan starts to smoke, put the chicken on the foil. Sprinkle with olive oil, salt and pepper, and add the lemon and lemon grass to the wok. Cover with a tight-fitting lid and leave to smoke for about 25 minutes, or until the chicken is tender. Set the cooked chicken aside to rest.

Blanch the asparagus in a tall saucepan of boiling water for 4 minutes, then plunge into ice-cold water to stop the cooking. Cut the asparagus lengthways down the middle, and in half crossways at an angle. Make 20 nori belts by cutting the nori into strips measuring 6cm by 1cm.

When the sushi rice has cooled down to about 28°C, mould it into 20 rice blocks (see pages 60-61). If you do not have a nigiri mould, the hand-shaped rice blocks should measure about 5cm long, 2cm wide and 2cm tall.

Slice the smoked chicken on the bias to give thin slices of similar size to traditional nigiri toppings. Apply a thin layer of wasabi to each slice of chicken and lay wasabi-side down on the rice, shaping them into nigiri (see pages 60-61). Balance a piece of white asparagus on top of each nigiri and secure with a nori belt. Serve with extra wasabi, pickled ginger and the teriyaki sauce.

Prepare the sushi rice following the method on page 15 and allow it to cool.

Meanwhile, cut the beef to a piece about 7cm wide and 2-3cm tall. Trim each end off the block so you have a blunt square to work with. Season the beef on each side. Heat the oil and butter in a non-stick pan. Sear the beef on all four long sides for 2 minutes per side, so the heat penetrates to a depth of 5-7mm on each side. Set aside to rest.

To make the horseradish and wasabi cream: in a small bowl mix the wasabi paste with the Philadelphia cream cheese and horseradish, then set aside.

When the sushi rice has cooled down to about 28°C, mould it into 16 rice blocks (see pages 60-61). If you do not have a nigiri mould, the hand-shaped rice blocks should measure about 5cm long, 2cm wide and 2cm tall.

Thinly slice the beef along the length of the piece (pieces should be about 3cm wide, so it may be necessary to cut at an angle). Apply a thin layer of wasabi to each slice and place on top of the rice blocks, wasabi-side down. Arrange the nigiri on serving plates and top with some spring onion and a dab of the horseradish and wasabi cream.

Dress each plate with a little salad of grated mooli and rocket leaves, topped with another dab of the horseradish and wasabi cream. Serve with extra wasabi, pickled ginger and soy sauce.

400g Prepared Sushi Rice (see page 15)
1 piece beef topside or sirloin, about 300g
sea salt and freshly ground black pepper
1 teaspoon olive oil
small knob of butter
$1/2$ teaspoon wasabi paste
2 spring onions, thickly sliced at an angle

for the fresh horseradish
and wasabi cream
$1/2$ teaspoon wasabi paste
100g Philadelphia Lite cream cheese
2 tablespoons finely grated fresh horseradish or good-quality bottled horseradish

to serve
grated mooli, rocket leaves, wasabi, pickled ginger, soy sauce

organic beef nigiri with fresh horseradish and wasabi cream

serves ● ● ● ●

The Japanese appreciate beef, particularly their famous Kobe beef, with its wonderful marbling. Britain has equally great organic sirloin and, as with Kobe beef, it commands a premium price. The beef in this recipe is all but raw, so needs to be of a very high standard. Ask a reliable butcher to give you a special cut of topside, ideally a block about 3cm tall, 7cm wide and 10cm long. Alternatively, cut a good steak to size. This nigiri makes a show-stopping starter.

crab gunkan with avocado and wasabi mayo

makes :::::

For this recipe I use green-skinned avocados as they keep their shape when sliced or diced; black-skinned varieties are better for dishes in which the avocado is mashed, such as guacamole. I do not believe that drizzling pre-cut avocado with lemon juice helps preserve its colour, therefore I only cut avocado 'to order', just before it is being served. When making this nigiri, be sure to choose good quality hand-picked crabmeat from a reliable supplier, to save yourself the hard labour of cleaning the crab.

200g Prepared Sushi Rice (see page 15)
50ml Feng Mayo (see page 44)
1 teaspoon wasabi powder
150g white crabmeat
a few strips of nori
1/2 ripe, green-skinned avocado

to serve
wasabi, pickled ginger, and soy sauce

Cook the rice according to the instructions on page 15. Meanwhile, if you have not already done so, make the Feng Mayo using the recipe on page 44. Dilute the wasabi powder in a few drops of cold water, add it to the mayo and place the sauce in a squeeze bottle ready for garnishing.

Carefully pick over the crabmeat to check for any remnants of shell or cartilage. Cut the nori into belts measuring 2.5cm by 8cm. Halve the avocado, then peel it and cut the flesh into tiny squares.

When the sushi rice has cooled down to about 28°C, mould it into ten rice blocks (see pages 60-61). If you do not have a nigiri mould, the hand-shaped rice blocks should measure about 5cm long, 2cm wide and 2cm tall.

Wrap a nori belt around each rice block so that they look like little boats. Seal the nori by pressing it together with a few grains of cooked sushi rice.

Fill the gunkan a quarter full with diced avocado, and the reminder with crabmeat. Decorate with a dot of wasabi mayo and a few pieces of diced avocado. Serve with soy sauce, pickled ginger and wasabi.

Tip: For the nori belts you can use off-cuts from making maki and therefore minimise wastage.

ikura gunkan

makes :::::

This is the most famous gunkan nigiri: simple salmon eggs inside a crisp nori wrapper. Japanese salmon eggs (ikura) are salted or marinated in soy. Any good quality salmon eggs are good for this recipe – as long as you are willing to pay the premium prices.

200g Prepared Sushi Rice (see page 15)
a few strips of nori
150g ikura (salmon eggs)
10 long chives, halved, or 20 short chives

to serve
wasabi, pickled ginger and soy sauce

Cook the rice following the method on page 15. Meanwhile, cut the nori into belts measuring 2.5cm by 8cm and cut the chives into 5cm pieces.

When the rice has cooled down to about 28°C, mould it into ten rice blocks (see pages 60-61). Wrap a nori belt around each rice block, sealing the edges with a few rice grains.

Carefully fill each gunkan boat with a heaped teaspoon of salmon eggs, then decorate each one with two short chives. Serve with wasabi, pickled ginger and soy sauce.

tuna tartar with wasabi tobiko

makes :::::

200g Prepared Sushi Rice (see page 15)
4 teaspoons Feng Mayo (see page 44)
200g tuna off-cuts, minced (see page 27)
1 tablespoon ponzu sauce
1 spring onion, very finely chopped
a few strips of nori
40g wasabi tobiko

to serve
wasabi, pickled ginger and soy sauce

Cook the rice using the method on page 15. Meanwhile, make the Feng Mayo according to the recipe on page 44.

Mix the minced tuna with the ponzu sauce, 2 teaspoons of the mayo and the spring onions. Cut the nori into belts measuring 2.5cm by 8cm.

When the rice has cooled down to about 28°C, mould it into ten rice blocks (see pages 60-61). Wrap a nori belt around each rice block, sealing the edges with a few rice grains.

Fill each gunkan with a heaped teaspoon of the tuna tartar and decorate with a dot of mayo and the wasabi tobiko. Serve with the wasabi, pickled ginger and soy sauce.

scallops seared in teriyaki sauce

makes ⦂⦂⦂⦂⦂

I use only the freshest scallops for this dish – not scallops kept in brine or frozen, as these tend to absorb 50 percent of their weight in water. The best way of telling the difference is that fresh scallops are smaller and have hint of grey, whereas brine-soaked or frozen scallops look bright white, almost as though they have been bleached.

200g Prepared Sushi Rice (see page 15)
50ml Simple Teriyaki Sauce (see page 44)
a few strips of nori
5 fresh hand-dived scallops

to serve
wasabi, pickled ginger and soy sauce

Cook the rice using the method on page 15. Meanwhile, make the teriyaki sauce as described on page 44 and decant it into a squeeze bottle ready for garnishing. Cut the nori into belts measuring 2.5cm by 8cm.

Clean the scallops, removing the corals. Rinse the muscle meat under a cold tap and cut in half.

When the sushi rice has cooled down to about 28°C, mould it into ten rice blocks (see pages 60-61). If you do not have a nigiri mould, the hand-shaped rice blocks should measure about 5cm long, 2cm wide and 2cm tall.

Wrap a nori belt around each rice block, sealing the seaweed with a few rice grains.

Fill each gunkan with half a scallop and drizzle with a little of the teriyaki sauce. Serve the nigiri with the wasabi, pickled ginger and soy sauce.

tamago

I think you will find this method for tamagoyaki (rolled Japanese omelette) much easier than the traditional technique. Nevertheless you still need to be patient – this dish should not be rushed, but performed in a calm, Zen-like state of mind.

Gently whisk together 6 organic eggs, 2 teaspoons sugar, 1 teaspoon mirin, 1 teaspoon sake and $1/2$ teaspoon light soy sauce, being careful not to add too much air to the mixture. Strain it into a jug to remove any threads of egg white.

1. Place a square tamago pan over a medium heat and use a brush to grease it lightly with sunflower oil.

2. Pour a quarter of the egg mixture evenly over the base of the pan and cook until the top has just set.

3. Using a spatula, fold the omelette lengthways four times, trying to keep the roll as neat and tight as possible.

4. Remove the cylinder of omelette from the pan and put it to one side on a plate. Lightly oil the pan and pour another quarter of the egg mixture over the base.

5. When the second layer of omelette has set, place the rolled omelette back in the pan and wrap the second layer of omelette around it to create a larger roll. Use the spatula to make it as neat as possible, then remove the omelette from the pan. Repeat with the remaining egg mixture.

6. Place the omelette in a bamboo mat and leave to cool for at least 30 minutes. Use a very sharp knife to cut the omelette into ten slices. The omelette can be made a day in advance and kept in the fridge overnight, which also makes it easier to cut.

tamago with red roasted peppers

makes ⦂⦂⦂⦂⦂

Filling Japanese omelette with Italian ingredients makes an astonishing vegetarian dish.

200g Prepared Sushi Rice (see page 15)
1 roasted red pepper, deseeded and finely sliced
1 teaspoon balsamic vinegar
10 long chives

for the omelette
6 medium organic eggs
2 teaspoon sugar
1 teaspoon mirin
1 teaspoon sake
$\frac{1}{2}$ teaspoon light soy
vegetable oil, for greasing

to serve
wasabi, pickled ginger and soy sauce

Cook the sushi rice according to the instructions on page 15. Meanwhile, put the sliced roast pepper a small bowl and dress with the balsamic vinegar.

Prepare the omelette mixture and begin cooking as shown on pages 80-81, pouring one-quarter of the egg mixture into the pan. Place the roast pepper strips in a line down the first sheet of omelette. When set, fold the omelette into a cylinder, making it as tight as possible, and remove it from the pan. Pour another quarter of the egg mixture into the pan and continue cooking as described on the previous page. When done, leave the omelette to cool down in a rolled bamboo mat for at least 30 minutes.

When the sushi rice has cooled to about 28°C, mould it into ten rice blocks (see pages 60-61). If you do not have a nigiri mould, the hand-shaped rice blocks should measure about 5cm long, 2cm wide and 2cm tall. When the omelette is cool, cut it into ten slices.

Place a piece of tamago on top of each rice block and tie a chive around it to secure. Serve the nigiri with wasabi, pickled ginger and soy sauce.

tamago with ricotta and spinach

Follow the recipe above but replace the roast pepper filling with this mixture: Cook 100g baby spinach leaves in a lightly oiled frying pan for a few minutes until wilted. Drain thoroughly to remove the excess liquid. Crumble 20g ricotta over the spinach and season with salt and pepper. Fill and complete the omelette as described above then leave to cool. After topping the rice blocks with the sliced omelette, tie a belt of nori around the nigiri to secure them.

avocado with chives and pressed spinach with sesame seeds

makes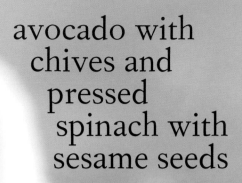

Although these sushi are suitable for vegan diets, all the ingredients widely available.

400g Prepared Sushi Rice (see page 15)
a few strips of nori

for the spinach topping
2 tablespoons olive oil
1 tablespoon sesame oil
500g baby spinach leaves
2 tablespoons black sesame seeds,
  toasted
sea salt and pepper

for the avocado topping
25 long chives
1 large green skinned avocado

to serve
wasabi, pickled ginger and soy sauce

Cook the sushi rice according to the method on page 15. Meanwhile, prepare the spinach topping: heat the oils in a wok over medium heat and, when smoking hot, add the spinach to the pan a handful at a time. Cook, stirring, until thoroughly wilted. Remove from the heat, add the sesame seeds and season with salt and pepper.

Place a rolling mat on a couple of layers of kitchen paper and place a piece of greaseproof paper on top. Put the spinach on the greaseproof paper and use the mat to press the spinach into a square log.

Hold the spinach log upright over the sink and gently squeeze out as much liquid as possible. Replace the paper towel and greaseproof paper with fresh sheets, then leave the spinach to rest in the rolling mat for 20 minutes.

For the avocado topping: cut the chives into 5cm pieces. Halve the avocado, discard the stone and peel off the skin. Slice each half into five pieces.

When the sushi rice has cooled down to about 28°C, mould it into 20 rice blocks (see pages 60-61). If you do not have a nigiri mould, the hand-shaped rice blocks should measure about 5cm long, 2cm wide and 2cm tall.

Cut the strips of nori into 20 belts measuring 6cm by 1cm. Take ten blocks of rice and place a slice of avocado on top of each. Add a bundle of trimmed chives and secure each nigiri with a nori belt.

Carefully cut the pressed spinach into ten slices. Place one on each of the remaining rice blocks and secure with a nori belt. Serve with wasabi, pickled ginger and soy sauce.

sushi-maki

We must thank Japan's gambling dens for sushi-maki. Card sharks who couldn't bear to leave the table took to wrapping their snacks in rice and nori. They could then graze while keeping their gaze fixed on the game, without the cards sticking to their fingers.

Clockwise from the top: Seared Salmon and Red Pepper Maki; Tuna, Spring Onion and Shiso Maki; Scallop, Chive and Shiso Maki; Avocado, Pesto and Chilli Maki; Salmon and Rocket Maki; Brown Rice, Avocado and Cucumber Maki

rolling sushi-maki

1 Trim each sheet of nori down by cutting a 3.5cm strip along the longest side to give a sheet measuring 15.5 x 20.5cm. Save the off-cuts for making gunkan nigiri and nori belts. Lay your first sheet of nori shiny-side down on a rolling mat and position it so that is close to you, near the edge of the work surface.

2 When the cooked sushi rice has reached a temperature of 28°C, gently spread about 125g of it over the nori, leaving a 1cm border along the side furthest from you free of rice. Be careful not to exert too much pressure on the rice as you spread it, as this may spoil the texture. Spread a line of wasabi paste along the rice about one-third of the way across it from you.

3 Arrange the maki filling on top of the strip of wasabi.

4 Using your thumbs to lift the bamboo mat and your index fingers to hold the filling in place, roll the sushi up and over to form a neat cylinder. Seal the roll with the uncovered border of nori.

5 Press the bamboo slats of the rolling mat along the sides of the sushi roll to shape it into a neat, square-sided maki. Set aside to rest for a few minutes.

6 Remove the sushi roll from the rolling mat and (unless the recipe says otherwise) trim off the rough ends. Finally, cut the roll into eight pieces.

mixed maki serves • • • •

Once you have mastered the basic maki-rolling technique using the simple combinations of fillings given here, feel free to try others. Some suggestions: minced raw tuna with shichimi powder and shiso; off-cuts of tamago with chives and baby spinach; roast red peppers with blanched asparagus; cucumber with pesto and sesame seeds. For any of these rolls, you could replace the white rice with brown (see page 96) if preferred.

600g Prepared Sushi Rice (see page 15)
1 teaspoon Simple Teriyaki Sauce (see page 44)
1 teaspoon Feng Pesto (see page 44)
$1/4$ green-skinned avocado
$1/2$ cucumber
$1/4$ red bell pepper
1 spring onion, green tops only
40g sashimi-grade salmon
40g cooked salmon
40g sashimi-grade tuna
2 hand-dived scallops
5 sheets nori
$1/2$ teaspoon wasabi paste
small handful of rocket leaves
small handful of shiso cress
5 long chives
2-3 pinches shichimi powder

to serve
wasabi, pickled ginger and soy sauce

Cook the sushi rice following the instructions on page 15. Meanwhile, if you have not already done so, prepare the teriyaki and pesto sauces using the recipes on page 44 and place each one in a squeeze bottle.

Cut the piece of avocado into three wedges. Quarter the piece of cucumber lengthways and remove the seeds. Cut the red bell pepper and the green tops of the spring onion into long, thin strips.

Trim any brown bits from the raw, sashimi-grade salmon and cut the flesh into strips. Cut the poached salmon and raw tuna into strips too, keeping them well separated.

Remove the intestines and corals from the scallops, then rinse them in cold water and pat dry with kitchen paper. Cut each scallop into three discs.

Trim each sheet of nori down by one-fifth. Place one sheet on a rolling mat shiny side down and spread about 120g of the cooled sushi rice over it, leaving a 1cm border at the top free of rice (see techniques on page 89). Be careful not to press too hard as this may ruin the rice.

Spread a line of wasabi paste across the very middle of the
rice. Lay the raw salmon strips and some rocket leaves on
top of this line. Hold the filling in place with your index
fingers and roll the nori sheet over to make a cylinder,
sealing the roll with the tab of uncovered nori. Use the
slats of the rolling mat to square up the roll and set aside
to rest for a few minutes.

Repeat the process with the remaining ingredients, using
the following combinations for subsequent sheets of nori:
tuna, spring onion and shiso; scallop, chives and teriyaki
sauce; poached salmon and red pepper; avocado, pesto
and shichimi powder.

Cut each maki roll into six pieces and serve with the
wasabi, pickled ginger and soy sauce.

Tip: for the cooked salmon you could use poached fish or
(as I have done in the picture on page 86) use leftovers
from making the seared salmon sashimi on page 22.

salmon skin with spring onions

makes

When you try this crisp filling for the first time it quickly becomes apparent why it is known as the 'bacon of the sea'. Ask your fishmonger to scale your salmon fillet before he skins it – the skin should be thrown in for free but as many people don't want it, you may have to remind him. Salmon skin freezes well too, so bear this in mind when buying salmon for other dishes. For extra flavour you can use the skin left over from marinating gravadlax; do not worry if there is a little meat on the back as this just adds to the flavour.

500g Prepared Sushi Rice (see page 15)
skin of 1 salmon fillet
salt and pepper
splash of olive oil
4 sheets nori
2 spring onions, finely chopped
60g mizuna leaves

to serve
wasabi, pickled ginger and soy sauce

Cook the sushi rice following the instructions on page 15. Meanwhile, cut the salmon skin into eight pieces and season with salt and pepper. Heat a generous splash of olive oil in a non-stick frying pan and fry the salmon skin until light golden. Set aside to drain on kitchen paper to remove any excess oil.

Trim each sheet of nori down by one-fifth. Place one sheet on a rolling mat shiny side down and spread about 125g of sushi rice over it, leaving a 1cm border at the top free of rice (see photographs on page 89). Be careful not to press too hard as this may ruin the rice.

Lay two pieces of fried salmon skin across the middle of the rice and top with a quarter each of the spring onions and mizuna leaves. Arrange the filling so that some of both the salmon skin and mizuna stick out at each end.

Hold the filling in place with your index fingers and roll the nori sheet over to make a cylinder and seal the roll with the tab of uncovered nori. Use the slats of the rolling mat to square up the roll and set aside to rest for a few minutes. Repeat with the remaining ingredients.

Cut each roll into eight pieces and arrange on a serving plate with wasabi, pickled ginger and soy sauce.

power lunch with edamame, wakame and tuna

serves ● ● ● ●

This is sushi for people on the go – I often reach for it myself if there is a busy afternoon ahead. The brown rice has complex carbs that release energy slowly into the bloodstream. Wakame is said to be good for the metabolism and cleanses the blood – the effect is thought to be doubled when it is served with a salad dressing made with healthy oil. To cook the wholegrain rice you need to briefly forget everything you have learned about sushi rice as it demands totally different treatment.

power lunch with edamame, wakame and tuna

300g frozen edamame

20g dried wakame

300g sashimi-grade tuna

1 green-skinned avocado, peeled and sliced

100g ikura (salmon eggs)

1 punnet shiso cress

small handful of coriander leaves

for the brown sushi rice mixture (makes about 640g)

300g long-grain brown rice

2 tablespoons poppy seeds

4 teaspoons extra virgin olive oil

4 teaspoons sushi vinegar

10g chives, finely chopped

sea salt and pepper

to serve

Japanese Vinaigrette (see page 42)

To cook the brown rice: first make a note of its volume in a measuring jug. Rinse the rice thoroughly under the tap and place in a heavy-bottomed saucepan. Add enough water to give 150 per cent of the volume of rice. Bring to the boil, cover and cook for 40 minutes over a low heat. Then remove the pan from the heat and set aside, still covered, for another 20 minutes.

Place the hot cooked rice in a bowl with the poppy seeds, olive oil, sushi vinegar and chives. Mix gently, then season with salt and pepper. Cover the bowl and leave to rest for 1 hour, or until the rice has cooled to room temperature.

Meanwhile, bring a kettle of water to the boil. Place the edamame in a heatproof bowl and cover with the hot water from the kettle. Leave to stand for 5 minutes, then drain and pod the beans.

Place the wakame in a small bowl and cover with cold water. Leave to rehydrate for 10 minutes, then drain.

Slice the tuna diagonally into 20 sashimi-style pieces, referring to the pictures on page 19 if necessary.

Divide the rice mixture among four noodle bowls or other large serving dishes. Top with the tuna sashimi, sliced avocado, wakame, salmon eggs and edamame. Garnish with shiso cress and coriander leaves and serve with a little dish of the Japanese vinaigrette.

Tip: in general this dish will work with any Japanese ingredients that take your fancy. You can also use fresh salmon, or a tartar mixture that uses up tuna trimmings from other recipes (see page 29).

salmon, rocket and pesto maki

makes

Peppery rocket complements salmon in any sushi roll, whether it's made with brown or white rice. This roll is a good way to use salmon off-cuts and is eternally popular.

500g Prepared Brown Sushi Rice
  (see opposite)
50ml Feng Pesto (see page 44)
150g sashimi-grade salmon
4 sheets nori
60g rocket

to serve
wasabi, pickled ginger and soy sauce

Cook the brown rice following the recipe on page 96. Meanwhile, if you have not already done so, prepare the pesto as described on page 44 and decant into a squeeze bottle. Trim the salmon, discarding any brown bits.

Trim each sheet of nori down by one-fifth. Place one sheet on a bamboo rolling mat shiny side down and spread about 125g of brown rice over it, leaving a 1cm border at the top free of rice (see pictures on page 89).

Place a row of salmon along the middle of the rice. Top with a line pesto and about a quarter of the rocket leaves. Hold the filling in place with your index fingers and roll the nori over to make a cylinder, sealing the roll with the tab of uncovered nori. Use the slats of the rolling mat to square up the roll and set aside to rest for a few minutes. Repeat with the remaining ingredients.

Cut each roll into six pieces, discarding the ragged ends. Arrange the maki on a plate and serve with wasabi, pickled ginger and soy sauce.

yellowtail and thai asparagus maki

makes

Here is an opportunity to use the off-cuts from other yellowtail dishes in this book. The rich, fatty fish works well with wholesome brown rice.

500g Prepared Brown Sushi Rice
  (see page 96)
16 spears Thai asparagus
salt
160g sashimi-grade yellowtail
4 sheets nori

to serve
wasabi, pickled ginger and soy sauce

Prepare the brown rice mixture following the recipe on page 96. While it is cooking, bring a kettle of water to the boil. Place the asparagus in a heatproof bowl. Cover with hot water from the kettle, add a little salt and set aside for a few minutes. Drain then plunge into ice-cold water to stop the cooking and help retain the colour.

Cut the yellowtail into small pieces.

Trim each sheet of nori down by one-fifth. Place one sheet on a rolling mat shiny side down and spread about 125g of brown rice over it, leaving a 1cm border at the top free of rice (see techniques on page 89).

Place a row of yellowtail along the middle of the rice and top with four spears of asparagus. Hold the filling in place with your index fingers and roll the nori over to make a cylinder, sealing the roll with the tab of uncovered nori. Use the slats of the rolling mat to help square up the roll and set aside to rest for a few minutes. Repeat with the remaining ingredients.

Cut each roll into six, discarding the ragged ends. Serve with wasabi, pickled ginger and soy sauce.

avocado, chive and sesame maki

makes

This vegetarian option for brown rice maki is simple and tasty.

500g Prepared Brown Sushi Rice
  (see page 96)
1 green-skinned avocado
4 sheets nori
20 long chives
80g sesame seeds

to serve
wasabi, pickled ginger and soy sauce

First prepare the brown rice mixtrue as described on page 96. Meanwhile, quarter the avocado, peel off the skin, then cut each piece to give two wedges.

Trim each sheet of nori down by one-fifth. Place one sheet on a rolling mat shiny side down and spread about 125g of brown rice over it, leaving a 1cm border at the top free of rice (see techniques on page 89).

Lay two wedges of avocado along the middle of the rice. Top with five chives and a sprinkling of sesame seeds.

Hold the filling in place with your index fingers and roll the nori over to make a cylinder, sealing the roll with the tab of uncovered nori. Use the slats of the rolling mat to square up the roll and set aside to rest for a few minutes. Repeat with the remaining ingredients.

Cut each roll into six pieces, discarding the ragged ends, and arrange on a plate. Serve with the wasabi, pickled ginger and soy sauce.

rolling inside-out maki

1 Trim each sheet of nori down by cutting a 3.5cm strip along the longest side to give a sheet measuring 15.5 x 20.5cm. Save the off-cuts for making gunkan nigiri and nori belts. Lay your first sheet of nori shiny-side down on a rolling mat and position it so that is close to you, near the edge of the work surface.

2 When the cooked sushi rice has reached a temperature of 28°C, gently spread about 150g of it over the nori, covering the whole sheet. Be careful not to press too hard as this may spoil the texture of the rice. Sprinkle the sesame seeds, or whatever mixture you are using to decorate the outside of the maki, evenly over the rice.

3 Quickly turn the square over so that the nori is uppermost. Arrange your chosen fillings across the middle of the nori.

4 Using your thumbs to lift the bamboo mat and your index fingers to hold the filling in place, roll the sushi up and over to form a neat cylinder. Seal the roll by tucking the top edge of the nori under the bottom edge – be sure to do this tightly so that the roll stays closed.

5 Press the bamboo slats of the rolling mat along the sides of the roll to shape it into a neat, square-sided maki. Set aside to rest for a few minutes.

6 Remove the roll from the bamboo mat. Use a sharp knife to trim off the rough ends, then cut each maki into eight pieces.

inside-out maki with crushed wasabi peas

makes

This maki came about by accident while I was teaching a sushi course in Denmark. It was the day after a public holiday and I could not find any decent fresh fish for love or money, so I devised this very tasty vegetarian sushi. Wasabi peas are dried peas coated in a wasabi-flavoured crust. Normally eaten as a snack, they are widely available in Asian stores.

600g Prepared Sushi Rice (see page 15)
50ml Feng Pesto (see page 44)
4 spears green asparagus
1 green-skinned avocado
100g wasabi peas
100g black sesame seeds, toasted
4 sheets nori
24 long chives
50g mizuna leaves
50g rocket leaves

to serve
wasabi, pickled ginger and soy sauce

Cook the sushi rice as described on page 15. Meanwhile, make the pesto using the recipe on page 44.

Blanch the asparagus in a pot of boiling salted water for 4 minutes, then drain and plunge into ice-cold water. Once cool, halve each spear down the middle.

Quarter and peel the avocado, then cut each piece into three wedges. Use a food processor to crush the wasabi peas coarsely, then mix them with the black sesame seeds.

Trim each sheet of nori down by one-fifth. Place one sheet on a rolling mat and spread 150g of sushi rice over it (see page 100). Sprinkle the sesame-wasabi mixture over the rice, then flick the square over so that the nori is uppermost.

Arrange the filling across the middle of the nori: lay two pieces of asparagus and six chives so that the ends stick out either side; add a line of pesto, three avocado wedges, a small handful of mizuna and a small handful of rocket.

Roll the maki tightly and seal by tucking the top end of the nori under the bottom end. Use the rolling mat to square up the maki and set it aside to rest for a few minutes while you repeat with the remaining ingredients.

Cut each roll into eight, arrange on a plate and serve with the wasabi, pickled ginger and soy sauce.

california sunset inside-out maki with crab and tobiko

makes

Globally, this is the most famous maki, but all too often made with crabsticks. Even in Japan some sushi bars will use them, which is strange as they come from large processing factories and are made from a dubious mix of white fish leftovers and artificial flavouring. For a real treat I recommend high quality picked crab claw meat. Yuzu-flavoured tobiko is optional in this recipe: wasabi or plum varieties would work as well.

600g Prepared Sushi Rice (see page 15)

50ml Feng Mayo (see page 44)

1 cucumber

1 green-skinned avocado

160g white crabmeat

4 sheets nori

100g mixed black and white sesame seeds

60g yuzu tobiko

to serve
wasabi, pickled ginger and soy sauce

Cook the sushi rice following the method on page 15. Meanwhile, prepare the mayo as described on page 44.

Cut the cucumber lengthways down the middle and set one half aside for use in other dishes. Use a spoon to scrape out the seeds, then cut the cucumber into four long sticks.

Quarter and peel the avocado, then cut each piece into three wedges. Carefully pick through the crabmeat, removing any shell or cartilage.

Trim each sheet of nori down by one-fifth. Place one sheet on a rolling mat and spread about 150g of sushi rice over it, covering the whole sheet (see page 100). Sprinkle the sesame seeds and tobiko over the rice, then flick the square over so that the black seaweed side is uppermost.

Arrange the filling across the middle of the nori: one cucumber stick, a line of mayo, three pieces of avocado and a quarter of the crabmeat.

Roll the maki tightly and seal by tucking the top end of the nori under the bottom end. Square up the sides and set aside to rest while you repeat with the remaining ingredients.

Cut each roll into eight pieces, discarding the ragged ends, and serve with the wasabi, pickled ginger and soy sauce.

vegetarian inside-out maki with pickles

makes

Most Japanese pickles will work in this recipe. Try sakurazuke (pink pickled mooli), takuwantoro (yellow pickled mooli), shibazuke (purple pickled aubergine), and kappa (Asian pickled cucumber), just to name a few of the possibilties.

600g Prepared Sushi Rice (see page 15)

1 cucumber

1 green-skinned avocado

4 sheets nori

100g mixed black and white sesame seeds

20 long chives

120g Japanese pickles, drained

to serve

wasabi, pickled ginger and soy sauce

Cook the sushi rice following the method on page 15.

Cut the cucumber lengthways down the middle and set one half aside for use in other dishes. Use a spoon to scrape out the seeds, then cut the cucumber into four long sticks.

Quarter and peel the avocado, then cut each piece into three wedges.

Trim each sheet of nori down by one-fifth. Place one sheet on a rolling mat and spread about 150g of sushi rice over it, covering the whole sheet (see page 100). Sprinkle the sesame seeds over the rice, then flick the square over so that the black seaweed side is uppermost.

Arrange the filling across the middle of the nori: one cucumber stick, three pieces of avocado, five chives and a quarter of the Japanese pickles.

Roll the maki tightly and seal by tucking the top end of the nori under the bottom end. Square up the sides and set aside to rest for a few minutes while you repeat the process with the remaining ingredients.

Cut each roll into eight pieces, discarding the ragged ends. Arrange the sushi on a plate and serve with the wasabi, pickled ginger and soy sauce.

san fran rainbow roll

makes

500g Prepared Sushi Rice (see page 15)
160g salmon sashimi block
160g tuna sashimi block
1 cucumber
4 sheets nori
20-40 long chives
120g sashimi-grade yellowtail off-cuts,
    finely chopped

to serve
wasabi, pickled ginger and soy sauce

First prepare the sushi rice following the method on page 15. Meanwhile, cut the salmon and tuna into 12 nigiri slices each (see the pictures on pages 19 and 26).

Cut the cucumber lengthways down the middle and set one half aside for use in other dishes. Use a spoon to scrape out the seeds, then cut the cucumber into four long sticks.

Trim each sheet of nori down by one-fifth. Place one sheet on a rolling mat shiny side down and spread about 125g of sushi rice over it, leaving a 1cm border at the top free of rice (see techniques on page 100).

Lay six of the nigiri slices, alternating the salmon and tuna, along the bottom half of the rice. Flick the whole square over so that the nori is uppermost.

Arrange the filling across the middle of the nori: one cucumber stick, 5-10 chives and a quarter of the yellowtail.

Roll the maki tightly into a cylinder and seal with the tab of uncovered nori. Use the slats of the rolling mat to square up the maki and leave to rest for a few minutes. Repeat with the remaining ingredients.

Cut each roll into eight pieces, discarding the ragged ends, and arrange on a plate. Serve with the wasabi, pickled ginger and soy sauce.

gravadlax with salmon, rocket and pesto

makes

Gravadlax needs eight to ten days to cure, so bear this in mind when you are planning to make this dish. Alternatively, you can use ready-made traditional dill gravadlax, or smoked salmon, making sure that each slice is only a few millimetres thick.

500g Prepared Sushi Rice (see page 15)
50ml Feng Pesto (see page 44)
4 sheets nori
320g gravadlax (see page 67)
120g sashimi-grade salmon off-cuts, finely chopped
50g rocket leaves

to serve
wasabi, pickled ginger and soy sauce

Cook the sushi rice according to the instructions on page 15. Meanwhile, prepare the pesto following the recipe on page 44 and place in a squeeze bottle. Cut the gravadlax into 24 nigiri slices following the technique on page 19.

Trim each sheet of nori down by one-fifth. Place one sheet on a rolling mat shiny side down and spread about 125g of sushi rice over it, leaving a 1cm border at the top free of rice (see page 100).

Lay six nigiri slices along the bottom half of the rice. Flick the whole square over so that the nori is uppermost.

Arrange the filling along the centre of the nori: a line of pesto, a quarter of the salmon and a handful of rocket.

Holding the filling in place with your index fingers, roll up into a cylinder and seal the maki with the tab of uncovered nori. Square up the sides of the maki and leave to rest for a few minutes. Repeat with the remaining ingredients.

Cut each roll into eight pieces, discarding the ragged ends. Arrange on a plate and serve with the wasabi, pickled ginger and soy sauce.

organic roast beef with horseradish cream, chives and cucumber

makes •••••••
••••••
••••••

Here is the maki version of my beef nigiri. It is a good option if you want to make something quick for a drinks party. Buy ready-roast organic beef that is nicely pink in the middle, and have the butcher cut each slice no more than a few millimetres thick.

500g Prepared Sushi Rice (see page 15)
100ml Fresh Horseradish and Wasabi Cream (see page 74)
1 cucumber
4 sheets nori
400g organic roast beef, about 20 slices
20 long chives

to serve
wasabi, pickled ginger and soy sauce

Cook the sushi rice according to the instructions on page 15. Meanwhile, prepare the horseradish and wasabi cream following the recipe on page 74.

Cut the cucumber lengthways down the middle and set one half aside for use in other dishes. Use a spoon to scrape out the seeds, then cut the cucumber into four long sticks.

Trim each sheet of nori down by one-fifth. Place one sheet on a rolling mat shiny side down and spread about 125g of sushi rice over it, leaving a 1cm border at the top free of rice (see techniques on page 100).

Lay five slices of beef so that they overlap along the bottom half of the rice. Flick the whole square over so that the nori is uppermost. Arrange the filling across the middle of the nori: a generous spread of horseradish and wasabi cream, one cucumber stick and five chives.

Roll tightly up into a cylinder and seal the maki with the tab of uncovered nori. Use slats of the rolling mat to square up the sides and leave to rest for a few minutes. Repeat with the remaining ingredients.

Cut each roll into eight pieces, discarding the ragged ends. Arrange on a plate and serve with the wasabi, pickled ginger and soy sauce.

tamago roll with roast bell pepper salsa

makes

On one hand this maki is designed to impress; on the other it's a cost-effective vegetarian sushi roll. Use a large tamago pan if possible, otherwise cook the tamago in a large non-stick frying pan and cut the individual sheets of omelette to size.

500g Prepared Sushi Rice (see page 15)
4 sheets nori
100g cream cheese
80 long chives

for the tamago sheets
6 organic eggs
2 teaspoons caster sugar
2 teaspoons mirin
2 teaspoons sake
pinch of salt
olive oil, for greasing

for the salsa
2 yellow bell peppers, roasted, deseeded
   and peeled
2 red bell peppers, roasted, deseeded
   and peeled
1 tablespoon red wine vinegar
1 tablespoon honey
1/2 teaspoon shichimi powder

to serve
wasabi, pickled ginger and soy sauce

Cook the sushi rice according to the instructions on page 15.

Prepare the tamago mixture following the techniques on pages 80-81. Cook as instructed, but instead of rolling the omelette, turn the individual sheets out onto a rolling mat as soon as they are set and leave them to cool.

For the salsa: finely dice the roast peppers and place in a bowl with the vinegar, honey and shichimi. Marinate for 5 minutes, then drain to remove the excess liquid.

Trim each sheet of nori down by one-fifth. Place one sheet on a rolling mat shiny side down and spread about 125g of sushi rice over it, leaving a 1cm border at the top free of rice (see techniques on page 100).

Lay a sheet of omelette on top of the rice. Flick the whole square over so that the nori is uppermost. Arrange the filling across the middle of the nori: a generous spread of cream cheese, 3 tablespoons salsa and 20 long chives.

Roll the maki tightly into a cylinder and seal by tucking the top end of nori under the bottom end. Square up the sides and leave to rest for a few minutes while you repeat the process with the remaining ingredients.

Cut each roll into eight pieces, discarding the ragged ends. Arrange them on a plate and serve with the wasabi, pickled ginger and soy sauce.

rolling temaki

Temaki are cone-shaped hand rolls traditionally eaten at the sushi counter as quickly as the sushi chef can produce them. They are also a perfect party piece. Invite your friends to make their own – all you need to do is prepare the ingredients and show them how. Any maki filling is suitable for temaki.

1 Cut the nori straight down the middle, so that each sheet gives two rectangular pieces. Lay the first sheet of nori shiny-side down on the work surface. Place 50g of cooked sushi rice in a round, flat circle on the left side of the nori. Then stick 2-3 rice grains in the bottom right-hand corner of the nori to help seal the temaki later.

2 Smear a dab of wasabi in the centre of the circle of rice.

3 Lay your chosen filling diagonally across the middle of the rice so that it sticks out at the top left-hand corner.

4 Lift the bottom left-hand bottom corner of the nori up and across the filling, rolling the temaki over into a cone.

5 Use the rice that you previously stuck in the bottom right-hand corner to seal the nori.

6 Hand the finished temaki straight to your guests, or place on a serving plate, and repeat the process with the remaining ingredients.

green temaki

makes ::::

400g Prepared Sushi Rice (see page 15)
1 green-skinned avocado
4 sheets nori
50g mizuna leaves
20-40 long chives
80g kappa or other Japanese pickles

to serve
wasabi, pickled ginger and soy sauce

Cook the sushi rice according to the instructions on page 15. Meanwhile, quarter and peel the avocado, then cut each wedge into two pieces.

Cut the nori straight down the middle, so you have eight half sheets in total. Lay one sheet of nori shiny-side down on a work surface and place 50g of cooled sushi rice in a round, flat circle on the left side. Stick 2-3 rice grains in the right bottom corner, to help seal the temaki later.

For each temaki use a handful of mizuna leaves, a wedge of avocado, some chives and one-eighth of the pickles and place the filling in the middle of the rice so that it sticks out at the top left-hand corner.

Lift the bottom left-hand bottom corner and roll the temaki into a cone using the rice in the bottom right-hand corner to seal the nori. Repeat with the remaining ingredients and serve with wasabi, pickled ginger and soy sauce.

yellowtail temaki with rocket, shiso and feng mayo

makes ∷∷

400g Prepared Sushi Rice (see page 15)
50ml Feng Mayo (see page 44)
4 sheets nori
50g rocket leaves
16 nigiri slices yellowtail
1 punnet shiso cress

to serve
wasabi, pickled ginger and soy sauce

Cook the sushi rice according to the instructions on page 15. Meanwhile, if you have not already done so, make the Feng Mayo and place in a squeeze bottle.

Cut the nori straight down the middle, so you have eight half sheets in total. Lay one sheet of nori shiny-side down on a work surface and place 50g of the cooled sushi rice in a round, flat circle on the left side. Stick 2-3 rice grains in the right bottom corner, to help seal the temaki later.

Place the filling in the middle of the rice so that it sticks out at the top left-hand corner. First a generous dot of mayo, then one-eighth of the rocket leaves, two slices of yellowtail nigiri and a cluster of shiso cress.

Lift the bottom left-hand bottom corner and roll the temaki into a cone using the rice in the bottom right-hand corner to seal the nori. Repeat with the remaining ingredients and serve with wasabi, pickled ginger and soy sauce.

tempura

Tempura is vegetables or fish coated with a light batter and deep-fried. Some believe the idea arrived in Japan with the Portuguese in the mid-15th century. A hundred years later tempura of sea bream wrapped in shiso leaf had become a very exclusive dish. Later the technique spread to street food stalls, where busy workers would pick up tempura for a quick bite. In Japan there are restaurants specialising in tempura. The most prestigious use pure untoasted sesame oil for frying, while cheaper establishments will use lesser quality toasted sesame oil mixed with a high proportion of other oils such as soya or corn oil. I like to use sunflower oil as it seems to give a lighter result.

Pesto tiger prawn tempura

making tempura

When it comes to deep-fried food, Western people tend to favour a golden batter, however Japanese tempura batter is paler in colour. To make 500ml of batter you will need 500ml of ice-cold water and 250g tempura flour (plus extra for dusting). Alternatively, start with 500ml of ice-cold water and whisk in 1 egg yolk, 40g cornflour and 250g self-raising flour.

1. Take your jug of ice-cold water and add the flour to the water. Never add the water to the flour.

2. Gently whisk the ingredients together so that the batter has the consistency of double cream with lots of little lumps of flour in it. The air bubbles and lumps of flour will help make the tempura crisp – as will placing the batter in the fridge for 30 minutes to set and chill.

3. Dust all the ingredients in tempura flour. This will ensure an even coating of batter.

4. Heat the oil to 180°C in a heavy wok or deep-fryer. Remove the cold batter from the fridge and dip the ingredients in it. Use tongs to transfer each piece quickly to the hot oil, gently moving the tempura back and forwards in the oil before letting it go to stop it dropping to the base of the pan.

5. Never fry more than six pieces of tempura at a time. This ensures that the temperature of the oil does not drop significantly when you add the ingredients, which would make the tempura absorb some of the oil and take too long to fry. It also helps prevent the tempura sticking together.

6. Leave the cooked tempura to drain on sheets of paper towel, then season with sea salt before serving.

Highly seasoned dipping sauces such as the two recipes here enhance the taste of tempura and help cut through the fattiness of the deep-fried batter. Other condiments commonly served alongside tempura are shown below. Grated mooli is particularly important as it aids digestion.

Kimchee base

Shichimi powder

Chopped pickled ginger

Chilli oil

Thai sweet chilli sauce

dipping sauces and garnishes

basic tempura dipping sauce
makes about 550ml

250ml soy sauce

250ml boiling water

2 tablespoons dashi powder

2 tablespoons caster sugar

1 tablespoon finely chopped ginger

1/2 teaspoon shichimi powder

Combine all the ingredients in a large measuring
jug. Pour into a squeeze bottle and store in the
fridge, where it will keep for up to 2 weeks.

vegetarian dipping sauce
makes about 550ml

250ml soy sauce

250ml boiling water

2 tablespoons good quality vegetarian stock

2 tablespoons caster sugar

1 tablespoon finely chopped pickled ginger

2 tablespoons mixed black and white sesame seeds

Combine all the ingredients in a large measuring
jug. Pour into a squeeze bottle and store in the
fridge, where it will keep for up to 2 weeks.

Finely grated mooli

Sea salt

Basic tempura
dipping sauce

Vegetarian
dipping sauce

vegetarian tempura

serves ● ● ● ●

Making a batch of vegetarian tempura is the perfect opportunity to master the technique before moving on to more pricey ingredients such as fish. In principle, any vegetable can be fried in tempura batter; this recipe contains some of my favourites.

500ml Basic Tempura Batter
(see page 118)

1 beetroot

1 yellow beetroot

1/4 butternut squash

2 large fresh shitake mushrooms

4 oyster mushrooms

2 baby aubergines

1 small courgette

1 small mild pepper, such as
sweet romano

2 litres sunflower oil, for deep-frying

tempura flour, for dusting

sea salt

to serve

400g Prepared Sushi Rice (see page 15)

4 teaspoons toasted sesame seeds

200ml Vegetarian Dipping Sauce
(see page 121)

100g mooli, finely grated

Make the tempura batter according to the recipe on page 118 and place in the fridge to chill.

The vegetables need to be cut into pieces of similar size so that they will cook evenly. Do not peel the beetroot or butternut squash, simply cut them into discs 1/2cm thick.

Trim the base off the shitake mushrooms, then cut them in half leaving the stalk attached. The oyster mushrooms can be left whole. Halve the baby aubergines, but leave the stalks intact (these are not edible but look attractive). Cut the courgette and pepper diagonally into ovals 1/2cm thick.

Heat the sunflower oil to 180°C in a deep-fryer or large heavy-based saucepan. Place the tempura flour in a bowl and remove the cold batter from the fridge. Working with one variety at a time, dust the vegetables with tempura flour then dip in the batter. Fry the root vegetables and aubergine for 21/2-3 minutes, and the peppers, courgette and both varieties of mushroom for 11/2 minutes.

Remove the cooked tempura to a tray lined with kitchen paper to drain. Season with salt.

Divide the cooked sushi rice into four portions and shape them into a triangle using an onigiri mould, or use another tool such as a round cutter. Place a portion of rice on each serving plate, garnish with sesame seeds and stack the tempura vegetables around the rice. Serve immediately with the dipping sauce and grated mooli.

chilli tuna tempura

salmon, dill and tobiko tempura

chilli tuna tempura

makes

Adding extra crunch or flavour to tempura batter makes a brilliant variation. The following recipe is perfect served as a snack with cold beer on a hot day.

250ml Basic Tempura Batter
   (see page 118)
1 tablespoon kimchee base
1 tablespoon shichimi powder
2 litres sunflower oil, for deep-frying
150g tuna sashimi block
tempura flour, for dusting
sea salt

to serve
100ml Thai sweet chilli sauce

Make a half quantity of the basic tempura batter on page 118, adding the kimchee base and shichimi powder to the flour. Put the batter in the fridge to rest and chill.

Heat the sunflower oil in a deep-fryer or heavy based saucepan to 180°C. Cut the tuna loin into 12 pieces approximately 1cm thick and turn them lightly in the flour.

When the oil is ready, dip the tuna in the cold batter and, working with six pieces at a time, fry for about 2 minutes, or until light golden. Transfer the cooked tempura to a tray lined with kitchen paper to drain. Season with sea salt and serve with the Thai sweet chilli sauce.

salmon, dill and tobiko tempura

This is my Scandinavian take on tempura. Follow the recipe above but instead of adding the kimchee base and shichimi to the tempura batter, gently stir in 25g finely chopped dill and 2 tablespoons yuzu tobiko just before you put the batter in the fridge to chill. Replace the tuna with salmon sashimi and serve the cooked tempura with 100ml Scandia Dill Dressing (see page 43).

pesto tiger prawn tempura

makes ∷∷∷

Here is a very refreshing Italian twist on tempura.

50ml Feng Pesto (see page 44)
250ml Basic Tempura Batter
  (see page 118)
2 litres sunflower oil, for deep-frying
12 raw tiger prawns, size 16/20
tempura flour, for dusting
sea salt

to serve
100ml Basic Tempura Dipping Sauce
  (see page 121)

First make the Feng Pesto and Basic Tempura Dipping Sauce according to their respective recipes. Transfer both to squeeze bottles.

Take a half quantity of the Basic Tempura Batter on page 118 and stir in 50ml of the pesto so that it is evenly distributed. Place the batter in the fridge to chill.

Heat the sunflower oil in a deep-fryer or heavy-based saucepan to 180°C. Meanwhile, peel prawns: twist off the heads, remove the jackets but leave the tails on. Slit along the backs and lift out the intestines. Rinse the prawns, pat dry with kitchen paper, then turn them lightly in the flour.

When the oil is ready, dip each prawn in the batter and fry in the hot oil for about 2 minutes, or until light golden. Do not cook more than six prawns at a time. Transfer the cooked tempura to a tray lined with kitchen paper to drain. Season with sea salt and serve with the dipping sauce.

Tip: when frying tiger prawns, carefully hold them by the tail end, keeping your hands clear of the hot oil, and move the prawns back and forth in the oil a few times to help make the tempura large and crisp.

extra-crunchy baby squid tempura with pickled cucumber

serves ● ● ● ●

Cornmeal provides the extra crunch to this tempura. The cucumber salad is a take on my grandma's old recipe which she always served with whole roasted chicken and new potatoes. But here you go – it has found its way into my Japanese cuisine.

500ml Basic Tempura Batter
  (see page 118)
100g cornmeal
1/2 tablespoon shichimi powder
12 baby squid
2 litres sunflower oil, for deep-frying
sea salt

for the pickled cucumber
10cm piece dried kelp
200ml sushi vinegar
100g caster sugar
1 cucumber

To start the cucumber salad, rinse the kelp under the tap, then place in a saucepan with the vinegar and sugar. Heat the mixture until it just reaches boiling point, then remove from the heat and set aside to cool.

Make the basic tempura batter according to the recipe on page 118, adding the cornmeal and shichimi to the flour and an extra 100ml cold water to the jug. Chill thoroughly.

To continue the cucumber salad: finely slice the cucumber on a Japanese mandolin then place in a mixing bowl. Lift the kelp from the vinegar mixture and pour the liquid over the cucumber. Leave to marinate for at least 30 minutes.

Working under running tap water, remove the hard membrane from each squid body (this looks like a piece of plastic). Use your index finger to remove any soft tissue or slime from inside the body. With a pair of scissors, cut between the eyes and squid head, detaching the tentacles. Discard the eyes and any slimy bits. Cut each squid body into three pieces. Rinse everything once more in cold water and pat dry with kitchen paper. Set aside in a bowl.

Heat the sunflower oil in a deep-fryer or heavy-based saucepan to 180°C. Turn the baby squid in the flour, then dip in the batter. Fry six pieces of the squid at a time for approximately 2 minutes, or until light golden.

Transfer the cooked tempura to a tray lined with kitchen paper to drain. Season with sea salt and serve with the pickled cucumber salad.

magic's coconut tempura prawns with mango and papaya salsa

Here is my fiancé David's Caribbean version of tempura. We often serve it as a nibble on hot summer days while guests are waiting for the real party pieces to come off the barbecue.

500ml Basic Tempura Batter
  (see page 118)
12 raw tiger prawns, size 16/20
2 litres vegetable oil, for deep-frying
tempura flour, for dusting
70g unsweetened desiccated coconut

for the mango and papaya salsa
1 large ripe mango
1 large ripe papaya
1 red onion, finely sliced
juice of 2 limes
3 tablespoons red wine vinegar
3 tablespoons caster sugar

First make the salsa: peel and deseed the mango and papaya, cutting the flesh into 1cm cubes. Combine the fruit in a mixing bowl with the red onion, lime juice, red wine vinegar and caster sugar and stir gently. Cover and place the salsa in the fridge to chill for at least 30 minutes.

Make the basic tempura batter according to the recipe on page 118 and leave it to rest in the fridge.

Remove the heads and jackets from the prawns, but leave the tails intact. Slit each prawn along its back and lift out the intestinal thread.

Heat the oil to 180°C in a deep-fryer or heavy-based saucepan. Place the flour and desiccated coconut in separate dishes. Remove the cold batter from the fridge.

Working one at a time, dust the prawns in the flour, dip in the batter, then roll the coated prawns in coconut before placing in the hot oil. Fry for 2 minutes or until light golden.

Transfer the cooked tempura to a tray lined with kitchen paper to drain briefly, then serve immediately with the mango and papaya salsa.

japanese-style fish and chips with cod and rémoulade

serves ● ● ● ●

This is my most ambitious fusion – Japan meets Britain with a Danish detour. The Danish influence is the tradition of serving fish and chips with rémoulade sauce; something that was totally forbidden me in my childhood and is unapologetically central to my Feng Sushi recipe. I console myself with the fact that a homemade rémoulade bears little or no resemblance to the store-bought stuff. Plus I use sweet potatoes instead of some of the starchy whites for the chips, so it's as near as you can get to a sin-free treat and something that no parent should feel bad about serving to children... occasionally...

The quantity of pickled vegetables in this recipe is much more than you'll need for one batch of rémoulade sauce, but it's the sort of thing that is impractical to make in smaller amounts. The vegetables keep well in their cooled pickling liquid in a tightly sealed jar in the fridge, and you can use them as an accompaniment to many other things. I use sustainable Icelandic cod for this dish but monkfish tail also works well.

japanese-style fish and chips with cod and rémoulade

1 fillet cod, about 600-700g, skinned

2 large sweet potatoes

2 large Maris Piper potatoes

3 litres sunflower oil, for deep-frying

for the pickles

2 large carrots

2 large courgette

400g cauliflower

400g broccoli

400g celery

400g butternut squash

300g caster sugar

small handful of whole black peppercorns

1 tablespoon mild curry powder

1 tablespoon turmeric

1 piece of kombu, or 1 bay leaf

sushi vinegar

3-4 tablespoons cornflour

for the rémoulade sauce

1 whole egg

2 egg yolks

4 teaspoons yuzu juice

4 teaspoons sushi vinegar

1 tablespoon caster sugar

100ml olive oil

200ml vegetable oil

200ml sweet chilli sauce

salt and pepper

To make the pickles: peel and cut all the vegetables into 1cm dice. Place in a large heavy-based saucepan with the sugar, spices and kombu. Add enough sushi vinegar to cover the vegetables completely. Bring to the boil and cook until the vegetables are cooked but still very crunchy.

Place a large colander on top of a large bowl and drain the vegetables, saving the liquid. Return all the liquid to the saucepan and bring it back to the boil. Dissolve the cornflour in a little cold water and gradually add it to the vinegar mixture to give a thick, smooth consistency (you may not need to use all the cornflour). Pour the sauce over the pickled vegetables, stir, and set aside to cool.

To make the rémoulade sauce: place the egg, yolks, yuzu juice, sushi vinegar and caster sugar in a food processor and blend until white and fluffy. Combine the two oils and add them to the mixture gradually, blending to give an even consistency, then pour in the sweet chilli sauce.

Take a quantity of pickled vegetables similar to the total volume of sauce and add it to the food processor. Pulse the mixture just enough to give a coarse, lumpy dipping sauce. Season to taste with pepper, salt and sugar.

Prepare the tempura batter: start with a jug of iced water and gradually add the combined flours until the mixture is lumpy and airy. Place in the fridge to chill.

for the batter
1 litre ice-cold water
400g Japanese tempura flour
100g plain flour
tempura flour, for dusting

Rinse the fish and pat dry with kitchen paper. Place the cod on a board and cut the fillet down the middle, following the line of the backbone. Trim off any flabby bits and discard. Cut the fillet diagonally into 1cm thick slices, working at a 45-degree angle so that each piece is cut on the bias. You should aim to have 16-18 pieces.

Cut both varieties of potatoes into chips. Keeping the batches separate, rinse them in cold water and leave to drain in a colander. Heat the oil to 180°C in a deep-fryer or large heavy-based saucepan. When the oil is ready, fry the Maris Piper potatoes for 2 minutes, then add the sweet potatoes and continue frying for a further 8 minutes. Drain the chips on kitchen paper and season with salt.

Dust the cod slices in flour, then dip them in the chilled tempura batter. Fry for 2-3 minutes or until light golden, then drain on kitchen paper and season with salt and pepper. Stack the chips on a serving plate, place the cod on top and drizzle with the rémoulade sauce before serving.

sushi with tempura

Sushi with tempura is the perfect balance of naughty and nice. Adding just a few pieces of crispy tempura to a maki roll or temaki gives the maximum effect without piling on the calories. These rolls are good to share, and when served in combination with other dishes allow you to enjoy flavourful deep-fried food while still keeping the meal lean.

shitake mushroom roll with chives and teriyaki sauce

makes ● ● ● ●
● ● ● ●
● ● ● ●

Shitake mushrooms, a good source of antioxidants, are categorised as a umami ingredient, foods with the 'fifth taste' that is found so often in Japanese cuisine. This inside-out maki roll with a deep-fried filling has plenty of flavour and texture.

4 teaspoons Simple Teriyaki Sauce
   (see page 44)
280g Prepared Sushi Rice (see page 15)
250ml Basic Tempura Batter
   (see page 118)
6 fresh shitake mushrooms
2 litres sunflower oil, for deep-frying
tempura flour, for dusting
2 sheets nori
50g mixed black and white sesame seeds
1 punnet shiso cress, leaves picked, some
   reserved for granish
10-20 long chives

to serve
grated mooli, wasabi paste, pickled ginger
   and soy sauce

If you have not already done so, make the teriyaki sauce as on page 44 and decant it into a squeeze bottle.

Cook the sushi rice as per the instructions on page 15 and, while the rice is boiling, make a half quantity of the tempura batter on page 118 and place in the fridge to rest.

Brush the shitake mushrooms clean with a pastry brush, trim away the base of the stalks, and cut the mushrooms in half lengthways leaving the stalk attached.

Heat the vegetable oil to 180°C in a deep-fryer or heavy based saucepan. Dust the shitake in flour, dip in the cold tempura batter, and fry for a few minutes until golden and crisp. Transfer the cooked tempura to a plate lined with kitchen paper to drain.

When the sushi rice is ready, roll into maki following the pictures on page 100 if necessary. Place a sheet of nori on a bamboo mat, spread 140g cooked sushi rice over the entire surface and sprinkle with the sesame seeds and most of the shiso cress. Flick the over the square so the seaweed is uppermost. In the middle of the maki, place a line of teriyaki sauce, shitake tempura and chives. Roll the maki tightly, sealing it by tucking the top end of the nori under bottom end. Repeat with the remaining ingredients.

Cut each roll into eight pieces, discarding the ends, garnish with the remaining shiso cress and serve with the traditional accompaniments.

tiger prawn inside-out roll with thai asparagus and feng mayo

makes

This is a gorgeous maki roll, probably the second most popular maki in the Western sushi world – California maki having a strong first position.

280g Prepared Sushi Rice (see page 15)

250ml Basic Tempura Batter
  (see page 118)

4 teaspoons Feng Mayo (see page 44)

1 small punnet Thai asparagus

4 raw tiger prawns, size 16/20

2 litres sunflower oil, for deep-frying

tempura flour, for dusting

2 sheets nori

50g mixed black and white sesame seeds

to serve

grated mooli, wasabi paste, pickled ginger
  and soy sauce

Cook the sushi rice as per the instructions on page 15 and, while the rice is boiling, mix a half quantity of the tempura batter recipe on page 118 and leave it to rest in the fridge.

If you have not already done so, make the Feng Mayo as described on page 44 and place it in a squeeze bottle.

Bring a saucepan of salted water to the boil. Blanch the asparagus for 1 minute, then plunge it into ice-cold water.

Peel the tiger prawns, removing the intestinal threads, then rinse and pat dry. Skewer the prawns from belly to tail to stretch them out and make the maki easy to roll.

Heat the vegetable oil to 180°C in a deep-fryer or heavy-based saucepan. Dust the prawns in flour, dip in the tempura batter and fry for a few minutes until golden and crisp. Transfer to a plate lined with kitchen paper to drain, then remove the skewers from the prawns.

When the sushi rice is ready, roll the maki, referring to the pictures on page 100 as necessary. Place a sheet of nori on a bamboo mat, spread 140g cooked sushi rice over the surface and sprinkle all over with the sesame seeds. Flick the square over so the seaweed is uppermost. In the middle of the square place a row of mayonnaise, asparagus and tiger prawn tempura. Roll the maki tightly, closing it by tucking in top end of nori under bottom end.

Cut the roll in eight pieces, discarding the ends, and serve with the traditional accompaniments.

tempura wild salmon temaki with ikura and yuzu tobiko

makes ●●●● ●●●●

Wild salmon deserves its place in the sushi world; nonetheless I find it safest to eat this beautiful fish cooked. As you are already 'pushing the boat out' for this dish I recommend finishing it off in style with a few ikura and tobiko 'sea pearls'.

400g Prepared Sushi Rice (see page 15)
250ml Basic Tempura Batter
  (see page 118)
50ml Feng Mayo (see page 44)
80g wild salmon
2 litres sunflower oil, for deep-frying
tempura flour, for dusting
4 sheets nori
100g mizuna leaves
40g ikura (salmon eggs)
40g yuzu tobiko

to serve
grated mooli, wasabi paste, pickled ginger
  and soy sauce

Prepare the sushi rice following the instructions on page 15. While the rice is cooking, make a half quantity of the tempura batter recipe on page 118 and leave to rest in the fridge. If you have not already done so, make the Feng Mayo as described on page 44 and place it in a squeeze bottle.

Cut the salmon sashimi style into eight pieces following the pictures on page 19 if necessary.

Heat vegetable oil to 180°C in a deep-fryer or heavy-based saucepan. Dust the salmon in flour, dip in the cold tempura batter and fry for a few minutes until golden and crisp. Drain on a plate lined with kitchen paper.

Cut each sheet of nori in half to give a total of eight pieces. When the sushi rice has cooled, make temaki following the pictures on page 112 if necessary. Lay one sheet of nori shiny-side down and place 50g of the sushi rice in a round, flat circle on the left side. Stick 2-3 rice grains in the right bottom corner, to help seal the temaki later.

Place the filling in the middle of the rice so that it sticks out at the top left-hand corner: use one-eighth of the mizuna, one piece of wild salmon tempura and a dot of mayo per temaki. Lift the left hand bottom corner of the seaweed and roll the nori into a cone, using the rice grains to seal the nori. Repeat with the remaining ingredients.

Place the temaki in tall glasses and garnish them with the ikura and yuzu tobiko, then serve with the traditional sushi accompaniments.

Roberto, an old Mexican chef, first introduced me to this combination. He'd often make sushi as he knew it from his homeland for staff who were tired of the healthy Japanese version and craved something richer. We nicknamed it the 'triple bypass batter' for its rich cream cheese and double-frying technique, but I've reinvented it here in a leaner incarnation featuring tuna. This dish is still no saint, but it is delicious to share and has proved a stellar hit with Feng Sushi customers.

First prepare the sushi rice following the method on page 15. While the rice is cooking, make the tempura batter following the recipe on page 118 and leave to rest in the fridge. Cut the tuna into six pieces, no more than $1/2$ cm thick but about 3cm in diameter.

Heat the vegetable oil to 180°C in a deep-fryer or heavy-based saucepan. Dust the tuna in the flour, then dip into the cold tempura batter and place in the hot oil. Fry for a few minutes until light golden. Set aside to drain on a plate lined with kitchen paper and sprinkle with sea salt. Remove the oil from the heat and set it aside, along with the remaining tempura batter.

Shape maki rolls referring to the pictures on page 89 as necessary. Spread half the cooled sushi rice over one sheet of nori. Spread generously with 40g cream cheese, 2 teaspoons kimchee base, half the chopped spring onion and three pieces of tuna tempura. Roll the maki very tightly – this will help it keep its shape while frying. Repeat the process to make a second roll.

Return the oil to 180°C. Cut each maki roll in half. Dust each piece in flour, dip in the remaining tempura batter and fry for 2 minutes. Drain briefly on kitchen paper, then carefully cut each maki roll into five pieces and serve them immediately with the traditional accompaniments.

240g Prepared Sushi Rice (see page 15)
500ml Basic Tempura Batter
   (see page 118)
100g yellowfin tuna
2 litres sunflower oil, for deep-frying
tempura flour, for dusting
sea salt
2 sheets nori
80g Philadelphia Lite cream cheese
4 teaspoons kimchee base
1 spring onion, finely chopped

to serve
grated mooli, wasabi paste, pickled
   ginger and soy sauce

deep-fried
tuna maki

makes

east|west
noodles and rice

There is nothing like Japanese noodles for simplicity: a few ingredients in a bowl and you have a magical meal. However I do think that efforts to reproduce authentic noodle dishes outside Japan often fail, so decided to take a different approach to the noodle section of Feng Sushi's menu. It became our playground. I was looking for soul food – nutritious dishes with deep flavours. Working with the chefs, we came up with a global tour de force, incorporating fine ingredients from various countries into Japanese cuisine.

Moroccan pumpkin ragout with soba noodle soup

Spaghetti this thin wheat pasta from Italy makes a reasonable substitute for Japanese wheat noodles, and is preferred for some fusion recipes.

Soba noodles in Japanese, soba means buckwheat as well as the noodles made from it. Soba noodles may be either a mixture of buckwheat and wheat flour, or 100 percent buckwheat flour, the latter being stronger in flavour, and healthier. Cook for 6-7 minutes in plenty of boiling water.

Chasoba soba noodles flavoured and coloured with green tea powder. Cook as for regular soba noodles, mixed with them if desired.

noodles

Thin udon noodles
made from wheat, these
dried noodles should be
cooked for 6-8 minutes
or until al dente.

Japanese noodles originated in China, but have been a staple
part of the Japanese diet for centuries. In Europe they were
known first and foremost from their use in Asian stir-fry
dishes, but they are now seen as a great alternative to pasta
and have become very popular. In fact good pasta can be used
as a substitute for Japanese wheat noodles. Ramen (Chinese-
style wheat noodles) will also work with most of the recipes in
this chapter, as will rice vermicelli. When it comes to gauging
quality, noodles are very similar to pasta; the mid-range and
organic brands tend to have a better flavour than cheaper
lines. Noodles sold in health food stores are often of superior
quality. I prefer noodles cooked al dente (tender with some
bite remaining) in a pot of salty boiling water and, once done,
like to give them a good rinse in cold water for extra shine,
before heating them through in the soup or sauce with
which they are to be served. If keeping cooked
noodles in the fridge I always dress
them in a little olive oil to
ensure they do not stick
together.

Somen noodles thin
wheat noodles that only
need 2 minutes cooking.

Thick udon noodles
these are precooked and
therefore very easy to
prepare. They need only a
couple of minutes boiling.

char-grilled baby squid, french beans and quails' eggs in somen soup

serves ● ● ● ●

There is something really bizarre about baby squid. The preparation is like a mini horror film, however it is easy to do, and they have a much tastier texture than their parents. Buy baby squid fresh: the frozen version is very expensive and less tender.

16 baby squid, with tentacles

300g french beans, trimmed

300g dried somen noodles

8 quails' eggs

100ml Simple Teriyaki Sauce
(see page 44)

4 tablespoons dashi powder

100ml olive oil

salt and pepper

2 teaspoons bonito flakes

Clean the squid in cold running water and remove the hard membrane from the bodies – this looks like a piece of plastic. Remove any soft tissue using your index finger. Cut between the eyes and tentacles, discarding the eyes and any slimy bits. Rinse in cold water, pat dry and set aside.

Bring a pot of salted water to the boil, add the beans and cook for 2 minutes. Remove the beans using tongs and plunge into ice-cold water. Drain and set aside. Cook the noodles in the same pot of boiling water for 2 minutes, then drain, rinse, and leave to rest in a colander.

Bring a small pan of salted water to the boil. Carefully lower the quails' eggs into the water and cook for 2 minutes. Drain and cool under the tap. Peel the eggs, cut in half, then set aside.

To make the soup, combine the teriyaki sauce, dashi and 1.5 litres of boiling water in a large saucepan or wok and bring to the boil. Add the noodles and reheat gently.

Meanwhile, divide the oil between two bowls and season each batch with salt and pepper. Add the squid to one and the beans to the other and turn gently to coat. Heat a griddle pan and, when it is smoking hot, cook the squid and beans until crisp and slightly charred.

To assemble the dish, divide the noodles and soup among four large bowls. Add the quails' eggs, squid and beans, and finally garnish with a small pinch of bonito flakes.

japanese style red curry with somen

serves ● ● ● ●

Supermarkets and Asian stores carry most of the ingredients for this dish. The Japanese version of red curry paste is simple to make, however you could substitute an authentic Thai brand. It's not worth trying to make a small quantity, so the recipe here gives about 200ml of curry paste, which will keep in a sterilised jar in the fridge for three months.

200g fresh shitake mushroom

200g mooli, about 15-20cm long

200g baby aubergines

200g butternut squash

200g okra

2 tablespoons vegetable oil

3 heaped tablespoons 'Japanese' Red Curry Paste (see below)

400g can coconut milk

50g creamed coconut block

4 kafir lime leaves

1 stalk lemon grass

2 teaspoons Thai fish sauce

300g dried somen noodles

a small bunch of coriander

for the 'japanese' red curry paste

3 small shallots

50g fresh ginger

3 large cloves garlic

3 red chillies

1 stalk lemon grass, or the grated zest of ½ a lemon

1 tablespoon dashi powder

1 tablespoon kimchee base

1 tablespoon cumin

1 tablespoon paprika

50ml extra virgin olive oil

To make the Japanese red curry paste: peel the shallots, ginger and garlic, deseed chillies and chop them all finely. Remove the outer layer of the lemon grass and cut the stalk into thin rings. Combine all these ingredients, plus the dashi, kimchee base, cumin and paprika, in a large mortar or food processor. Start grinding the ingredients to a thick paste, adding the oil gradually. Set aside.

Brush the shitake clean then slice them, leaving the stalks on. Peel the mooli and cut into 5cm-long julienne. Cut the baby aubergines into quarters, leaving the stalks on. Halve the butternut squash lengthways and scrape out the seeds and pith. Cut lengthways again to give four pieces, then cut into ½cm slices. Trim the okra if necessary.

Heat the wok, add the vegetable oil and, when hot, fry the curry paste for a few minutes to enhance the flavours. Mix in the coconut milk, creamed coconut and 1 litre of boiling water. Add all the vegetables, plus the kafir lime leaves, lemon grass, and fish sauce and simmer for 10 minutes.

Meanwhile, in a large pan of boiling water, cook the somen for 2 minutes. Drain, then rinse in cold water and divide among four large noodle bowls. Ladle the red vegetable curry over the noodles and serve garnished with coriander.

Tip: for a special dinner party version of this dish, add 500g of raw, deveined tiger prawns at the same time you add the vegetables. Leave the tails on for colour and flavour.

wakame coriander sauce, pancetta and soba

serves ● ● ● ●

Wakame sauce is based on tofu and absolutely fantastic! It is versatile beyond belief and can be served with almost any spuds, pasta, noodles or meats. The super-healthy way to serve it is with brown rice or mooli salad if you are detoxing or dieting; tofu is a perfect source of vegetable protein. However in this recipe I have added a little naughtiness in the form of a good Italian pancetta.

300g chasoba (green tea soba noodles), or a mixture of 150g chasoba and 150g soba noodles
2 tablespoons vegetable oil
200g pancetta, finely diced

for the wakame sauce
20g dried wakame seaweed
120g coriander sprigs
1/2 bunch spring onions, roughly chopped
1 large clove garlic, peeled
20g pickled ginger, or fresh ginger, peeled
200g firm tofu
40ml olive oil
4 teaspoons soy sauce
4 teaspoons sesame oil
1 tablespoon runny honey
1 tablespoon dashi powder
salt and pepper

To make the wakame sauce: put the seaweed in a small bowl, cover with cold water and set aside to rehydrate.

Place the coriander in a food processor with the spring onions, garlic and ginger. Break the tofu into chunks and add to the machine. In a small measuring jug combine the olive oil, soy sauce, sesame oil, honey and dashi with 40ml of boiling water. Switch on the food processor and gradually add the liquid, blending until the sauce has the consistency of thick mayonnaise. Transfer the sauce to a mixing bowl. Drain the wakame, stir it into the sauce, and season to taste with salt and pepper.

Bring a pot of boiling salted water to the boil and cook the noodles for 6-7 minutes until they are tender but still have some bite. Drain the noodles in a colander.

Meanwhile, heat 1 tablespoon of vegetable oil in wok and cook the pancetta gently until light golden and just crisp. Transfer to a piece of kitchen paper for a few minutes to absorb the excess fat, and discard the oil in the wok.

Return the wok to a medium heat and add 1 tablespoon of fresh oil. Add the cooked noodles, pancetta and, finally, the wakame sauce, stirring constantly until the ingredients are hot through. Serve immediately.

spaghetti with chilli jam, cashews and peppers

serves ● ● ● ●

Chilli jam takes several hours to cook, however it is a very therapeutic process and perfect for rainy Sundays when you are pottering around at home. This versatile flavouring brings instant depth to many dishes, from pasta, rice and noodles to fish and poultry. The recipe is derived from one in Australian chef Christine Manfield's excellent book Stir.

300g dried spaghetti

a splash of olive oil

1 large red onion, thinly sliced

2 heaped tablespoons chilli jam

100g raw cashew nuts

2 large red peppers, deseeded and thinly sliced

50g rocket leaves

salt and pepper

for the chilli jam

350g large red chillies, roughly chopped

100g birds' eye chillies, roughly chopped

2 large brown onions, roughly chopped

4 cloves garlic, roughly chopped

250ml sunflower, grapeseed or vegetable oil

20g tamarind paste

35g palm sugar

Make the chilli jam at least one day in advance. Combine the chillies, onions and garlic in a food processor and blend, gradually adding the oil to make a paste. Pour into a wide, heavy-based saucepan and cook gently over a low heat for 6-7 hours, or until the paste is thick and dark red, stirring every half hour to prevent sticking or burning.

Meanwhile, in a small bowl, steep the tamarind paste in 75ml hot water. Use a teaspoon to break up the paste as much as possible then set aside for 20 minutes, stirring occasionally. Sieve the mixture to give 75ml of tamarind liquid. Dissolve the palm sugar (grate it first if necessary) in the tamarind then, when the chill paste is thick and dark red, add the tamarind mixture to the pan and continue cooking for a further hour or so, stirring occasionally. Leave the chilli jam to cool down, then store in a sterilised jar in the fridge, where it will keep for up to 3 months.

Bring a pot of salted water to the boil and cook the pasta according to the packet instructions. Drain and set aside.

Place a wok over a medium heat. Add a splash of olive oil and fry the onion until soft. Add 2 heaped tablespoons of chilli jam and stir until the onions are well coated. Add the cashews and red peppers and stir-fry for a few minutes. Finally add the cooked spaghetti and rocket and stir until hot through. Season with salt and pepper and serve.

wild mushroom ragout with udon and shaved parmesan

serves ● ● ● ●

The shitake mushroom is one of the undisputed heroes of Japanese cuisine, adding flavour and texture to almost any dish. Both dried and fresh shitake are now widely available in the West. The dried version needs to be reconstituted in water; fresh shitake cost a few pennies more, but are worth it for the taste. In this recipe you can use any wild mushrooms available locally, such as pied a mouton, oyster, morel, pied bleu, or trompette de la mort, to name a few. Mushrooms are a sensitive bunch, so the best way to clean them is to brush gently with a pastry brush. However, first cut off the dirty ends, leaving as much of the stalks on as possible as these are full of flavour.

300g flat dried udon noodles

100g parmesan cheese, cut into flakes

for the mushroom ragout

2 tablespoons olive oil

1 large onion, finely chopped

200g mixed wild mushrooms, roughly chopped

200g brown chestnut mushrooms, quartered

100g fresh shitake mushrooms, thinly sliced

125ml mirin

125ml sake

2-3 tablespoons cornflour

100g curly parsley sprigs, finely chopped

50g chives, roughly chopped

salt and pepper

To make the ragout: heat the olive oil in a wok and fry the chopped onion until golden. Add the prepared mushrooms and turn them gently in the oil, cooking for 8 minutes. Add the mirin and sake, cover with a lid and leave to simmer over a gentle heat for 20 minutes, stirring occasionally.

Meanwhile, cook the udon in a pot of boiling salted water for 7-8 minutes until al dente, or just cooked. Drain the noodles in a colander.

Dissolve the cornflour in 200ml of cold water. Add the slaked cornflour gradually to the mushroom ragout until it thickens – you may not need it all. Stir in the fresh herbs and season to taste with salt and pepper.

Remove half the ragout from the wok and set aside in a bowl. Add the noodles to the wok and turn them in the ragout until they have heated through. Divide the noodles among four large bowls, top with the remaining ragout and plenty of parmesan cheese.

moroccan pumpkin ragout with soba noodle soup

serves ● ● ● ●

This recipe is Japan-meets-North-Africa, which admittedly sounds like a very odd fusion of ingredients. Nonetheless it is the best comfort food for those first winter days, when I realise that hibernation is again upon us and I long for energy-giving food. The ragout tastes better after a few days in the fridge, so it's a good idea to make a double portion.

800g pumpkin

1 tablespoon cumin powder

1 tablespoon coriander powder

1/2 tablespoon shichimi or other chilli powder

1/2 tablespoon garam masala

100ml olive oil

2 shallots, finely chopped

2 cloves garlic, finely chopped

500ml tomato juice

70g sultanas

70g pine nuts

1 stick cinnamon

salt and pepper

300g dried soba noodles

4 tablespoons dashi powder

100ml Simple Teriyaki Sauce (see page 44)

Peel, deseed and cube the pumpkin.

Toast the cumin, coriander, shichimi and garam masala in a dry frying pan over a low heat until fragrant. Immediately transfer to a small dish and set aside.

Working in two batches, heat half the olive oil in a large wok over medium heat. Add half the shallots and garlic and fry until softened. Add half the toasted spices and half the pumpkin and fry for another 5 minutes, stirring to coat the pumpkin with the spice mixture. Transfer the mixture to a large pot and repeat with the remaining olive oil, shallots, garlic, spices and pumpkin.

Add the tomato juice and 200ml cold water to the pot, then mix in the sultanas, pine nuts, cinnamon stick and some salt. Cover and simmer for up to 1 1/2 hours, stirring every 15 minutes. When all the liquid has evaporated and the mixture is a rich dark colour, the ragout is ready. Season to taste with salt and pepper.

Shortly before the ragout is finished cooking, bring a pot of salted water to the boil and cook the soba noodles for 6-7 minutes until al dente, or just cooked. Meanwhile, make the soup: combine the dashi powder, teriyaki sauce and 1.5 litres of boiling water in a saucepan and bring to the boil.

When the noodles are ready, drain them and divide among four large noodle bowls. Carefully pour the soup over each portion and top with the ragout before serving.

udon moules marinière with baby plum tomatoes and fresh herbs

serves ● ● ● ●

Moules Marinière is one of the best-recognised shellfish dishes in the world and surely deserves this Japanese interpretation.

1.5kg mussels

600g frozen chunky udon noodles

2 tablespoons olive oil

2 shallots, finely chopped

2 garlic cloves, finely chopped

100g flat-leaf parsley sprigs, finely chopped

175ml dry white wine

2 tablespoons dashi powder

200g baby plum tomatoes, halved

50ml double cream

salt and pepper

50g basil leaves, torn

Scrub the mussels using a scouring pad and plenty of cold water. Pull off any beards. Tap any open mussels sharply – if they do not close they are dead and should be discarded.

Place the frozen udon noodles in large bowl and cover with cold water. Put a large kettle of water on to boil.

Heat the olive oil in a large saucepan and gently fry the shallots and garlic until light golden. Stir in the parsley, then add 300ml of boiling water from the kettle, and the white wine. Put the cleaned mussels in the saucepan, cover and cook for 3-4 minutes, shaking the pan occasionally to ensure that they cook evenly. The mussels are done when they are all open. Using a slotted spoon, remove them to a plate and set aside.

Add 1 litre of boiling water to the cooking juices in the pan, then stir in the dashi powder and halved tomatoes. Cook for a few minutes, then stir in the cream and season to taste with salt and pepper.

Divide the udon noodles among four large bowls. Ladle the soup over the noodles, top with the mussels and garnish with torn basil leaves. The dish is ready to serve.

teriyaki salmon with warm soba salad

serves ● ● ● ●

This is a Feng classic – my best-selling special of all time. After seven years I am tempted to take it off the menu, but staff have threatened me with strike action, so fond are they of this dish. It is fast, simple and tasty. For this recipe I use Loch Duart salmon which not only is heavenly raw, but also cooks perfectly. Ask for the salmon skin to be left on. You will need about half a side for four people. As you can see from the picture, I like to cut it differently from the traditional way of presenting salmon steak. To do this, halve the side lengthways along the line of the spine, then cut each piece diagonally into portions.

300g soba noodles, or a mixture of
   150g soba and 150g chasoba
   (green tea soba noodles)
olive oil, for frying
4 salmon fillets, about 140g each
1 large red onion, finely chopped
2 garlic cloves, finely chopped
100g pine nuts
100g rocket leaves

to serve
200ml Simple Teriyaki Sauce
   (see page 44)

First prepare the teriyaki sauce according to the method on page 44. Preheat the oven to 180°C/Gas 4. Bring a large pan of salted water to the boil. Cook both varieties of soba togther until al dente (or tender but with some bite remaining) then drain and set aside in a colander.

To cook the salmon: pour a good splash of olive oil into a large frying pan and place over a high heat. Place the fillets in the oil skin-side down and fry for 2-3 minutes. Season with salt and pepper, then turn the fillets over and season again. Continue cooking for another 2-3 minutes. Transfer the salmon to a baking tray and place in the oven for 6-8 minutes, or until the salmon is just cooked through.

Pour a little olive oil into a wok and fry the onion and garlic until golden. Add the pine nuts, rocket and cooked soba noodles and stir until all the ingredients are hot through.

Divide the noodle mixture among four large plates and place the cooked salmon carefully on top. Drizzle each portion with the teriyaki sauce before serving.

First wash the rice following the instructions on page 15, then leave in the sieve to dry for 30 minutes.

Meanwhile, make a half quantity of the tempura batter as per the recipe on page 118 and place in the fridge to rest. Clean the baby squid (see page 146) and place in the fridge.

Put a kettle of water on to boil. Place the dashi powder in a large jug and cover with 1 litre of boiling water from the kettle, stirring to dissolve.

Heat the olive oil in a wok and fry the shallots, garlic, shitake and pine nuts until golden. Add the sushi rice and cook, stirring, for a few minutes to ensure that all the grains are well coated. Ladle about 100ml of the hot dashi stock into the wok and stir until the liquid has been absorbed. Repeat with another ladle of dashi stock, stirring until it has been absorbed. Continue this process of adding stock and stirring until the rice is cooked but the grains still have a little bite.

Add the teriyaki sauce and plum wine and stir until absorbed. Season to taste with salt and pepper, then cover, remove from the heat and set aside in a warm place.

To prepare the baby squid tempura: heat the vegetable oil to 180°C in a large heavy-based saucepan or electric deep-fryer. Meanwhile, cut the body of each squid into 3 pieces, so that you have chunky rings. Turn rings and the tentacles in a bowl of tempura flour, then dip in the prepared batter and fry for 1-2 minutes, or until golden. Drain the squid on kitchen paper and season with salt.

Divide the risotto among four shallow serving bowls and top with the rocket leaves and grated parmesan. Serve with a dish of the baby squid tempura on the side.

300g raw sushi rice
2 tablespoons dashi powder
2 tablespoons olive oil
2 shallots, chopped
2 garlic cloves, chopped
6 fresh shitake mushrooms, finely chopped
50g pine nuts
50ml Simple Teriyaki Sauce (see page 44)
50ml plum wine
salt and pepper
50g rocket leaves
50g parmesan cheese, coarsely grated

for the baby squid tempura
500ml Tempura Batter (see page 118)
8 baby squid
tempura flour, for dusting
2 litres vegetable oil, for deep-frying

japanese style risotto with baby squid tempura

serves ● ● ● ●

On certain days the low-carb diet needs to be put aside for old-style soul food such as this dish, which combines the best Japanese ingredients and traditional Italian cooking.

desserts

Japanese cuisine does not include desserts
as we in the West generally know them.
Maybe it is because the Japanese meal is
so perfect that it does not need a rich, heavy
ending. The standard dessert offered in sushi
bars is a simple scoop of green tea ice cream,
very much an acquired taste but nevertheless
gaining popularity worldwide. Here are my
interpretations of Japanese desserts, all very
grown up in their flavours – strong, savoury,
bitter and sweet. With the exception of the
Rice Krispie Layer Cake, they should
be served in small portions.

Dark chocolate, brazil nut and nori maki with Espressotini

poached pears with shiso and cream cheese in pink maki

serves ● ● ● ●

This dish is perfect for the picnic basket and absolutely divine at brunch with a glass of chilled champagne. I first used 'pink sheet', which is made from soy beans instead of seaweed, when I was casting about for something child-friendly on the menu. The children really liked it; the adults loved it. These make a great light meal for a hot summer's day.

2 ripe pale-skinned pears
5 tablespoons mirin
100ml sake
2 tablespoons caster sugar
4 pieces pink soy bean sheet
500g Prepared Sushi Rice (see page 15)
100g Philadelphia Lite cream cheese
seeds from 2 pomegranates
1 punnet shiso cress

Cut the pears into eighths, put in a saucepan with the mirin, sake and sugar. Bring to the boil, lower the heat and leave to simmer for about 20 minutes. When the pears are cooked through, drain in a sieve and leave to cool.

Using one of the 'pink sheets' in place of nori, trim it by one-fifth and place on a rolling mat as described on pages 88-9. Spread 125g of the sushi rice evenly across the sheet, leaving a border of about 2cm clear along the top. Using a spatula, spread a generous layer of cream cheese across the rice, then add pieces of the poached pear and sprinkle with sprigs of shiso cress.

Holding the filling in place with your index fingers, roll the maki into a neat cylinder and use the clear tab of pink sheet to seal it. Repeat the process with the remaining pink sheets, rice, cream cheese and pear.

Use the sides of the rolling mat to square up the maki and leave each one to rest for a few minutes. Remove from the rolling mat, trim off the rough ends, then cut each roll crossways into three pieces.

Arrange three pieces on each plate, scatter with the pomegranate seeds and garnish with shiso before serving.

green tea cheesecake

serves ••••
••••

I use ginger biscuits instead of digestives to make the base for this very dense but refreshing cheesecake because their flavour complements the green tea very well.

200g good quality ginger biscuits

60g butter, plus extra for greasing

75ml double cream

3 tablespoons green tea powder
  (matcha), plus extra for dusting

225g full fat cream cheese

3 tablespoons caster sugar

1 egg

1 egg yolk

200ml crème fraîche

Preheat the oven to 180°C (Gas 4) and butter an 18-20cm diameter spring-form cake tin. Crush the biscuits in a food processor and place in a mixing bowl. Gently melt the butter and add to the biscuit crumbs, mixing well. Press the crumbs into the base of the tin using your knuckles to form a firm layer, then chill for about 10 minutes to help it set. Bake for 10 minutes or until the base is light golden. Remove from the oven and set aside to cool.

Reduce the oven temperature to 150°C (Gas 2). In a small saucepan, heat the double cream gently and mix the green tea powder into it. (Do not let the cream go over 85°C or the mixture will split.) In a large mixing bowl, beat the cream cheese and sugar together. Add the egg and egg yolk, then the green tea mixture.

Pour the cheese mixture over the biscuit base and bake in the lower part of the oven for 30 minutes. Turn off the oven and leave the cheesecake to cool down in the oven for at least an hour before transferring it to the fridge. Serve with the crème fraîche, sprinkled with some additional green tea powder to decorate.

dark chocolate, brazil nut and nori maki

makes ● ● ● ●
● ● ● ●
● ● ● ●

Dark chocolate and nori is a special combination best enjoyed with a strong coffee or Espressotini (see below) after a satisfying meal. Use top quality chocolate because in this recipe a little goes a long way.

200g good quality 70% dark chocolate
15g unsalted butter
1/2 shot espresso, or other strong coffee
100g brazil nuts
1 sheet nori

Fill a small saucepan with water to a depth of about 5cm and place a metal bowl on top. Place over a moderate heat. Break up the chocolate and add to the bowl so that it melts gently. Add the butter and coffee, stirring constantly to ensure a smooth finish. Remove from the heat.

Roughly chop the brazil nuts and add them to the melted chocolate. Leave to rest for 10 minutes to harden a little.

Trim down the nori sheet by one-fifth and place on a rolling mat shiny side down. Place all of the chocolate mixture in the middle and gently roll into a square-sided maki roll (see technique page 88-9). Set the chocolate maki aside in the rolling mat in a cool place to rest for a few hours.

Use a sharp knife to cut the chocolate nori into twelve small pieces and serve as little bites with hot coffee or chilled Espressotini (see recipe below).

espressotini

makes ● ● ● ●

a handful of ice cubes
8 shots of espresso, of a strong small pot of cafetière coffee
4 shots vodka
4 shots coffee liqueur

Place the ice cubes in a jug or cocktail shaker. Add the coffee, vodka and liqueur and shake well. Pour into tall glasses and serve with the Dark Chocolate, Brazil Nut and Nori Maki (above), Rice Krispie Layer Cake (pages 166-7), or simply as an after-dinner drink in place of dessert.

Make the ice cream one day in advance. Place 500ml of the cream in a saucepan with the yolks and sugar. Split open the vanilla pods, scrape out the seeds, and add to the pan with the pods. Place over a moderate heat and, using an electric whisk, whisk the mixture while heating it to a temperature of 80°C exactly (use a thermometer). Transfer to a plastic container and freeze immediately. When the mixture is solid, cut into large chunks and blend in a food processor until the lumps turn to soft ice. Meanwhile, whip the remaining 500ml cream until stiff. Fold the soft ice into the whipped cream and freeze again for 24 hours or so.

To make the Rice Krispie layer cakes: grease a 40 x 30cm baking tray. Melt the butter in a small saucepan over a medium heat. Add the marshmallows and stir until melted, then mix in the honey. In a large bowl combine the Rice Krispies and sesame seeds. Add the marshmallow mixture and stir until well combined. Pour into the baking tray and spread out evenly with a buttered spoon. Place a piece of greaseproof paper over the top and sit something heavy, such as a phone book, on top. Set aside.

For the coulis: combine the berries, mirin or sake, and sugar in a small saucepan. Add just enough water to cover and simmer over a medium heat for 10 minutes. Sieve the mixture into a bowl, pressing the berries against the mesh of the sieve to extract as much liquid as possible. Return the coulis to the pan and place over a medium heat. In a small bowl, blend the cornflour with a little cold water and gradually stir into the coulis, so that it thickens to the consistency of double cream. Pour the sauce into a squeeze bottle and set aside.

Using a 7cm pastry ring, cut 8 discs from the Rice Krispie cake. Place one on a serving dish, add a scoop of ice cream and drizzle with coulis. Top with another Rice Krispie disc. Repeat with the remaining ingredients, then finish with berries.

30g unsalted butter, plus extra for greasing
150g white marshmallows
2 tablespoons honey
150g Rice Krispies, preferably organic
70g white toasted sesame seeds
a few berries, to decorate

for the ice cream
1 litre whipping cream, preferably organic
8 large egg yolks
150g caster sugar
2 vanilla pods

for the fruit coulis
100g raspberries
100g blackberries
50ml mirin or sake
50g caster sugar
1-2 tablespoons cornflour

rice krispie layer cake with fynen vanilla ice cream

This dessert is my tribute to my mother's amazing Fynen vanilla ice cream, for which she always uses top quality vanilla pods. Fynen is the island in Denmark where I grew up and is well known for its dairy products. The recipe here makes 1 litre so there is plenty left over for other treats. I've combined it with a layer cake – another Fynen speciality – made of soft biscuits of sesame, marshmallow and Rice Krispies.

serves • • • •

black sesame and maple syrup ice cream

serves ● ● ● ● ● ●

If you serve this ice cream once it will be expected again and again, and you'll find guests won't go home without it! It makes heavenly, happy 'afters' served with a small, strong cup of espresso made from the very best, freshly ground beans. I find one large scoop tends to suffice as it it's so dense with seeds and flavour that any more would be gluttonous.

150ml organic cream
250ml full fat organic milk
60ml organic maple syrup
4 egg yolks
50g caster sugar
100g toasted black sesame seeds

Combine the cream, milk and maple syrup in a saucepan and heat the mixture to just under boiling point.

In a large mixing bowl, whisk together the egg yolks and sugar. Slowly pour the hot milk mixture over the egg yolks, whisking continually, then return the custard mixture to the saucepan. Heat very slowly and carefully, stirring constantly to ensure the mixture does not curdle.

When it reaches 74°C exactly, transfer the mixture to a jug and leave to cool. Once it has reached room temperature, place the jug in the refrigerator to chill thoroughly.

Use a mortar and pestle, or the small bowl of a food processor, to grind half the sesame seeds. Add them, plus the remaining whole sesame seeds, to the cold custard and pour into an ice cream machine.

Churn the mixture until almost frozen, then transfer it to a plastic container and freeze until solid. If you don't have an ice cream maker, pour the mixture straight into the plastic container and place in the freezer, giving it a stir every 30 minutes or so until frozen.

Once made the ice cream keeps for up to a month (like it is going to last that long...). To serve, simply place a large scoop in a beautiful bowl.

japanese ingredients used in this book

Dashi a stock made of shavings of dried bonito, a fish of the tuna family. Dashi has natural flavour enhancing properties and is the base of much Japanese cooking, from sauces and soups to noodles.

Edamame young green soy beans. These are typically served in the pod, with sea salt or mirin dipping sauce, as an appetizer or snack. However you will often find them podded and used in salads.

Ginger, pickled known as gari in Japanese, pickled ginger is served with sushi and sashimi to cleanse the palate between different flavours. It can also be used as an ingredient in sauces and salads.

Kimchee base kimchee are Korean pickled vegetables traditionally served with every meal,. Kimchee base is a bright red, ready-made product popular in Japan as a convenient way to make pickled vegetables. It looks much like a spicy tomato sauce but is made of garlic, chilli, ginger, vinegar and salt. Also suitable as a sauce for dipping, in this book it is often used as a flavouring ingredient too.

Kombu also known as kelp, this variety of seaweed is used as a flavour enhancer in sauces, marinades and sushi vinegar.

Mirin sweet cooking sake, also used in marinades, sauces and tamago (Japanese omelette).

Miso paste a fermented paste of soy beans, sometimes with barley or rice, and salt. It is used in soups, salad dressings and marinades. The fermented soy protein tenderises meat or fish after 2-3 days of marinating. Miso is very nutritious, high in protein (14 per cent) and comes in white, red and dark brown varieties. White miso is the softest and mildest, red miso is rounder in its flavour, while the dark variety is rich and deeply flavoured. Miso paste is often mixed with sugar, mirin and sake to provide extra flavour and to give dishes a caramelised finish.

Mizuna this salad leaf originated in Japan but is now also grown in Italy. Mizuna has a crisp, peppery taste, like mild rocket leaves.

Mooli often called daikon or Chinese radish, this large white radish is integral to Japanese cuisine as an aid for digestion. Finely grated mooli is always served with raw fish and tempura to help the body digest the fatty components, however it is becoming more common in salads. Be sure to grate it very finely in long shreds.

Nori sheets of pressed seaweed, mostly kelp. Toasted nori is used for making maki and temaki sushi. Very high in iodine, fibre and totally non-fat, like all seaweed it can be categorised as a superfood. Nori flakes are also sold for sprinkling over food as a seasoning.

Ponzu sauce a mix of evaporated sake. soy sauce and the juice of ponzu, which is a fragrant Japanese citrus fruit. Typically served as a dipping sauce, it can also be used as a marinade and an ingredient in modern desserts.

Rice vinegar vinegar made from rice. It is the main ingredient of sushi vinegar, but also used in marinades and dressings. Vinegar has an important position in Japanese cuisine and is considered a body cleanser so is often used in soft drinks and natural health products.

Sesame oil is extracted from sesame seeds. It has a strong, distinctive flavour and a very high burning point. Sesame oil is often mixed with corn or vegetable oil for frying tempura and is a frequent inclusion in dressings and marinades. Remember sesame is categorised as a nut and anyone suffering from nut allergies may have a reaction to it.

Sesame seeds available in white and black varieties, these are served toasted as a topping for vegetables and rice, and are also frequently used in sushi.

Shichimi Japanese seven-spice chilli powder. Traditionally served as a table condiment with noodles, it can also be used to give a spicy kick to sushi rolls.

Shiso in Japan large shiso leaves are traditionally served with sashimi and temaki, however as they are at present only imported to Europe by airfreight, I prefer to use the smaller shiso cress, punnets of which come from Holland by road and sea. Shiso cress looks like mini basil leaves and has an aniseed flavour and fragrance reminiscent of Thai basil. It is perfect with everything, including desserts.

Shitake mushrooms the best known of the Japanese fungi. They are often sold dried, to be reconstituted in hot water, however fresh shitake mushrooms are now widely available as they are grown all over Europe, including Britain, and the fresh mushroom is much preferred.

Soba noodles buckwheat noodles. Can be made from a mixture of wheat and buckwheat, or with 100 percent buckwheat, the later being the healthiest option. Buckwheat is a complex carbohydrate and good for the metabolism. Soba is used in soups, salads as well as noodle dishes.

Somen noodles very thin wheat noodles most commonly used in soup noodle dishes.

Soy sauce the grandfather of Japanese ingredients, served with or used in almost all Japanese cuisine. It is brewed from soy beans and wheat, and has a low alcohol content of two percent. I prefer to use the soy sauce brewed in Europe under licence to Kikkoman (Japan's leading manufacturer) because imported soy arrives by sea and suffers when crossing the Equator: the alcohol evaporates in the heat, making the soy sauce thick and a little bitter. Soy sauce is seen as the salt of Asian cuisine, and dishes seasoned with soy sauce should not need additional salt.

Sushi vinegar I prefer using ready-mixed sushi vinegar as it ensures consistency throughout our restaurants. My preferred brand is Mitsukan, but you can certainly mix your own: gently heat 60ml rice vinegar with 100g caster sugar, 2 teaspoons salt and a 10cm piece kombu seaweed. When the sugar has dissolved, leave the mixture to cool down to room temperature and remove the kombu.

Tempura flour often called tempura-ko, this specialist flour is made of wheat and corn flour. It has a very light texture and is essential for light, crisp tempura.

Teriyaki sauce a thick sauce used with grilled fish or meat. It can be bought ready made, but is easy to make yourself (see page 44).

Tobiko flying fish roe, often flavoured with yuzu, wasabi or ume (plum), available in Japanese stores. Masago is a cheaper alternative: the eggs are smaller and often artificially coloured.

Tofu also known as bean curd, tofu is made of soy beans and very high in protein. It is highly versatile and can be eaten raw, fried, steamed, braised, or puréed to give a base for sauces such as the wakame sauce on page 149.

Udon thick wheat noodles popular at street food stalls in Tokyo.

Wakame a type of seaweed sold dried and reconstituted in cold water before use. Wakame is high in iodine and fibre and a good inclusion in soups and salads.

Wasabi Japanese horseradish. Traditionally found growing wild by rivers on mountainsides, it is now cultivated on the banks of streams. The fresh root is grated and served as a condiment for sashimi and sushi. Wasabi powder should be mixed to a thick paste with cold water. Ready-made wasabi pastes are also readily available.

Wasabi peas spicy snacks made from dried peas coated with a strong, wasabi flavoured crust. Traditionally eaten as a snack, they are excellent crushed and used as an ingredient in sushi.

Yuzu juice juice made from the yuzu, a Japanese citrus fruit with a fragrant aroma. It is an excellent ingredient for dressings and marinades. If not available, yuzu juice can be replaced with freshly squeezed grapefruit.

where to buy japanese ingredients

Shopping for Japanese ingredients has become much easier over the last decade as the cuisine has gained in popularity. Basic ingredients for making sushi – rice, sushi vinegar, nori, wasabi, pickled ginger and soy sauce – are widely available in larger supermarkets, food halls, and health food stores. Other ingredients commonly used in Japanese cooking, such as sesame seeds, mirin, sesame oil, fresh shitake mushroom and mooli, are also readily available in the above places, and all the other vegetables used in this book can be purchased from good greengrocers or large supermarkets. However, when it comes to raw fish, I must emphasise that supermarket fish is not sushi-grade. Instead use a good local fishmonger with a fine reputation and remind the person behind the counter that you are going to be serving the fish raw in sushi and sashimi.

For more specialised Japanese ingredients such as shichimi, tempura flour and wasabi peas, there are quite a few places in London and other cities with an excellent choice of imported products. When shopping at Asian stores that offer a broad range, I always recommend going for the mid-priced lines as these are good quality yet reasonably priced. I believe you have to be a serious connoisseur to go for the most expensive products, an extra spend I do not bother with as I would not be able to tell the difference. Note that very often Thai, Chinese and other specialist Asian stores carry Japanese products too.

Below are some of my favourite shops, plus a few other recommendations.

The Japan Centre
212 Piccadilly, London W1 (020 7434 4218) www.japancentre.com

Oriental City
399 Edgware Road, Colindale, London NW9 (020-8200-0009)

Atari-Ya Foods
7 Station Parade, Noel Road, London W3 (020 8896 1552) www.atariya.co.uk
Branches at 595 High Road, London N12 (020 8446 6669)and 15-16 Monkville Parade, Finchley Road, London NW11 (020 8458 7626).

Lotte Shopping
26 Malden Road, New Malden, Surrey (020 8942 9552).

Miura Foods
44 Coombe Road, Kingston, Surrey (020 8549 8079) www.miurafoods.com
Branch at 5 Limpsfield Road, Sanderstead, South Croydon (020 8651 4498).

Jasmin Food Shop
Stanton House Hotel, The Avenue, Stanton Fitzwarren, Swindon, Wiltshire (01793 861 777) www.stantonhouse.co.uk

Mai Bai's
4 Bamford Road, Didsbury, Manchester (07795 160272)

Oki-Nami
12 York Place, Brighton, East Sussex (01273 677 702) www.okinami.com

Midori
19 Marlborough Place, Brighton, East Sussex (01273 601 460)

Setsu Japan
196a Heaton Road, Newcastle upon Tyne (0191 265 9970)

Akaneya
81 Northumberland Avenue, Reading (0118 931 0448)

For online shopping

Mount Fuji (01743 741169) www.mountfuji.co.uk
Goodness Direct (0871 871 6611) www.goodnessdirect.co.uk

Australia and New Zealand

Tokyo Mart
27 Northbridge Plaza, Sailors Bay Road, Northbridge, NSW (02 9958 6860)

Fuji Mart
34A Elizabeth Street, South Yarra, Victoria (03 9826 5839)

Fuji Mart
Shop 1, Southport Park Shopping Centre, cnr Ferry and Benowa Roads, Southport, Queensland (07 5591 6211)

Made in Nippon
313 Queen Street, Auckland, New Zealand (09 377 1891)

index

Entries in **bold** indicate photographs.

acknowledgements

First I would like to thank my business partner Jeremy Rose for supporting me, believing in my abilities as a chef and helping to get this book published. Feng Sushi has provided me with a framework to develop and try new and interesting things, therefore I also would like to thank Chris McFadden our financial backer for his support and active role with Feng Sushi. The staff at Feng Sushi – in particular the excellent team of head chefs I work with on a daily basis – are all to thank for the success Feng Sushi has become. Without their hard work we would never be where we are today. Thanks to all of Feng Sushi's main suppliers: Tazaki Food, Aberdeen Sea Products and Leanards for their lovely produce. I would also like to thank Tanis Taylor who helped with the original pitch for this book. Special thanks to Lars, and all the talented people at Quadrille, for working so hard on this book. Finally thank you to my fiancé David for his support, brutally honest criticism and always cooking and serving me a lovely meal at the end of a long day.

First published in 2006 by
Quadrille Publishing Limited
Alhambra House
27-31 Charing Cross Road
London WC2H 0LS

Text © 2006 Silla Bjerrum
Photographs © 2006 Lars Ranek
Design and layout © 2006 Quadrille Publishing Ltd

Editorial director Anne Furniss
Creative director Helen Lewis
Project editor Jenni Muir
Photographer Lars Ranek
Food styling Silla Bjerrum
Designer Claire Peters
Production Ruth Deary

The rights of the authors have been asserted.
All rights reserved. No part of this book may be reproduced, stored in a retrieval system or transmitted in any form or by any means, electronic, electrostatic, magnetic tape, mechanical, photocopying, recording or otherwise, without the prior permission in writing of the publisher.
Although all reasonable care has been taken in the preparation of this book, neither the publisher, editors nor the authors can accept any liability for any consequences arising from the use thereof, or the information contained therein.

Cataloguing in Publication Data: a catalogue record for this book is available from the British Library.

ISBN-13 978 184400 335 8
ISBN-10 184400 335 3

Printed and bound in China